A Philosophy
of International Law

New Perspectives on Law, Culture, and Society

ROBERT W. GORDON AND MARGARET JANE RADIN, SERIES EDITORS

A Philosophy
of International Law

Fernando R. Tesón

WestviewPress

A Division of HarperCollins*Publishers*

New Perspectives on Law, Culture, and Society

Copyright © 1998 by Westview Press, A Division of HarperCollins Publishers, Inc.

Published in 1998 in the United States of America by Westview Press, 5500 Central Avenue, Boulder, Colorado 80301-2877, and in the United Kingdom by Westview Press, 12 Hid's Copse Road, Cumnor Hill, Oxford OX2 9JJ

A CIP catalog record for this book is available from the Library of Congress.
ISBN 0-8133-1131-4 (hc)
ISBN 0-8133-6864-2 (pbk)

The paper used in this publication meets the requirements of the American National Standard for Permanence of Paper for Printed Library Materials Z39.48-1984.

10   9   8   7   6   5   4   3   2   1

To Bettina, Fernando, and Marcelo, with love

Contents

Acknowledgments

Many people supported me during the several years in which this book took shape. I would like to thank my colleagues at Arizona State University, especially Jeffrie Murphy, Cynthia Ward, and the participants in the Moral, Political, and Legal Philosophy Discussion Group. Their criticisms and comments helped enormously and allowed me to avoid many mistakes. In particular, my conversations with fellow Kantian Jeff Murphy were instrumental in motivating me to write the book in the first place. I thank also John Rawls, David Wippman, and Lea Brilmayer for helpful criticisms to chapters 4, 5, and 6 respectively. I owe a debt of gratitude to colleagues at my summer institution (winter in the South), the Universidad Torcuato Di Tella in Buenos Aires: Guido Pincione, who exercised an important influence in my thinking and Horacio Spector, whose philosophical acumen is such that he never said anything that didn't make me change my position.

I wish to thank my research assistant Michelle Paz Soldán for putting the manuscript in impeccable camera-ready form. Special thanks go to my institution, Arizona State University College of Law, for its unfailing support for my scholarly efforts.

Finally, I thank the love and support of my wife Bettina, my boys Fernando and Marcelo, and my family in far-away Buenos Aires. Their help cannot be measured in simple words.

Fernando R. Tesón
Tempe, Arizona, Thanksgiving 1997

1

The Kantian Thesis

Introduction

This book defends the view, first developed by Immanuel Kant, that international law and domestic justice are fundamentally connected.[1] Despite the recent prominence of the international law of human rights, the dominant discourse in international law fails to recognize the important normative status of the individual. Traditional international legal theory focuses upon the rights and duties of states and rejects the contention that the rights of states are merely derivative of the rights and interests of the individuals that reside within them. Accordingly, international legitimacy and sovereignty are a function of whether the government politically controls the population rather than whether it justly represents its people. The traditional view of international law suggests a dual paradigm for the ordering of individuals: one domestic, the other international. Justice and legitimacy are, on this view, conceptually separate. It may well be that domestic systems strive to promote justice, but international systems only seek order and compliance.

International law thus conceived, however, is incapable of serving as the normative framework for present international relations.[2] Although it is understandably hard for lawyers to forsake the statist assumptions of classic international legal discourse, new times call for a fresh conceptual and ethical language.[3] A more liberal world needs a more liberal theory of international law.[4] Liberal theory commits itself to *normative individualism*, to the premise that the primary normative unit is the individual, not the state; thus it can hardly be reconciled with the statist approach.[5] The end of states and governments is to benefit, serve, and protect its components, human beings; the end of international law must also be to benefit, serve, and protect human beings, and not its components, states and governments.[6] Respect for states is merely derivative of respect for persons. In this way, the notion of sovereignty is redefined: the sovereignty of the state is dependent upon the state's domestic legitimacy; therefore the principles of international justice must be congruent with the principles of internal justice.

In this book I propose the reexamination of the traditional foundations of international law. These traditional foundations are illiberal and authoritarian because they unduly exalt state power. All exercise of power must be morally legitimate. Roughly, an exercise of power is morally legitimate when it is the result of political consent and respects the basic rights of the individuals subject to that power. If international law is to be morally legitimate, therefore, it must mandate that states respect human rights as a precondition for joining the international community. Immanuel Kant was the first to defend this thesis, and for that reason I will call it the Kantian theory of international law. In this first Chapter I examine in depth Kant's international theory as put forth in his famous essay *Perpetual Peace*. Kant's view was that no lasting peace could be achieved without nation-states being internally free. The Kantian thesis, then, is that a morally legitimate international law is founded upon an *alliance of separate free nations, united by their moral commitment to individual freedom, by their allegiance to the international rule of law, and by the mutual advantages derived from peaceful intercourse.*

Kant is usually regarded as the pioneering advocate of an international organization capable of securing a lasting peace. Commentators have justly praised Kant as the one philosopher who, in his effort to contest the then prevailing views upholding the absolute right of governments to wage war, foreshadowed modern conceptions of international law associated with the United Nations.[7] The novelty of his proposals explains why Kant's contribution has been regarded as *avant la lettre* political advocacy for the United Nations and peaceful world order.[8] Nevertheless, Kant accomplished far more. He developed a subtle, rich, and innovative theory of international law, one that was so much ahead of its time that even admirers were blind to its importance. Kant's originality stems not only from having predicted the rise of a global international organization, but, more important, from having been the first to show the strong links between international peace and personal freedom and those between arbitrary government at home and aggressive behavior abroad. He unveiled, for the first time, the connection between domestic freedom and the foundations of international law, thus foreseeing the human rights revolution of the twentieth century.

I offer here a modern reconstruction of Kant's thesis.[9] I believe that the interpretation of Kant suggested in this book is accurate whether one wants to confine oneself to the text of *Perpetual Peace* or whether one views his discussion of international law against the backdrop provided by Kant's general moral theory.

Subsequent chapters examine and reject various alternatives to the Kantian thesis. In Chapter 2 I challenge statism, that is, the view that states are the central unit of analysis in international relations and that, as such, they enjoy presumptive international legitimacy. In Chapter 3 I attack positivism, that is, the jurisprudential view that international law is created only by the consent of states. Chapter 4 discusses the doctrine of John Rawls, who, while coming close to the view defended here, is still too deferential to nonliberal conceptions of politics. Chapter 5 addresses self-determination, that is, the question of when a group has the right to form an independent state. Chapter 6 examines the feminist critique of international law.

The Requirement That States Be Liberal Democracies

The first principle of international ethics embodied in the first definitive article of *Perpetual Peace* is: "The civil constitution of every nation should be republican."[10] The requirement of a republican form of government must be read in conjunction with the second article: "The law of nations shall be based on a federation of free states."[11] The first two articles prescribe that international law should be based upon a union of republican states.[12] Kant asserts that adherence to these requirements will result in an alliance of free nations that will maintain itself, prevent wars, and steadily expand.[13] Contrary to predominant belief in his time, and to conventional current legal thinking, international law and the peace it intends to secure can only be based upon a union, an alliance, of states that protect freedom internally and whose governments are representative. Kant for the first time linked arbitrary government at home with aggressive foreign policies. An international community that attempts to secure peace forever cannot countenance tyrannical regimes because, as Kant tries to show, such regimes are not just despotic: they are also aggressive.

By *republican* Kant means what we would call today a liberal democracy, that is, a form of political organization that provides for full respect for human rights. Kant explains at some length the sense in which he understands "republican constitution."[14] According to Kant, a republican state is defined by a constitution based upon three principles. First, the principle of freedom of all members of society[15] that entails, according to Kant, the liberal principle of respect of individual autonomy and the government's (relative) neutrality of ends:

> No one can compel me (in accordance with his belief about the welfare of others) to be happy after his fashion; instead, every person may seek happiness in the way that seems best to him, if only he does not violate the freedom of others to strive toward such similar ends as are compatible with everyone's freedom under a possible universal law.[16]

One can hardly overemphasize the importance of this highly innovative Kantian thesis. Kant includes freedom (respect for individual autonomy under the rule of law) as the first tenet of international ethics. He is not committing the fallacy of transposing the notion of individual freedom into the conceptual framework of nationalism: freedom here is not the right *to* a nation-state but primarily claims *against* it—claims against fellow citizens and against the government established by social contract to implement social cooperation.

In order to understand Kant's discussion of the principle of freedom in the republican constitution, it is necessary to analyze in some detail Kant's categorical imperative. In his writings on moral philosophy, Kant attempted to demonstrate the possibility of human freedom and autonomy in the face of the deterministic laws of nature.[17] Only a free and autonomous being is capable of acting morally and can be said to have dignity and be worthy of respect. Thus, Kant's primary aim in the *Groundwork* was "to seek out and establish the supreme principle of morality."[18] This he calls the categorical imperative, a universal law that all rational beings can make and act upon for themselves as free, self-determining agents whose actions are morally good.[19] Kant offers three different formulae of the categorical imperative yet contends that they are "at bottom merely so many formulations of precisely the same law."[20]

The first formula is the most abstract. It emphasizes the impartiality and universal nature that moral principles ought to exhibit: "Act only on that maxim through which you can at the same time will that it should become a universal law."[21] While initially this formula seems empty of content, there is good reason for that. Kant insists that moral philosophy must have an a priori foundation, which in turn necessarily must be formal.[22] In this way, the violation of the categorical imperative is not only morally reprehensible but irrational and self-contradictory.[23] Additionally, while this maxim is formal, it is not entirely devoid of content, for it enjoins us to "act autonomously and respect the right and obligation of everyone else to do the same."[24] From the standpoint of a theory of international law, the first version of the categorical imperative provides crucial support for the universality of human rights.

The emphasis on the agent's autonomy and respect for the autonomy of others leads naturally to the second version, the formula of respect for the dignity of persons: "Act in such a way that you always treat humanity, whether in your own person or in the person of any other, never simply as a means, but always at the same time as an end."[25] This second formula is a specification of the first in that here Kant identifies the class of moral agents: all human beings. The term "humanity" denotes the "functional complex of abilities and characteristics that enables us to set ends and make rational choices."[26] Because rationality defines the moral agent and because the categorical imperative requires universalization, we must presuppose rationality in the persons on whom the agent's behavior impinges. Kant's crucial step in the argument is that this rationality makes persons objects that are worthy of respect, ends in themselves. Things are instrumental and have only extrinsic value. Human beings, on the other hand, have *intrinsic* value. In Kant's words: "Now I say that many, and in general every rational being, *exists* as an end in himself, *not merely as means* for arbitrary use by this or that will: he must in all his actions, whether they are directed to himself or to other rational beings, always be viewed *at the same time as an end*."[27]

The consequences for *political* philosophy of this view of respect for the dignity of human beings as the ultimate basis for the moral justification of our conduct are self-evident. If in our everyday behavior we should never consider fellow human beings merely as means, it follows a fortiori that the constitution of the state, an artificial creation to serve human needs, must embody and incorporate a formula of respect for persons—a bill of human rights.[28] Thus, in the Kantian vision, mechanisms for guaranteeing traditional civil and political rights, which act as barriers against the abuse of state power, form the basis of a republican constitution because such mechanisms implement the respect for autonomy and dignity of persons.[29]

It would be a serious mistake, however, to conclude that the Kantian notion of freedom entails only negative duties—the duties of others to leave me alone to pursue my own happiness in accordance with my ideal of individual excellence. While Kant was against what he called "paternal government,"[30] the second version of the categorical imperative, that is, the formula of respect for the dignity of persons, entails positive duties as well.[31] We must go beyond negative duties to make human beings our end, both by striving for our own virtue and by acting justly and benevolently toward others.[32] A modern reconstruction of Kantian political theory should make room for what we would call today positive socioeconomic rights alongside the traditional negative, civil and political rights.[33] Respect for the dignity of persons requires, in addition to respecting their moral space, doing our best to secure an adequate level of material well-being for every member of society. Two reasons militate in favor of recognizing socioeconomic rights by domestic and international law. First, socioeconomic rights allow individuals fully to flourish and develop their uniquely human potential.[34] Second, a certain material well-being is necessary for persons fully to enjoy their civil and political rights and thus to value and take advantage of liberty to its full extent. In an ideal society individuals are not only free; for them, liberty has high and roughly equal worth.[35]

The second defining principle of a republican, constitutional system is independence. By this Kant means that all legal acts (or dependence of all subjects) must derive from a single common legislation.[36] The legitimacy of a legal act therefore depends upon whether it is in harmony with the constitution, procedurally and substantively. Kant's formulation resembles the juridical definition of a state developed by Hans Kelsen.[37] Kelsen's system provides a valuable counterpoint to Kant's understanding of a legitimate republican regime. For Kelsen, all legal acts must derive from a single hypothetical basic norm that in turns legitimizes the first positive norm, the constitution. However, such derivation provides only formal legitimacy because the basic norm has no prior, or objective, status. The basic norm is "presupposed to be valid. . . . It is this presupposition that enables us to distinguish between individuals who are legal authorities and other individuals whom we do not regard as such, between acts of human beings which create legal norms and acts which have no such effect."[38]

Kant's system also mandates the obedience to law that depends upon a single constitution. However, Kant's constitution, unlike Kelsen's basic norm, is not presupposed to be valid, but is rather the result of a rational choice by free agents as expressed in the legitimate social contract that requires that every citizen be a colegislator.[39] The validity of the constitution proceeds from the exercise of the rational cognitive faculties by the members of the body politic. Individual members of the state will insist that the principles of the constitution, which is a material maxim,[40] comports with the categorical imperative. The constitution ceases to be valid when it no longer reflects this aggregate rationality. Thus, allegiance to the state by individuals is based upon their rationally believing that such allegiance is right, and a rational individual will not adhere to an irrational constitution. This requirement of a dependence of all upon a common constitution is yet another instance of Kant's strong reliance on, and reverence for, the idea of law.[41] For him, to justify an institution means that it has to have a legally protected status.[42] This means, domestically, that both freedom and subjection to the power of the state are legally regulated: freedom under law and coercion under law, or freedom and coercion according to reason.[43] In a lengthy footnote, Kant explains that external lawful freedom means "the authority not to obey any external laws except those which I have been able to give my consent."[44] Only in the *Rechstaat*, that is, under the rule of law, is allegiance to the law rational.

This is the place to notice a major weakness in Kant's political theory: his thesis of rational allegiance to the law is not easily reconciled with his strong opposition to a right to revolution.[45] The proposition that citizens may revolt (as a last resort) against arbitrary power when the sovereign has broken the agency contract follows logically from any liberal political theory.[46] Perhaps Kant was trying to make a purely formal point, namely that for citizens to have a *legal right* to revolution is self-contradictory.[47] Nevertheless, Kant's views on civil disobedience and revolution are inadequate, both in terms of his own moral theory and in terms of the common-sense judgments of ordinary morality.[48] If government breaches the social contract, then the people may dismiss the government, by violence if all other means have failed.

The recognition of the right to resist tyranny is extremely important in international law. Beyond the consequences for the law of international human rights itself, it has consequences for the theory of humanitarian intervention. If citizens did not have a right to revolt against their tyrants, foreigners a fortiori would not have a right to help them, even by non coercive measures, in the struggle against despotism. Humanitarian intervention can be defended as a corollary to the right to revolution: victims of serious human rights deprivations, who have rationally decided to revolt against their oppressors, have a right to receive proportionate transboundary assistance, including forcible help.[49]

The third principle is the principle of equality of all as citizens, that is, equality before the law.[50] The requirement of equality follows analytically from Kant's definition of law. Law is universal in form, and so every person has exactly the same rights as every other person.[51] Kant reaffirms his long-standing rejection of nobility or birth as the basis for assigning rights and duties under a republican constitution. Despite the fact that his writings were hardly accessible to the public, Kant reveals himself, in his historical context, as the philosopher of the ordinary people. Indeed, Kant's entire moral philosophy can be understood as a protest against distinctions based on morally irrelevant criteria such as wealth, rank, and privilege, and perpetuated by religious and political force and fear.[52] Kant's idea of society based upon a republican constitution is one that combines respect for individual autonomy with the need for social order. It applies equally to classical laissez-faire as well as to welfare states in the modern European tradition.

Kant reaffirms this idea in his commentary to the first definitive article: "The sole established constitution that follows from the idea of an original contract, the one on which all of a nation's just [*rechtliche*] legislation must be based, is republican."[53] In a somewhat detailed discussion of the forms of government as opposed to forms of rulership, Kant asserts that the form of government is either republican or despotic. Form of government has to do, for Kant, with the way in which the state employs its sovereign power. Republicanism means separation of powers; whereas despotism exists when "the ruler independently executes laws that it has itself made."[54]

The Kantian thesis, then, can be summarized as follows: observance of human rights is a primary requirement to join the community of civilized nations under international law. It follows that there cannot be federation or peace alliance with tyrannical states. If the international community constituted by the law of nations is going to preserve peace, it cannot accept tyrants among its members. Domestic freedom is a primary credential required from any state for it to become a legitimate member of the international community. Yet an important qualification is in order here with respect to the question of democratic representation. In principle, both respect for human rights and democratic representation must obtain in order to fulfill the requirements of international law. The main requirement of the first definitive article, however, is that *domestic freedom*, that is, human rights, be observed within each state. Normally respect for human rights entails, and results in, representative government of the kind found in liberal democracies. Thus, for example, we may conjecture that an originally unrepresentative monarchy that nevertheless respects human rights will naturally mature into a constitutional monarchy, much like those found in Western Europe today. Therefore, for the purpose of international law the central requirement is respect for human rights. Governments that respect those rights, even if they are not representative in form, are entitled to a *presumption* of agency. Individuals who are free are presumed to consent to their government, much as citizens in a liberal democracy are presumed to consent to the electoral system that brought their government to power, even if they did not vote for that government. It follows that governments that fully respect human rights are deemed to represent their citizens internationally.[55] I discuss this matter further in Chapter 2.

The justice of the domestic constitution, required by the first definitive article, is what makes a state internationally legitimate. This moral standing of the state is also illustrated by the second preliminary article, which provides that "no state having an independent existence, whether it be small or great, may be acquired by another state through inheritance, exchange, purchase, or gift." For Kant a state is not a possession, a piece of property, and since, like a tree, the state has its own roots, "to incorporate into another nation as a graft, denies its existence as a moral person, turns it into a thing, and thus contradicts the concept of the original contract, within which a people [*Volk*] has no rights."[56] At first blush, Kant seems to conceive of the state in a holistic way as a moral person, with rights and duties above and beyond the individuals who make up the state.[57] Such a view regards states as deserving respect because they are autonomous moral beings and enjoy sovereignty in their own right. I believe that this interpretation misunderstands Kant's argument. Kant maintains that a state is not a mere piece of territory but rather a civil society created by a social contract. Indeed, he emphasizes several times in the same paragraph the nature of the state as a society of men and how acquisition of the state violates that association.[58] The dichotomy established is between the state as a moral-political entity created by autonomous persons and the state as a mere piece of territory that can be bought and sold, not between rights of the state versus rights of individuals, where the community would hold a preeminent position at the expense of the individual. The state, for Kant, has moral standing *qua* the creature of a social contract.

Kant's international ethics follow from the categorical imperative. Just as individuals may not use human beings as mere means to an end, so foreigners (and especially governments) may not use the persons that form another state by disrupting their free civil association in order to pursue the foreigners' own ends such as national glory, exercise of political power, material enrichment, or the aggrandizement of territory. All communities freely constituted are deserving of respect because they come into existence as a result of the rational exercise of free choice by autonomous agents. Thus, a government is not deserving of respect per se but only insofar as it is the agent empowered by free individuals to make the law (legislative power), apply the law (executive power), and adjudicate claims among citizens (judicial power).[59] The state is the institution created to implement social cooperation grounded on the respect for liberty and must be respected (its territory and people should not be used at will) precisely for that reason. Failure to do so would be to deny the validity of the categorical imperative.

The Kantian thesis maintains that even the clearest instances of international behavior can be analyzed under its individualist premises. Take aggression: the reason to condemn aggression is that the aggressor is using citizens of the victim state as mere things; in Kant's words, "the subjects are thus used and consumed like things to be handled at will." Kant is not thinking about protecting governments, unless they are legitimately appointed by their people. In spite of his metaphorical description of the state as a moral person, Kant is no Hegel.

The emphasis on the individual rather than the state is also apparent in his commentary to the third definitive article, where Kant writes that "originally no one had a greater right to any region of the state than anyone else."[60] Such a statement is hardly compatible with the idea of the state as the primary moral unit. Kant never loses sight of the categorical imperative (second version): persons should always be treated as ends in themselves, not merely as means.[61] Here we have the sketch of a liberal theory of self-determination; one that relies not on mystical properties of the state or the prerogatives of enlightened rulers but, properly, on the rational pursuit of freedom by autonomous agents.[62]

But why must states guarantee internal freedom in order to be legitimate members of the international community? For if peace is the overall purpose of international law (as Kant himself seems to think) one could simply require that as long as international peace and stability are secured, it does not matter how states are internally organized, or at least not so much as to make it a requirement for an enduring system of international law. This argument has been repeatedly made; indeed, it is one of the tenets of the school of thought called Realism, and some commentators even embrace a statist (or Realist) reading of Kant.[63] All we can aspire to, it is argued, is balance of power, or peace. Except as an occasional political tool, concern for freedom or human rights does not belong in the realm of international relations because there is no centralized authority, no super-state, which alone can guarantee the rights of the subjects. There are of course several variations of this theme, and subtle Realists would not discard the importance of human rights and democracy altogether.[64] But characteristically, Realists regard such concern as subservient to the national interest.[65] They see national interest as an interest of the state that endures regardless of political and socioeconomic changes within the state and extends over and above individual interests and the internal organization of the state.[66] Conventional political theory, they argue, addresses mostly relations between government and governed (usually centering around individuals and their claims against the state) and is therefore incapable of accounting for the national interest as the key component of foreign policy. Only an international theory built around the state as the primary actor can do the job. The consequence of this approach is, of course, to overlook or downplay human rights in the study, formulation, and implementation of international law and policy.

In *Perpetual Peace* and elsewhere, Kant tried to show a necessary link between peace and freedom. He was challenging precisely the Realist assumption, just described, denying that link. The Kantian theory of international law provides two arguments for its central thesis (that liberal democracy and respect for human rights are the basic requirements of a just international order): one empirical, the other, normative. I will examine them in turn.

Freedom and Peace: The Empirical Argument

Kant's work on international law begins with the premise that peace is the fundamental purpose of international law. Under normal circumstances war is an intrinsic evil that must be avoided. Kant does not furnish separate arguments for this maxim,[67] and his views on war are indeed complicated.[68] Kant believed that an international order could be established only when governments freely abjured their right to make war on each other, despite his emphasis on the idea of coercion to sustain the law within a state.[69] From the peace premise he attempts to design international law so that peace will be forever secured.

Kant gives several reasons why peace is likely to be achieved when individual rights and political participation are secured. His central argument is that if the people are self-governed then citizens on both sides on any dispute will be very cautious in bringing about a war whose consequences they themselves must bear.[70] Those who will be eventually exposed to the horrors of the conflagration will decide whether or not to go to war. This central theme can be expanded in several directions.

In a liberal state the government is elected and rotates periodically. These two factors are a crucial restriction on the power of the government to initiate war, both for reasons of self-interest (incumbency) and outright political and logistical limitations. In contrast, it is relatively easy for a despot to start a war. As Kant points out, the tyrant does not suffer the consequences; his privileges and prerogatives remain intact.[71] Crucially, the despot does not benefit from objective advice and debate. He rules by force, which means that within his own *entourage* he is feared and vulnerable to adulation. Advisers are not likely to tell the tyrant the harsh truths but rather only what he wants to hear. More generally, because a despotic regime does not tolerate freedom of expression, public opinion has no significant impact on the government's decisions; consequently there is no opportunity for public debate on the moral and prudential reasons to make war. Psychologically, insulation of tyrannical rulers from criticism and debate fuels in them a sense of megalomania. Tyrants acquire a feeling of invincibility. They become accustomed to getting away with murder (literally) internally; and they no doubt reach a point of self-delusion where they become convinced that they can get away with external aggression as well.[72]

From an institutional standpoint, the separation of powers inherent in a liberal democracy creates a system of mutual checks that complicates and encumbers governmental decisions about war.[73] No all-powerful sovereign exists who can by himself initiate hostilities. For Kant the notion of autonomy inherent in the republican form of government implies that a multiplicity of decision-makers will participate in decision to make war. The lawmaker does not administer the law. Thus, liberal constitutions attempt to impose institutional limits on power, including foreign relations power, through the checks and balances inherent in the separation of powers and through freedom of speech—notably freedom of the press.

Another reason for the increased likelihood of enduring peace among free republics is that in a liberal democracy citizens will be educated in the principles of right and therefore war will appear to the citizens as the evil that every rational person knows it is, at least when war is not waged for liberal causes.[74] Kant had a rich and exciting theory of cosmopolitan education, the main theme of which is that we must cultivate universal virtues that will prevail over the bellicose instincts that we also have.[75] Unlike the authors of some of the modern peace education projects,[76] Kant saw clearly that peace education aimed only at inculcating fear of war (and of nuclear weapons, etc.) was insufficient. Fear alone is demoralizing and may cause surrender to a tyrant, not action on behalf of a morally good and peaceful world.[77] A cosmopolitan education should include, among many other things, education on the principles that underlie a just constitution from a cosmopolitan perspective, that is, on the value of human rights generally, not only as they relate to *our* constitution.[78] Because this kind of moral education empha- sizes rationality as a universal trait of persons, it will induce citizens in a liberal democracy to see individuals in other nations as deserving of equal respect and thus treat them as ends in themselves, not as mere objects for the satisfaction of local preferences.

The final reason why liberal states are likely to be peaceful is that liberal democracies foster free trade and a generous system of freedom of international movement of persons that Kant calls the Cosmopolitan Law.[79] Kant remarks that by observing a rule of hospitality for foreigners facilitating commerce with indigenous peoples "distant parts of the world can establish with one another peaceful relations that will eventually become matters of public law, and the human race can gradually be brought closer and closer to a cosmopolitan institution."[80] Kant reaffirms this idea by observing that peoples' mutual interest unite them against violence and war, for "the spirit of trade cannot coexist with war."[81] He was cognizant that "peace to do business"[82] is a nonmoral reason to want peace but that such economic incentives provide an additional argument for maintaining international peace. Free trade and freedom of movement are sufficiently linked to the principles of a liberal constitution to make leaders in liberal democracies much more prone to weigh economic costs before initiating a war.[83] There is no question that free trade is a strong, if not dispositive, influence over external behavior. Free trade inclines diplomacy toward peace because international business transactions require stability and predictability to be successful. Kant's views have been confirmed by the success of the European Union and even by the global system of international trade regulated by GATT and similar institutions. It is not by coincidence that the European Union requires democracy as a condition of membership, as does the more recent Mercosur, the South American free market agreement.[84]

Research by Michael Doyle and R.J. Rummel bolsters Kant's argument for the causal link between domestic freedom and peace.[85] These modern versions of Kant's argument have shown that Kant's prediction of a gradual expansion of the liberal alliance has been confirmed by events of the last 200 years, notably the last 45 years. These authors' research has conclusively demonstrated, in my view, that Kant was essentially right. Events since the publication of these articles provide splendid supplementary confirmation of the Kantian thesis.[86]

Liberal states show a definite tendency to maintain peace among themselves, while nonliberal states are generally prone to war. The historical data since 1795 shows that even though liberal states have become involved in numerous wars with nonliberal states, liberal states have yet to engage in war with one another.[87] Doyle concedes that liberal states have behaved aggressively toward nonliberal states, but he attributes this fact precisely to the difference in regimes.[88] Conversely nonliberal states have behaved aggressively among themselves. Therefore, only a community of liberal states has a chance of securing peace, as Kant thought. Should people ever fulfill the hope of creating such a liberal international community, the likelihood of war would be greatly reduced.

Alternative hypotheses have not been forthcoming to explain the liberal peace. I have not seen serious challenge to the evidence provided by Doyle and Rummel. Doyle, for example, shows that constitutionally secure liberal states have never engaged in war with one another.[89] Writers who take issue with this view contest only the thesis (held by Rummel but not by Doyle) that liberal democracies are *generally* peace-prone, regardless of the nature of the other regimes.[90] But everyone concurs in the factual assertion that war rarely, if ever, occurs among democratic states.[91] To be sure, there are some difficult cases.[92] Yet even if those cases are treated as genuine instances of war between liberal states, the correlation is still so strong that it cries for an explanation. The argument is not that war between liberal states is impossible but that it is highly unlikely. Kant warns that there will be regressive wars and setbacks in the establishment of the liberal alliance but that the alliance will expand and solidify with time.[93]

Some commentators have challenged the plausibility of the causal connection between freedom and war. This view treats the correlation as spurious, either the result of pure coincidence or, more likely, of an underlying common factor unrelated to the nature of the domestic regimes. Diana Meyers has taken such a position: while she agrees that liberal states by and large have maintained peaceful relations, she raises questions about the explanation offered by Kant and Doyle.[94] Meyers offers two considerations to deny the premise that liberal democracies provide mechanisms through which aggregated self-interest is translated into national policy.[95] First, state bureaucracies often distort public opinion, and thus "liberal democracy does not in any straightforward way place state action under the control of majority interests."[96] The second related objection is that people are deceived about their self-interest, therefore expressed preferences may militate for or against peace.[97] Public opinion in a liberal democracy (the argument goes) may also be bellicose. Neither a free press nor a constitutional system with checks and balances has prevented leaders of liberal democracies to wage aggressive wars for spurious liberal causes.[98]

This reply to Kant and Doyle is unconvincing. The general skeptical position about liberal democracies (that they do not provide a true outlet to majority opinions and preferences) proves too much: that there is no real difference, in any respect (not just in the formulation of foreign policy or the initiation of wars) between liberal democracies and despotisms. While threats to popular participation posed by bureaucracies should be a matter of concern, that does not equate all political systems in terms of the degree to which popular will is expressed. Liberal democracies provide improved mechanisms for political participation (to put it mildly) than do tyrannies. While there are surely hard cases, free political systems and despotic ones can be distinguished. We draw the distinction precisely in terms of how human rights are protected, how the citizen's interests are served, and the degree of their participation in the political process.

More importantly, this objection misses Kant's central point: peace is likely to be maintained only among liberal societies, and consequently the likelihood of world peace will increase as the liberal alliance expands. All the examples offered of liberal aggression involve confrontations against nonliberal states. The point of the Kantian theory, however, is that the difference in regimes is the cause of instability. Liberal states do engage in aggressive behavior against nonliberal states, but this fact cannot support the claim that official duplicity could serve just as well to rationalize an attack on a bothersome liberal state.[99]

The argument seems to be that the psychology of power is the same regardless of political systems and, therefore, both tyrannical and democratic rulers are equally prone to deceiving the people and waging war for dishonorable reasons such as the ruler's self-aggrandizement. But the Kantian hypothesis is precisely that in a liberal democracy there are intrinsic limitations on the ability and discretion of governments to deceive and manipulate. The psychology of power may be the same across political systems, but there is little question that in a liberal society institutional constraints are more likely to prevent bad governments from doing too much damage, both at home and abroad. So it is not enough to say that democratic governments are also capable of deceit and manipulation: the very point of democratic institutions is to keep political power (with all its corrupting potential) under check.[100]

Other commentators accept the evidence but attempt to explain the liberal peace by different hypotheses. The Realist school of thought in international relations has long maintained that the causes of war have to do with prudential reasons that affect all state actors equally in the international arena. Those reasons are not related to the difference in regimes. Doyle summarizes the Realist theory of war:

> Specific wars . . . arise from fear as a state seeking to avoid a surprise attack decides to attack first; from competitive emulation as states lacking an imposed international hierarchy of prestige struggle to establish their place; and from straightforward conflicts of interest that escalate into war because there is no global sovereign to prevent states from adopting that ultimate form of conflict resolution.[101]

Thus, the Realist explains peace through purely prudential reasons that motivate state decision-makers. Realists downplay the importance of the difference in domestic regimes and emphasize features of states and governments that derive from the condition of international anarchy.[102]

Realists have failed to explain the undeniable peace that has reigned among liberal states for so long. The suggestion that states with similar regimes (liberal or not) have peaceful relations conflicts with the evidence regarding relations among feudal, communist, and fascist societies.[103] To say that the liberal peace only reflects the absence of deep conflicts of interest among liberal states simply begs the question of why liberal states have fewer or less fundamental conflicts of interest with other liberal states than liberal states have with nonliberal, or nonliberal states among themselves.[104]

But let us concede, *gratia argumentandi*, that the real reason for peace is the similarity in regimes, so that a community of despotic states could equally maintain peace. In that case, since peace is our ultimate goal and since uniformity of regimes is the only guarantee for peace, we have a choice of designing international law either requiring respect for human rights or requiring despotism. And on any defensible theory of morality, if that is our choice, we would prefer an international legal system that required states to secure human rights and political representation and thus be uniform on the side of liberty.

There is a strong factual correlation between internal freedom and external peaceful behavior toward similarly free societies; the causal dynamics that underlie the correlation seem very plausible; and those who disagree with this explanation have failed to provide convincing alternative explanatory hypotheses. The conjecture that internal freedom is causally related to peaceful international behavior is as safe a generalization as one can make in the realm of political science. Kant's empirical argument therefore shows that, if only for instrumental reasons (the desire to secure peace), international law must require full respect for human rights.

Freedom and Peace: The Normative Argument

The second Kantian argument for including a requirement of respect for human rights and democracy as a foundational principle of international law is even more straightforward: governments should be required by international law to observe human rights because that is the right thing. Kant commentators have overlooked the fact that Kant expressly offers this argument along with the empirical one. In *Perpetual Peace*, Kant defends the universal requirement of human rights and democracy as grounded in "the purity of its origin, *a purity whose source is the pure concept of right*."[105] The empirical argument is then offered in addition to the normative one. Writers who felt uncomfortable with Kant's first definitive article have attacked the plausibility of the empirical argument[106] without realizing that it was just a reason given to reinforce the main reason, which alone suffices: that a global requirement of a republican constitution logically follows from the categorical imperative.[107] Thus, Kant's complete argument for democracy and human rights as a requirement of international law is far stronger than his critics thought. The normative argument is addressed to those who rank justice over peace; the empirical argument, to those who rank peace over justice.

Protecting human rights is the reason why governments exist in the first place,[108] and because the reasons that support internal freedom are universal (they derive from the categorical imperative) they should be engrafted in the law of nations which also purports to be universal. Because Kantianism relies on universal traits of persons (their rationality), it is incompatible with relativism. It is not possible to defend at the same time Kant's theory of human nature and morality, and the view that liberal democracy and respect for persons is good only for certain societies. The categorical imperative is universal and holds for every civil society regardless of history and culture. Liberal democracies, ranging from laissez-faire states to welfare states, are the only ones that secure individual freedom, thereby allowing human beings to develop their potential fully. Therefore, the only way in which international law can be made fully compatible with the freedom of individuals to pursue and act upon rational plans of life is if it contains a strong obligation for governments to respect human rights. International law must be congruent with individual autonomy, the trait, for Kant, that sets human beings apart from other species.

Kant insists that pure ethics, or pure duty, be separated from historical and cultural contingencies. The whole enterprise of moral philosophy, for Kant, is based on that part of practical knowledge that is pure (the same word he uses in the quoted sentence in *Perpetual Peace*), perceived by human beings a priori, independently from their experiences and traditions.[109] The nonrelative character of Kantian philosophy is easy to see in the realm of *individual* or personal morality. Indeed, the examples that Kant gives are of this type.[110] Yet there is every reason to extend Kant's moral universalism to *political* morality as well. The contingent division of the world into discrete nation-states does not turn political freedom (in the sense discussed above) from an ethical imperative into a mere accident of history. Just as rational, albeit fallible, beings are capable of selecting the morally correct action out of a pure sense of duty, so are the same rational beings creating the law of nations capable of selecting the morally correct form of political organization.

International law is concerned, at least in part, with incorporating those rules and principles that are deemed just on a global scale. First among them is the principle of a republican constitution proposed by Kant. This is not generated by a desire to impose an idiosyncratic system of values to groups in other parts of the globe who have different traditions. The republican constitution (the liberal-democratic society), far from being idiosyncratic, is *objectively* right. It is not tied to empirical circumstance or historical accident. The republican constitution derives from the categorical imperative, from the exercise of rational faculties by autonomous agents capable of articulating the pure concept of right, as Kant expressly says in *Perpetual Peace* on this very issue. To be consistent with justice, therefore, international law must include the requirement that states respect human rights. An international legal system that *authorizes* individuals to exercise despotic political power (as classic international law does) is morally deficient in a fundamental way. It loses sight of ethics as concerned with Kant's "kingdom of ends," where the basic commonality of the human race, regardless of national borders, is defined by this aptitude to become members of the same moral

community where individuals are always treated with dignity and respect.[111] Such
is the notion that the international law of human rights attempts to vindicate.[112] In
the Kantian vision, human rights are not mere privileges graciously granted by
individuals in power (for example, by agreeing to international human rights
convention). They are constitutive of the international definition of a legitimate
nation-state.

The Problem of Authority and Enforcement

Kant's "Second Definitive Article" provides that international law must be
based on a federation of free states. Kant refers first to international law. We have
seen already how important the idea of law is for Kant. Domestically, the just civic
constitution results, as in Locke, from citizens surrendering their unlimited freedom
in the state of nature in order to create the rule of law, the *Rechtstaat*, which alone
can rationally secure individual freedom. The moral and civilized nature in us thus
overcomes our evil instincts of lawlessness and destruction. We accept coercion
and the idea of law and order to secure freedom for all.[113] Only then can we pursue
the higher forms of life that define our essential humanity.

The human propensity to master our evil nature with reason[114] and reliance on
law holds internationally as well. Governments, even in times of Kant's international state of nature, want to see their actions, no matter how self-interested and
destructive, as legally justified. Far from reaching a skeptical conclusion from this
crude reality of world politics, Kant saw this reliance on legal discourse as
evidence of rationality: "The homage that every nation pays (at least in words) to
the concept of [law] proves . . . that there is in man a still greater, though presently
dormant moral aptitude to master the evil principle in himself (a principle he cannot
deny) and to hope that others will also overcome it."[115]

Therefore, according to Kant, the international order logically ought to mirror
the domestic order; just as individuals would choose to create a civic constitution
to solve the problems posed by the ruthless state of nature, so too would the same
individuals, organized in nation-states, agree upon a system of international law to
solve the problems posed by the international state of nature.

The analogy to domestic ordering raises the question of whether a successful
system of international law must also be centralized into a super-state with a world
government. This question is, of course, an old acquaintance of international
lawyers: the view that there cannot be international law without an international
sovereign has long since been discredited in international legal circles.[116] In
addition, the controversy over whether international law is "really" law seems to
be primarily semantic.[117] Yet the objection is still worth examining, for it could
well be that critical reflection will lead us to reconsider world government as a
better alternative.[118]

In order to fully understand Kant's proposed solution to this dilemma, one must
remember that Kant was writing at a time when war was the main method of
settling international disputes and when the right of princes to make war was not

seriously in dispute.[119] Politicians, scholars, and other educated persons living in that climate of international lawlessness were his audience. Therefore, the idea of an international legal system that would outlaw war was revolutionary. Of course, today the presumption is against the right to make war, not in favor of it, and so many of Kant's arguments and assumptions might seem to us outmoded or taken for granted.

Both Hobbes and Rousseau faced the problem of authority before Kant. Hobbes, of course, thought that international relations were the state of nature *par excellence*.[120] Some commentators of Kant's work followed his argument to its seemingly logical conclusion: they read "federation" in the modern sense, as meaning a federated republic with a unified sovereign.[121] These commentators argued that just as a constitutional government is the answer to the problems of social cooperation, freedom, and order within civil society, so too world government should be the answer to similar problems internationally. Others believed that world government is what Kant should have argued for and that anything less is either useless, because it does not solve the problem of the international state of nature, or logically inconsistent with Kant's own arguments in *Perpetual Peace* and elsewhere.[122]

Most modern commentators, however, agree that Kant did not support world government.[123] Not only does Kant expressly disavow the creation of a centralized world government,[124] but the Third Definitive Article, establishing the Cosmopolitan Law, or the rules of free trade and universal hospitality, is inexplicable outside the context of a world of independent nation-states.[125] The Kantian answer to this problem is to propose instead an alliance of separate states that respect their citizens and one another and are thus in the best position to engage in beneficial cooperation. The international distribution of authority proposed by Kant is thus quite close to the modern international legal system: states have rights and duties under international law because they represent autonomous moral beings. However, there is no world sovereign to enforce those norms; enforcement is decentralized. Kant was ahead of modern international law in requiring that states observe human rights as a precondition for joining the alliance.

Quite apart from textual evidence, and notwithstanding the serious problem of the lack of centralized enforcement, there are good reasons to prefer an organization of separate states subject to international law to a centralized world government. Kant defended separate states not only because he thought that in this way his proposal would be more realistic but because he thought that such a system was morally justified.[126]

First, he decided that world government presents too great a threat to individual freedom. Liberty is better secured when political power is relatively diluted. Kant wrote:

> [A world consisting of separate nations] is rationally preferable to [its] being overrun by a superior power that melds them into a universal monarchy. For laws

invariably lose their impact with the expansion of their domain of governance, and after it has uprooted the soul of good a soulless despotism finally degenerates into anarchy.[127]

Kant was aware that while world government may be an attractive idea in theory, it carries the danger of degenerating first into a world tyranny and ultimately back into international anarchy.[128] Under a centralized world government, resisting the tyranny of a corrupt leadership would present an overwhelming logistical problem for individuals struggling to reestablish human rights and representative democracy. Freedom fighters would not have safe refuge or the fiscal and political support of independent representative governments. And neither would free states exist to moderate the excesses of despots through diplomacy and coercive intervention when appropriate.[129]

Second, a system of separate states allows individuals to associate with those that share their same culture, customs, history, and language. Such a system is more likely to respect the individuals' community interests and contribute to the affirmation of their self-respect that ultimately leads to the flourishing of individual autonomy. From a practical standpoint, a decentralized system minimizes conflicts originating as a result of cultural differences.

Kant supports his view with a curious argument, mixing a Hobbesian perspective with a sort of evolutionary determinism.[130] He argues that nature has used war as an instrument to force people to live in all sections of the globe and eventually to reach the situation of separate nations in a state of (potential) war. In contrast, nature has used the same features that divide peoples—differences in language and religion—to create an "equilibrium of the liveliest competing powers" that alone can control the danger of the deceptive peace that despotism brings—as he writes, "in the graveyard of freedom."[131] Despite Kant's dubious deterministic parlance,[132] the argument is based on Kant's original theory of the "asocial sociability" of human beings.[133]

In the international arena, the Kantian analysis shows how decentralized enforcement can take the place of a world police force and underscores the subtlety of international mechanisms to secure compliance.[134] Of course, the idea that communities with a strong sense of cultural identity should be allowed to be autonomous is a relative assessment. It springs from the empirical conjecture that if subject to world government, different groups and minorities would tend to see their claims for identity ignored by a huge bureaucracy, whereas local government might appear to be more responsive to such claims. Yet by no means must all cultures live under separate governments; there are a number of successful examples of multicultural states. Furthermore, cultural differences should not preclude nations from voluntarily merging into larger political units, such as the European Union. Finally, principles of respect for individual human rights trump the right to self-determination.[135]

Kant argues for the maintenance of separate nation-states as a balance between the dangers to freedom posed by centralized world government and the state of nature.[136] An alliance of liberal democracies subject to international law will provide the exact point of equilibrium for world order. Compliance will hopefully be achieved gradually by operation of subtle decentralized systemic mechanisms.[137]

If a morally justified international law is the result of such a liberal alliance, what is the legal status of those states that are not liberal democracies? First, tyrannical governments are outlaws. However, they are not outside the law of nations. Like domestic criminals, they are still bound by elementary principles, such as the rules that prohibit crimes of aggression and war crimes. While outlaw governments do not benefit from the rights conferred by membership in the alliance, they retain some rights. For example, if they are accused of human rights violations or war crimes, they have a right to be tried by an independent and impartial tribunal in accordance with well-established international rules.[138]

Second, a liberal theory of international law seeks to protect individuals. Therefore, actions, even by legitimate governments, that violate the rights of individuals in tyrannical states are prohibited. Citizens in undemocratic states lack representation, but they have not lost their rights. It follows that agreements creating obligations that benefit individuals should be respected. Such agreements include conventions inspired by considerations of humanity and, in some cases, treaties that establish boundaries. However, agreements that dictators enter into to benefit themselves are binding neither upon members of the alliance nor upon the citizens of the tyrannical state. Because dictators do not represent their people, they cannot create obligations for their subjects. Such agreements are sometimes respected, not because of the traditional principle *pacta sunt servanda* but rather for prudential reasons or because they protect oppressed individuals.

Similarly, a liberal theory of international law must account for the role of force and war. Force may be used in defense of persons and, derivatively, in defense of representative governments and states.[139] Because members of the liberal alliance are in compliance with the First Definitive Article, force will never need to be used to exact compliance with their international obligations. However, force will sometimes have to be used against nonliberal regimes as a last resort in self-defense or in defense of human rights. Liberal democracies must seek peace and use all possible alternatives to preserve it. In extreme circumstances, however, violence may be the only means to uphold the law and to defend the liberal alliance against outlaw dictators that remain nonmembers. Such, I believe, is the proper place of war in the Kantian theory.

However, Kant seems to disagree. In his commentary to the Sixth Preliminary Article, Kant dismisses the idea that there could be a just war. War, Kant writes, is "a sad necessity in the state of nature [where] the outcome of the conflict (as if . . . it were the so-called 'judgment of God') determines the side on which justice lies."[140] Kant was troubled by the impossibility of rationally making a judgment of right prior to the conflict itself because in international relations there is "no tribunal empowered to make judgments supported by the power of law."[141] Kant returns to the theme of justice as identified with law and legal adjudication. Because in the international arena there can be no courts backed by force, there can be no rational decision about the justice of a particular war.[142]

How can we reconcile the extreme pacifism voiced in these passages with Kant's acceptance of a decentralized law of nations and with the analysis of the causes of war as intimately related to the difference in regimes? As to the first point, Kant's argument for rejecting the possibility of a just war proves too much. For if the absence of international courts with compulsory jurisdiction means that no war can ever be just, then there can be no law of nations at all. There would be no courts to render enforceable judgments about *any* disputes among nations. There seems to be an inconsistency here. We saw that in the addendum entitled "On the Guarantee for Perpetual Peace" Kant accepted a definition of international law that did not require a sovereign power, courts, legislators, or police—in short, world government.[143] Perhaps Kant fell prey to his obsession with the definition of law in *civil society*, which indeed requires courts rendering decisions backed by the power of the state. In his discussion of international authority, in contrast, Kant addressed the difficulty and dangers of creating world government by accepting the notion of decentralized enforcement. Yet decentralized enforcement means that, while war is absolutely banned within the alliance, force will sometimes need to be used by individual states or members of the alliance acting in concert against enemies of the alliance. Therefore, a war of self-defense by a democratic government and its allies against a despotic aggressor is a just war.[144]

The central difficulty with Kant's rejection of just war is the status of tyrannical regimes that have not yet joined the alliance. If the analysis in this chapter is correct, the difference in domestic regimes will be a permanent threat to peace. Perhaps one could devise principles of political prudence designed to moderate the historical intolerance of liberal governments toward despots,[145] but there are at least two thorny problems with Kant's view. The first, already mentioned, concerns the reaction of liberal democracies against aggressive despots. There is no doubt that democratic governments should retain their right of self-defense,[146] which in Kantian terms is nothing more than the defense of persons by their government against foreign attack.[147] Second, similar perplexities arise in the case of intervention to stop serious violations of human rights in other states. Kant's Fifth Preliminary Article provides that "no nation shall forcibly interfere with the constitution and government of another."[148] In a very succinct commentary, Kant justifies this precept by saying that "generally, the bad example that one free person furnishes for another . . . does not injure the latter."[149] For example, a tyrant who tortures his citizens does not injure citizens in neighboring nations.

Leaving aside for the moment the inconsistency of this view with the universalist thrust of Kant's thesis, there remains the question whether such an absolute rule of nonintervention can be reconciled with Kant's First Definitive Article, the requirement that states be liberal democracies. A possible answer would be that nations join the alliance voluntarily, not as a result of intervention, however benign, by liberal members of the alliance.[150] Voluntary adherence to the alliance means allowing citizens in nonliberal states to resolve their differences among themselves, through their own efforts. In this way, citizens of a nonliberal state could eventually upgrade their society, as it were, so it could become a liberal democracy and qualify as a member. Only through the unfolding of such a process of self-determination will a decision to join the liberal alliance be voluntary; members of the alliance should patiently wait until that occurs spontaneously and not force the process by intervening.

This reading of Kant is certainly possible. A reading more consistent with the rest of Kant's views, however, is that the nonintervention principle is dependent upon compliance with the First Definitive Article. Internal legitimacy is what gives states the shield of sovereignty against foreign intervention. Since morally autonomous citizens hold rights to liberty, the states and governments that democratically represent them have a right to be politically independent and should be shielded by international law from foreign intervention.[151] The liberal version of nonintervention and self-determination thus emphasizes respect for human rights and true representation. Political legitimacy is thus seen as the proper foundation of state sovereignty.[152] The question of internal legitimacy must be resolved prior to the question of nonintervention.[153] Noninterventionism, therefore, follows from whatever theory of internal legitimacy one adopts. If the only just political arrangement is the republican constitution, state sovereignty reacquires its shielding power only in states that have adopted and implemented such a constitution. Sovereignty is to be respected only when it is justly exercised.[154] This suggests that Kant's Fifth Preliminary Article (the prohibition of forcible intervention) might be misplaced. If the protection against intervention is a consequence of domestic legitimacy, then nonintervention holds *only* among liberal states, and therefore the nonintervention principle should be seen as a definitive precept that governs the liberal alliance, not as a step that must be taken before the alliance is formed.

It follows from these considerations that citizens in a liberal democracy should be free to argue that, in some admittedly rare cases, the only morally acceptable alternative is to intervene to help the victims of serious human rights deprivations.[155] However, even if Kant is correct on the issue of humanitarian intervention, his rejection of the possibility of just wars is not consistent with the normative individualism underlying the rest of his theory of international law.[156] While aggression by members against other members of the alliance will be banned forever, in some cases democratic nations must resort to self-help to enforce their rights against outsiders.[157] At the very least, Kant's view does not account for the case of aggression by despots against members of the alliance. More generally, Kant's reason for rejecting just wars—that there are no courts to determine the justice of the cause—is unconvincing. Kant himself advocates an international law among separate nations that entails a decentralized system of authority. Judgments on the legality of wars are no different from judgments of legality generally, so if there are no courts available for the former, there are no courts available for the latter. Yet Kant's whole purpose is precisely to show that a law of nations, and judgments of legality in conformity with it, are possible notwithstanding such a decentralization of power.

A Note on the Organization of Perpetual Peace

The essay *Perpetual Peace* was published in 1795 and was one of Immanuel Kant's last philosophical works.[158] It is a relatively short essay that was meant for popular reading.[159] Kant was not very good at writing for the general public, however, and the essay suffers as a consequence: the arguments are at times too concise, and the writing often is obscure. Nonetheless, Kant's genius pervades the essay.[160] The essay had immediate success, and Kant's authority was frequently invoked throughout the nineteenth and twentieth centuries by advocates of pacifism and internationalism.[161] While there are many interpretations of *Perpetual Peace*, almost all commentators agree that in this short essay Kant made a subtle, rich, and lasting contribution both to the theory of international law and to the causes of justice and peace. The essay is undergoing an unexpected revival, having been invoked by Mikhail Gorbachev in his speech accepting the Nobel Peace Prize.[162]

Perpetual Peace contains six Preliminary Articles, three Definitive Articles, and two long Addenda, the most important of which is "On the Guarantee of Perpetual Peace." The text of the articles with their headings is as follows:[163]

First Section Which Contains the Preliminary
Articles for Perpetual Peace Among Nations
1. No treaty of peace that tacitly reserves issues for a future war shall be held valid.
2. No independent nation, be it large or small, may be acquired by another nation by inheritance, exchange, purchase, or gift.
3. Standing armies shall be gradually abolished.
4. No national debt shall be contracted in connection with the foreign affairs of the nation.
5. No nation shall forcibly interfere with the constitution and government of another.
6. No nation at war with another shall permit such acts of war as must make mutual trust possible during such future time of peace: Such acts include the use of *Assassins (percussores), Poisoners (venefici), breach of surrender, instigation of treason (perduellio)* in the other opposing nation, etc.

Second Section Which Contains the Definitive
Articles for Perpetual Peace Among Nations
1. The civil constitution of every nation should be republican.
2. International law[164] shall be based on a federation of free states.

3. The Cosmopolitan Law shall be limited to conditions of universal *hospitality*.

The structural organization of *Perpetual Peace* raises two questions, the answer to which may provide insight into Kant's intent: one, why is the essay put in the form of articles like a treaty; and two, what meaning, if any, should we give to the categories of "preliminary" and "definitive" articles? The selection of the articles format might indicate that Kant intended to offer a programmatic formula for peace rather than a philosophical analysis of the nature of international law and relations. Indeed, he wanted politicians to follow his advice—he specifically (and not without irony) enjoins governments to take advice from the philosophers.[165] Thus, the articles format, at least in part, suggests that Kant wanted to draft a model treaty of some sort,[166] with specific provisions to be honored by all signatories. However, he only partially succeeded: *Perpetual Peace*, as written, seems to suffer from a fundamental methodological ambiguity. While the essay can be viewed as an unattainable moral ideal to which states ought to aspire in their international relations,[167] *Perpetual Peace* is better viewed as an attempt to explicate international moral principles—the principles of right that should underlie the relations among nations. Kant was a philosopher, not a mere pamphleteer.[168] There is a call for political action, to be sure: it is the one that flows naturally from his normative theory of international law. Thus, the essay is both conceptual and normative; it attempts to draw applied international law principles from an understanding of the underlying philosophical nature of international relations.

The second organizational question is the meaning of the categories "preliminary" and "definitive." Some commentators have defined the preliminary articles as those that, if honestly adhered to, might well have maintained the peace among any eighteenth century powers that agreed to them, or as a statement of international law as it ought to be; whereas the definitive articles are the main political presuppositions and safeguards without which no eighteenth century state could seriously be expected to adhere to the earlier articles.[169] For these writers, the preliminary articles are part of the solution, not a statement of the preliminary progress that nations must make before beginning the work for establishing an enduring peace.[170]

The reader may think that this debate is highly formalistic, exegetic, and overly textual. Not so: one's interpretation of the purpose of structuring the essay in preliminary and definitive articles conditions one's interpretation of the work as a whole. Commentators in the Realist tradition, who emphasize the primacy of the state as the international actor, exalt the preliminary articles.[171] Indeed, the key progovernment rule, nonintervention, is embodied in one of the preliminary articles. In addition, Kant's commentary ostensibly relies on the analogy of the state as a moral person, which is a favorite device of Realists. In contrast, each of the three definitive articles enshrines in different ways the primacy of individual freedom and the logically consistent unity of purpose of international and domestic law.

The Realist interpretation seems dubious. According to Kant no perpetual peace can be achieved without states being internally free and without such states agreeing on an alliance or federation; therefore, it does not seem that adherence to the preliminary articles alone would have sufficed to maintain peace even among the eighteenth century European powers. The better interpretation of the preliminary articles is that they are those urgent agreements that should enter into force if the state of nature among states is to end; they are the most pressing stages to reach if we want subsequently to proceed with the lasting solution.[172]

In contrast, the substantive solutions, the institutional features of an effective and just international organization, are contained in the definitive articles. When Kant wrote "definitive" he meant what the word implies: a structure providing the final and conclusive solution to the problem of international relations. The preliminary articles do not even provide for the peace desired, which is included in the Second Definitive Article. Moreover, the definitive articles, which (as conceded by one of the above mentioned commentators) contain Kant's most original political thinking,[173] are preceded by a very important paragraph. There Kant wrote:

> The state of peace among men living in close proximity is not the natural state (status naturalis); instead, the natural state is a one of war, which does not just consist in open hostilities, but also in the constant and enduring threat of them. The state of peace must therefore be *established*, for the suspension of hostilities does not provide the security of peace, and unless this security is pledged by one neighbor to another (which can happen only in a state of *lawfulness*), the latter, from whom such security has been requested, can treat the former as an enemy.[174]

The most natural interpretation, then, is that the definitive articles are the foundation of perpetual peace; they contain the institutional arrangements that directly reflect the precepts of international justice; they are the ones that are designed to eliminate war from the face of the earth for all time.[175]

The preliminary articles are the first steps that governments must take to end international lawlessness, those points that must be agreed upon first by them in order subsequently to agree upon the definitive principles of international law. Two important preliminary articles are the nonintervention principle and the principle that a state may not be acquired by conquest, inheritance, or other means. Here Kant is trying to lay down the preliminary conditions conducive to the definitive peace. They are the norms that are designed to govern the intermediate status of international relations, after the lawless state of nature is ended but before the definitive law of nations is established.[176] The preliminary articles will not suffice to guarantee peace unless the definitive articles are agreed upon. Yet the important point to remember is that they are meant to be permanent; they are preliminary but not provisional. Standing armies must disappear; peace treaties should not contain reservations for future wars; states should not intervene in other states; states should not be acquired by conquest; abject means of conducting war should be permanently prohibited. These provisional rules will acquire their full effectiveness and meaning once all states turn into liberal democracies.

Conclusion and Suggestions for Reform

The Kantian theory is not limited to a rarified philosophical domain. The theory yields practical solutions in many fields. First, the theory suggests the creation of compulsory judicial mechanisms to settle controversies arising from the three Definitive Articles: an International Court of Human Rights, the International Court of Justice, and an International Court of Trade (roughly corresponding to Kant's three Definitive Articles). Second, the Kantian theory also necessitates amendment of the conditions of admission and permanence in the United Nations. Articles 4 and 6 of the Charter of the United Nations should be amended to include the requirement that only democratic governments that respect human rights should be allowed to represent members and that only democratic states will be accepted as new members.[177] Third, the law of treaties must undergo important changes. Representatives of dictators must be disenfranchised for the purposes of expressing the state's consent to be bound by the treaty.[178] Fourth, the law of diplomatic relations should be amended to deny diplomatic status to representatives of illegitimate governments.[179] Finally, the law of recognition should prohibit recognition of illegitimate governments, along the lines suggested by Woodrow Wilson in the beginning of this century[180] and by the International Court of Justice for South Africa in the *Namibia* opinion.[181] These and other reforms will have to be worked out in detail, and many variations consistent with the Kantian theory are possible.

One of the most remarkable developments since the end of World War II has been the exponential growth of individual liberty—the impressive expansion of human rights and democracy to societies that had been excluded from the benefits of freedom. This extraordinary and, for many, unexpected development disproves the claim that human rights and democracy are just the luxury of industrial societies and lends credence to the assumption that every rational person, regardless of historical or cultural circumstance, is apt to value and pursue freedom both as an intrinsic good and as the necessary means to formulate and act upon rational plans of life.

This enlightened moral and political global reality is ill-served by the traditional model of international law. The model promotes states and not individuals, governments and not persons, order and not rights, compliance and not justice. It insists that rulers be permitted to exercise whatever amount of coercion is necessary to politically control their subjects. Yet the reasons to prefer a world of free nations are strong enough to place the burden of proof on international lawyers who cling to the traditional statist paradigm that privileges power-holders and ignores people.

Perhaps there is no necessary link between the political triumph of human rights and democracy and the theoretical foundations of international law and politics. Perhaps all we can say is that the wind is blowing now in the directions of individual freedom and that the historical cycle will before long see nations return to despotism and gross injustice. It is indeed possible that the optimism caused by the triumph of human rights is hasty and that the celebration is therefore premature.[182] Yet if the tide is going to turn against individual freedom, it will be the product of human design, not of the forces of nature pushing us around. It follows that we have to construct and defend our world institutions if we want them to last.

International law can make an important contribution in this respect. We must rethink and reconstruct international law in a way that incorporates and recognizes that the ultimate aim of international institutions is to foster the development of each individual's full potential as an autonomous human being, to protect freedom. This is so even if pessimist forecasters are right that we should expect significant setbacks to freedom in the years to come. Moreover, international law does not merely describe international behavior, so that our conceptual model would be more or less statist depending on the progress or restriction of human rights around the world. Rather, international law purports to set standards of international behavior. Judgments of legality are evaluations of diplomatic history according to that standard. It is insufficient to verify that many governments ignore the precepts of justice and conclude that justice should be discarded. The better view includes moral analysis as an integral part of international law. The alternative positivist paradigm, by clinging to the deceptively simple notion of the unrestrained practice of states as the touchstone for legitimacy, ends up surrendering to tyranny and aggression, the evils that international law was intended to control in the first place.

With any luck, the community of free nations envisioned by Kant will expand gradually and maintain itself, as it has done for the past 200 years, and the aim of perpetual peace will be achieved the moment when the liberal alliance comprises every civil society. It is never too late to replace the grim view of a world order in which naked political power is the standard of legitimacy with Kant's inspired cosmopolitan vision of moral progress in which tribute is paid to the definitive traits of humanity—freedom and reason.

In the following chapters I discuss and reject two traditional assumptions of international law: statism (Chapter 2) and positivism (Chapter 3). I then turn to specific problems faced by the Kantian thesis: modern social contract theory (Chapter 4); self-determination (Chapter 5); and feminism (Chapter 6).

Notes

1. Immanuel Kant's most important work on international relations is "To Perpetual Peace: A Philosophical Sketch" [1795], in *Perpetual Peace and Other Essays* 107 (Ted Humphrey trans., 1983) [hereinafter Perpetual Peace]. See also, Immanuel Kant, "Idea For A Universal History with A Cosmopolitan Intent" [1794], in *Perpetual Peace and Other*

Essays 29, 34–39 (Ted Humphrey trans., 1983) [hereinafter Universal History]; Immanuel Kant, "On The Proverb: That May Be True In Theory, But Is Of No Practical Use" [1793], in *Perpetual Peace and Other Essays* 61, 85–89 (Ted Humphrey trans., 1983) [hereinafter Theory and Practice]. The best summary of Kant's moral theory by Kant himself is Immanuel Kant, "Groundwork for the Metaphysics of Morals," in *The Moral Law* (H.J. Paton trans., 1948) [hereinafter Groundwork]. A very useful secondary source for Kant's moral theory is Roger J. Sullivan, *Immanuel Kant's Moral Theory* 384–396 (1989).

2. I am referring to the liberal revolutionary changes in the last twenty-five years, including the Iberian Peninsula in the 1970s; Latin America (led by Argentina) in the mid-1980s; and Central Europe, including the Soviet Union, since 1989. See generally Dankwart A. Rustow, "Democracy: A Global Revolution," *Foreign Affairs* (Fall 1990), at 75. On Latin America, see generally, *Democracy in Developing Countries: Latin America* (Larry Diamond et al. eds., 1989); on Europe, see *Vents D'Est: Vers L'Europe Des Etats De Droit* (Pierre Grémion & Pierre Hassnser eds., 1990).

3. I have discussed the statist paradigm in Fernando R. Tesón, *Humanitarian Intervention: An Inquiry Into Law and Morality* (2d ed. 1997) chapters 3 and 4 [hereinafter Humanitarian Intervention]. See also Anthony D'Amato, "The Invasion of Panama Was a Lawful Response to Tyranny," 84 *American Journal of International Law* 516 (1990); W. Michael Reisman, "Sovereignty and Human Rights in Contemporary International Law," 84 *American Journal of International Law* 866 (1990).

4. The word "liberal" is notorious for its multiple meanings in politics and political theory. I mean "liberal theory" here simply as a theory of politics founded upon individual freedom, respect for individual preferences, and individual autonomy. As such, it encompasses a broad spectrum of actual political positions, from social democrats to libertarians.

5. For a survey of the different meanings of "individualism," see Steven Lukes, *Individualism* 45–124 (1973). The notion of individualism defended in the text is both methodological and normative. Methodological individualism contends that social science explanations should only be made in terms of individuals. Normative individualism insists that our moral concepts should be referred in the last analysis to individual rights and interests (this is *not* to be confused with ethical egoism, which is a substantive moral doctrine).

6. Sir Karl Popper made this observation more than 50 years ago. See 1 Karl R. Popper, *The Open Society and Its Enemies* 288 (2d ed. 1966).

7. For a comparison between Kant's proposals and the precepts of the United Nations Charter, see Carl J. Friedrich, *Inevitable Peace* 33 (1948) (the United Nations Charter in many respects mirrors Kant's conditions for world order). See also Wolfgang Schwarz, "Kant's Philosophy of Law and International Peace," 23 *Philosophy and Phenomenological Research* 71, 76–78 (1962).

8. On this, see A.C. Armstrong, "Kant's Philosophy of Peace and War," 28 *Journal of Philosophy* 197 (1931). See also W.B. Gallie, *Philosophers Of Peace and War* 11–12 (1978). While I depart from Gallie on important points, his chapter on Kant is, in my view, excellent, and I have greatly benefitted from reading it.

9. There are two ways of examining an author: The strict-constructionist approach (what the author really meant) and the reconstructionist approach (how the author's written words can be interpreted to achieve the philosophically favored result). The treatment of Kant in this paper is a mixture of both approaches.

10. Kant, *Perpetual Peace*, supra note 1, at 112.

11. Id. at 115.

12. Thus, the first article is contained in the second: "federation of *free* states." See Friedrich, supra note 7, at 45. The redundancy (having the first and second articles separate) is important to underscore the crucial role of domestic legitimacy in the system of international law proposed by Kant.

13. Kant, *Perpetual Peace*, supra note 1, at 117–118.

14. The requirements of a republican constitution, merely summarized in *Perpetual Peace*, are put forth in Kant, *Theory and Practice*, supra note 1, at 71–84.

15. Id. at 112.

16. Id. at 72.

17. Within the general framework of Kant's critical program, the categorical imperative is the solution to the third antinomy of pure reason, to wit, the apparently irresolvable conflict between the ideas of freedom and causal determinism. Immanuel Kant, *Critique of Pure Reason* 409–15 (A445/B473–A451/B479) (Norman K. Smith trans., 1929); Immanuel Kant, *Critique of Practical Reason* 3–8 (4–8) (Lewis W. Beck trans., 1956) [hereinafter Critique of Practical Reason]; Kant, *Perpetual Peace*, supra note 1, at 123–129.

18. Kant, *Groundwork*, supra note 1, at 60. Kant defines the categorical imperative and explicates the complex ideas contained within it in the *Groundwork*. In his two later works on moral philosophy, *Critique of Pure Reason* and *The Metaphysics of Morals*, Kant demonstrates the binding force of the categorical imperative on human beings who are only imperfectly rational and employs the categorical imperative to derive the whole system of human duties. It is important to note that, for Kant, the categorical imperative cannot be proved but can be deduced from pure practical reason. In the *Critique of Practical Reason*, Kant presents this deduction and demonstrates "the unity of practical and theoretical reason in [the] common principle" that is the categorical imperative. Id. at 59. See Kant, *Critique of Practical Reason*, supra note 17, at 43–51 (42–50).

19. Kant, *Groundwork*, supra note 1, at 98–103.

20. Id. at 103. Paton identifies five interrelated but distinct formulations of the categorical imperative in the *Groundwork*. H.J. Paton, *The Categorical Imperative: A Study in Kant's Moral Philosophy* 129–130, 133–198 (1971).

21. Id. at 88.

22. See Kant, *Groundwork*, supra note 1, at 55; Sullivan, supra note 1, at 151–153.

23. See Kant, *Groundwork*, supra note 1, at 90; Sullivan, supra note 1, at 151–153. Most philosophers agree that Kant has provided a *necessary* condition for the validity of moral judgment. See, e.g., Marcus G. Singer, *Generalization in Ethics: An Essay in the Logic of Ethics, with the Rudiments of a System of Moral Philosophy* 34 (1971) (explaining that generalization is presupposed in every genuine moral judgment). However, commentators have expressed doubts on whether Kant has provided a *sufficient* condition for such validity. Many principles which we intuitively regard as unacceptable comply with the formal requirement of this first version of the categorical imperative.

24. See Sullivan, supra note 1, at 165–166.

25. Kant, *Groundwork*, supra note 1, at 96 (footnotes omitted).

26. Sullivan, supra note 1, at 193; cf. Kant, *Groundwork*, supra note 1, at 105 ("So act in relation to every rational being (both to yourself and to others) that he may at the same time count in your maxim as an end in himself"). Kant here attempts to demonstrate how the second version is logically equivalent to the first.

27. Kant, *Groundwork*, supra note 1, at 95.

28. See Kant, *Theory and Practice*, supra note 1, at 72.

29. The second version of the categorical imperative is not just a logical equivalent of the first. Rather, it adds substance to the formal requirements for moral judgment. Cf. John Rawls, *A Theory of Justice*, 251 n.29, 251–257 (1971) (arguing that one should avoid interpretation of Kant's writings as merely providing formal elements of moral theory). See also Jeffrie G. Murphy, *Kant: The Philosophy of Right* 60–86 (1970) (arguing that Kant's moral point of view is not strictly formal but contains ends, purposes, and values); Onora O'Neill, *Acting on Principle: An Essay on Kantian Ethics* 59–93 (1975) (discussing practical application of categorical imperative). For a defense of the Rawlsian reading of Kant, see Arnold I. Davidson, "Is Rawls a Kantian?" 66 *Pacific Philosophical Quarterly* 48 (1985).

30. See id. at 73.

31. See Sullivan, supra note 1, at 194.

32. See id. at 194; see also Louden, "Kant's Virtue Ethics," 61 *Philosophy* 473 (1986).

33. The best modern reconstruction of Kant in this sense is, of course, Rawls, supra note 29.

34. For an analysis of the place of socioeconomic rights in Rawlsian theory, see Frank I. Michelman, "Constitutional Welfare Rights and A Theory of Justice," in *Reading Rawls* 319 (Norman Daniels ed., 1973). I cannot pursue here the important question of priority between positive and negative duties, and between civil-political rights and socioeconomic rights. However, the Kantian theory of international law in principle upholds the priority of civil and political rights. See Rawls, supra note 29, at 243–251.

35. On this, see Norman Daniels, "Equal Liberty and Unequal Worth of Liberty," in *Reading Rawls* (Norman Daniels ed., 1973).

36. See Kant, *Perpetual Peace*, supra note 1, at 112; Kant, *Theory and Practice*, supra note 1, at 75–77.

37. See, e.g., Hans Kelsen, *General Theory of Law and State* 181–192 (Anders Wedberg trans., 1961).

38. Id. at 115.

39. Kant, *Theory and Practice*, supra note 1, at 75–76.

40. See, e.g., Kant, *Groundwork*, supra note 1, at 71 ("reverence is the assessment of a worth which far outweighs all the worth of what is commended by inclination, and the necessity for me to act out of *pure* reverence for the practical law is what constitutes duty, to which every other motive must give way because it is the condition of a will good *in itself*, whose value is above all else").

41. See, e.g., Kant, *Groundwork*, supra note 1, at 66.

42. See Kant, *Perpetual Peace*, supra note 1, at 127–131; see also Gallie, supra note 8, at 22.

43. See the summaries of Kant's philosophy on this point in Sullivan, supra note 1, at 247–252; see also Kenneth N. Waltz, *Man, the State, and War* 331–333 (1959).

44. Kant, *Perpetual Peace*, supra note 1, at 112–113.

45. See, e.g., Kant, *Theory and Practice*, supra note 1, at 79–80; see also Lewis W. Beck, "Kant and the Right of Revolution," 32 *Journal of the History of Ideas* 411 (1971); Sullivan, supra note 1, at 244–245.

46. See, e.g., John Locke, "An Essay Concerning the True Origin, Extent, and End of Civil Government" [1690], in *Social Contract* 124 (E. Baker ed., 1948).

47. Kant gives the following reason to deny the right to revolution: "For suppose they had such a right, and, indeed, that they opposed the judgment of the nation's leader, then who would determine on which side the right lies? Neither of them can serve as judge in his

own case. Thus, there would have to be still another head above the head to decide between the latter and the people—and that is contradictory." Kant, *Theory and Practice*, supra note 1, at 79. This is not his only reason, however. His other reasons are his obsession with the danger of reverting to the lawless state of nature, and the prudential reason that since revolution is violent, citizens living under an unjust regime must never give up hope that liberal reforms can occur peacefully. See the excellent summary in Sullivan, supra note 1, at 244–245.

48. See id. at 245.

49. See Tesón, supra note 3, at 87–88; see D'Amato, supra note 3 (arguing similarly).

50. See Kant, *Perpetual Peace*, supra note 1, at 112; Kant, *Theory and Practice*, supra note 1, at 73–75.

51. This is not inconsistent with the sorts of inequalities in wealth and power that arise in every society from a combination of talent, industry, and luck. See Sullivan, supra note 1, at 256.

52. See id. at 197.

53. Kant, *Perpetual Peace*, supra note 1, at 112.

54. Id. at 114.

55. This is very different from Michael Walzer's assertion that *all* governments are presumed to represent their people unless they render themselves guilty of genocide or similar atrocious and widespread crimes. See Michael Walzer, "The Moral Standing of States," 9 *Philosophy and Public Affairs* 209 (1980).

56. Kant, *Perpetual Peace*, supra note 1, at 108.

57. This is the view of several commentators. See F.H. Hinsley, *Power and the Pursuit of Peace* 66–67 (1963). See also Thomas L. Carson, "Perpetual Peace: What Kant Should Have Said," 14 *Social Theory and Practice* 173, 183–184 (1988); and Sullivan, supra note 1, at 257. I have argued at length against this view of the state in Tesón, supra note 3, at 21–94.

58. Kant, *Perpetual Peace*, supra note 1, at 108.

59. See, inter alia, Kant, *Theory and Practice*, supra note 1, at 71–84. Accord, Gallie, supra note 8, at 22. For Kant, existence of effective governments requires that most of the subjects obey its laws because they think it right to do so.

60. Kant, *Perpetual Peace*, supra note 1, at 119. Kant also suggests here, along the same lines, that all men have a "common ownership of the earth's surface." Id.

61. For the first version of the categorical imperative see Immanuel Kant, "The Metaphysical Foundation of Morals" [1785], in *The Philosophy of Kant* 170 (Carl J. Friedrich trans., 1949); For the second version of the categorical imperative see id. at 178. See also Sullivan, supra note 1, at 193–211. Kant scholars have debated whether the second version of the categorical imperative is logically equivalent to the first, or whether it adds instead substantive content to the formal requirements for moral judgement. I follow the modern reading presented by John Rawls, that insists that one should avoid an interpretation of Kant's writings as merely providing the formal elements of moral theory. See Rawls, supra note 29, at 251–257, n.29. See generally Jeffrie G. Murphy, *Kant: The Philosophy of Right* (1970). For a defense of the Rawlsian reading of Kant, see Davidson, supra note 29.

62. I outline such a theory of self-determination in Chapter 5.

63. See the discussion at the end of this chapter.

64. See, e.g., Stanley Hoffmann, *Duties Beyond Borders, On the Limits and Possibilities of Ethical International Politics* (1981).

65. Classical works in the Realist tradition are Hedley Bull, *The Anarchical Society: A Study of Order in World Politics* (1979); and Waltz, supra note 43. For an extended critical discussion of the Realist view, see Marshall Cohen, "Moral Skepticism and International Relations," 13 *Philosophy and Public Affairs* 299 (1984).

66. For full references to Realist literature, see infra Chapter 2.

67. Kant writes that "reason absolutely condemns war as a means of determining the right and makes seeking the state of peace a matter of unmitigated duty." Kant, *Perpetual Peace*, supra note 1, at 116. Elsewhere Kant wrote that moral reason "voices its irresistible veto: there should be no war." Kant, *Groundwork*, supra note 1, at 354; Sullivan, supra note 1, at 256 (citing same passage). Cf. Gallie, supra note 8, at 9 (opening section of *Perpetual Peace* a *tour de force*, without any preliminary discussion of why or in what circumstances war is an unacceptable evil).

68. As we shall see, Kant had peculiar views (not all negative) about the role that war has played in the *Design of Nature*.

69. See Gallie, supra note 8, at 20.

70. Kant, *Perpetual Peace*, supra note 1, at 113.

71. Id. Kant writes that the ruler does not act here as a fellow citizen, but as the nation's owner. Id. Kant's prudential reasons are always permeated by the theme of the categorical imperative: never use persons simply as means, which of course applies with even more strength to the government.

72. I suggested this explanation of the Malvinas war, see Fernando R. Tesón, Book Review, 81 *American Journal of International Law* 112 (1987).

73. See Kant, *Perpetual Peace*, supra note 1, at 114; Michael W. Doyle, "Kant, Liberal Legacies, and Foreign Affairs, Part I," 12 *Philosophy and Public Affairs* 205, 228 (1983) [hereinafter Liberal Legacies, Part I].

74. See id. at 229.

75. See id. at 116. See also Joseph M. Knippenberg, "Moving Beyond Fear: Rousseau and Kant on Cosmopolitan Education," 51 *Journal of Policy* 809, 815–819 (1989).

76. See generally *Education for Peace and Disarmament: Toward a Living World* (Douglas Sloan ed., 1983).

77. See Knippenberg, supra note 75, at 810.

78. Kant writes that cosmopolitan education is aimed at the universal good and the perfection for which humanity is destined. Knippenberg, supra note 75, at 815 (citing Immanuel Kant, *Education* 15 (Annette Churton trans., 1960)).

79. See Kant, *Perpetual Peace*, supra note 1, at 118–119, 125. See also Doyle, *Liberal Legacies Part I*, supra note 73, at 231–232.

80. Kant, *Perpetual Peace*, supra note 1, at 118.

81. Id. at 125.

82. "For among all those powers (or means) that belong to a nation, financial power may be the most reliable in forcing nations to pursue the noble cause of peace (though not from moral motives)." Id.

83. One could expand this theme by saying that liberal citizens tend to be more cosmopolitan and less nationalistic, (except where the issue is the defense of freedom), precisely because they place the individual as the origin and end of political arrangements.

84. For the European Union, see 1978 Bulletin of the European Communities, No. 3, at 5; for the Mercosur agreement, see *New York Times*, Aug. 12, 1986, at A20.

85. See Doyle, *Liberal Legacies, Part I*, supra note 73; Michael W. Doyle, "Kant, Liberal Legacies, and Foreign Affairs, Part II," 12 *Philosophy and Public Affairs* 323 (1983)

[hereinafter Liberal Legacies, Part II]; Michael W. Doyle, "Liberalism and World Politics," 80 *American Political Science Review* 1151 (1986); Michael W. Doyle, "Liberal Institutions and International Ethics," in *Political Realism and International Morality* 185 (Kenneth Kipnis & Diana T. Meyers eds., 1987); R.J. Rummel, "Libertarianism and International Conflict," 27 *Journal of Conflict Resolution* 27 (1983).

    86. See D'Amato, supra note 3.

    87. See Doyle, *Liberal Legacies, Part I*, supra note 73, at 209–217.

    88. See Doyle, *Liberal Legacies, Part II*, supra note 85, passim.

    89. See Doyle, *Liberal Legacies, Part I*, supra note 73, at 213.

    90. See Chan, "Mirror, Mirror on the Wall: Are the Freer Countries More Pacific?" 7 *Peace Research Society Papers* 31 (1984); Melvin Small & J. David Singer, "The War Proneness of Democratic Regimes, 1816–1965," 1 *Jerusalem Journal of International Relations* 50 (1976) (critiquing Rummel's earlier work); Erich Weede, "Democracy and War Involvement," 28 *Journal of Conflict Resolution* 649 (1984). As indicated above, Doyle concedes (and the evidence seems to show) that liberal states behave aggressively toward nonliberal states.

    91.   See David Garnham, "War-Proneness, War-Weariness, and Regime Type: 1916–1980," 23 *Journal of Peace Research* 279 (1986); authors cited supra, note 90. For another challenge to Rummel's methodology, see Jack Vincent, "Freedom and International Conflict: Another Look," 31 *International Studies Quarterly* 103 (1987); but see R.J. Rummel, "On Vincent's View of Freedom and International Conflict," 31 *International Studies Quarterly* 113 (1987).

    92. The two hard cases are the 1812 war between England and the United States and World War I. As to the first, arguably the United States became a liberal republic only after 1865; as to the second, Doyle's explanation is that Imperial Germany, although largely a liberal republic for domestic issues, did not allow any popular participation in foreign affairs decisions. See Doyle, *Liberal Legacies, Part I*, supra note 73, at 216–217 n.8.

    93. See Kant, *Perpetual Peace*, supra note 1, at 118.

    94. See Diana T. Meyers, "Kant's Liberal Alliance: A Permanent Peace?" in *Political Realism and International Morality* 212 (Kenneth Kipnis & Diana T. Meyers eds., 1987).

    95. Id. at 215. See also Hinsley, supra note 57, at 71. After writing that "it is impossible to overlook the lameness of this conclusion" [i.e. that republican forms of government are more likely to lead to international peace], Hinsley downplays Kant's emphasis on internal freedom and emphasizes instead the freedom of the state and the "Design of Nature" as Kant's main causes of peace. I believe that Hinsley's view on this point is empirically implausible and unfaithful to *Perpetual Peace* and to Kant's philosophy generally.

    96. Meyers, supra note 94, at 215.

    97. Id.

    98. Id. at 216. The example used is the Vietnam war.

    99. See id.

    100. There are countless real and counterfactual examples to illustrate the Kantian hypothesis. My favorite one is: there would have been no Malvinas war between the United Kingdom and Argentina had there been a democratic government installed in Buenos Aires. While there is no indication that irredentist sentiments have subsided in Argentina, the two countries (with Argentina now a member of the liberal alliance) are pursuing peaceful means to solve the conflict. See, e.g., "UK–Argentine Joint Statement on Relations and a Formula on Sovereignty with Regard to Falkland Islands, South Georgia, and South Sandwich Islands," 29 *International Legal Materials* 1291 (Sept. 1990); see also "BBC Summary of

World Broadcasts," *The Monitoring Report, Part 4* (Dec. 29, 1990) (Argentine Foreign Minister downplaying British Prime Minister comparison of Iraqi invasion of Kuwait with 1982 Argentine invasion of Malvinas).

101. Doyle, *Liberal Legacies, Part I*, supra note 73, at 219. As Doyle notes, this tradition goes back to Thucydides and Hobbes. Id. and authors cited supra note 90. Other Realist explanations of the liberal peace discussed and rejected by Doyle are based on hegemony or equilibrium, along the lines suggested by Raymond Aron. The liberal peace persisted in the inter–war period when there was no hegemony. Doyle, *Liberal Legacies, Part I*, supra note 73, at 223. Doyle also points out that hegemonic control is overestimated in both the pre-war and post-war periods. It is argued that in a situation of international equilibrium aggressive attempts at hegemony will deter wars. But bipolar equilibrium is insufficient because it only explains peace among the polar powers, not proxy or regional wars. Id. at 224.

102. Id.

103. Id.

104. Id.

105. Kant, *Perpetual Peace*, supra note 1, at 113 (my emphasis).

106. See, e.g., Hinsley, supra note 57, at 66.

107. Kant makes this argument clear in *Perpetual Peace* itself, and it can of course be found in other texts (most particularly in Universal History, supra note 1) and, as a logical corollary, it can be gleaned from Kant's general moral theory. See references supra note 1.

108. See Fernando R. Tesón, "International Obligation and the Theory of Hypothetical Consent," 15 *Yale Journal of International Law* 99–120 (1990).

109. See Kant, *Groundwork*, supra note 1, at 54–56. Asks Kant: "Do we not think it a matter of the utmost necessity to work out for once a pure moral philosophy completely cleansed of everything that can only be empirical and appropriate to anthropology?" Id. at 56.

110. See id. at 84–86.

111. See Kant, *Groundwork*, supra note 1, at 95–96.

112. State-oriented international lawyers persistently disregard the fact that the respect for human dignity was a major purpose of the international organization after 1945. See, inter alia, United Nations Charter preamble.

113. See Kant, *Perpetual Peace*, supra note 1, at 111–12 n.† ("For by entering into civil society, each person gives every other . . . the requisite security").

114. See Gallie, supra note 8, at 16 ("The intensity of feeling which Kant focused upon this hope for Reason in human life is unparalleled in the history of political thought, anyhow since Plato").

115. Kant, *Perpetual Peace*, supra note 1, at 116. The word "law" has been substituted for "right" in this Article.

116. See, e.g., Anthony D'Amato, *International Law: Process and Prospect* 1–26 (1987) (rejecting idea that international law must be centrally enforced to be considered law); W. Michael Reisman, "Sanctions and Enforcement," in *International Law Essays* 381, 386 (Myres S. McDougal ed., 1981) (discussing community and group sanctions as distinguished from state-imposed); see also Eiichi Fukatsu, "Coercion and the Theory of Sanctions in International Law," in *The Structure and Process of International Law* 1187 (R. St.J. Macdonald & Douglas M. Johnston eds., 1983) (discussing diplomatic, economic, and military coercion by individual state as international law sanctions).

117. See Glanville L. Williams, "International Law and the Controversy Concerning the Word Law," 22 *Britain Year Book of International Law* 146, 158–162 (1945).

118. See Carson, supra note 57, at 184–191 (arguing that "ultra-minimal" world government could preserve world peace).

119. For an account of international law allowing the right of states to wage war prior to the United Nations Charter see 2 Lassa Oppenheim, *International Law* 177–178 (H. Lauterpacht ed., 7th ed. 1952); see also Hubert Thierry et al., *Droit International Public* 538–541 (1975) (discussing development of ideas of pacifism and just war from early Christianity to absolute monarchies of the 18th century). Kant has numerous references in his writings to international lawlessness and the international state of nature. See, e.g., Kant, *Perpetual Peace*, supra note 1, at 115–116; Kant, *Theory and Practice*, supra note 1, at 67; see also Waltz, supra note 43, at 334 (discussing Kant's conception of states in international system).

120. See Hinsley, supra note 57, at 51 (citing Thomas Hobbes, *On Dominion*, Chapter 13). The problem of authority confounded Rousseau. Consequently his works contain some inconsistencies about the appropriate resolution. See id. at 46–51 (discussing Rousseau's works on international relations).

121. See, e.g., Friedrich, supra note 7, at 45.

122. See Carson, supra note 57, at 179–184.

123. See Hinsley, supra note 57, at 62–70; Gallie, supra note 8, at 20–21; Waltz, supra note 43, at 335–337; Jean-Michel Besnier, "Le Droit International Chez Kant et Hegel," 32 *Archives De Philosophie Du Droit: Le Droit International* 85, 91 (1987).

124. See Kant, *Perpetual Peace*, supra note 1, at 117.

125. See id. at 118–119.

126. See Hinsley, supra note 57, at 63.

127. Kant, *Perpetual Peace*, supra note 1, at 125.

128. After suggesting the possibility that nations might consider world government, Kant writes: "But they do not will to do this because it does not conform to their idea of the [law] of nations, and consequently they discard in *hypothesis* what is true in *thesis*." Id. at 117; see also Gallie, supra note 8, at 23–24 (discussing Kant's rejection of both peace-by-empire and peace-by-federation).

129. See Terry Nardin, *Law, Morality, and The Relations of States* 238–239 (1983).

130. See Kant, *Perpetual Peace*, supra note 1, at 120–125.

131. Id. at 125.

132. Why should the champion of free will talk about the Laws of Nature forcing people to do things? Besnier rightly criticizes Kant's abuse of the notion of the Design of Nature. See Besnier, supra note 123, at 93–94 (calling the argument "*la ruse de la nature*"); see also Robert K. Faulkner, "Liberal Plans for the World: Locke, Kant, and World Ecology Theories," *International Journal of World Peace* (March 1990) at 61, 77–79 (critiquing Kant's "strangely ruthless humanitarianism" that assumes war will eventually dictate progress toward a rational world).

133. See George Modelski, "Is World Politics Evolutionary Learning?" 44 *International Organizations* 1, 2–6 (1990) (Kant's historicist argument confirmed by recent studies on nature of international cooperation); Hinsley, supra note 57, at 72 (Kant's international philosophy combined "the historical sense, the moral element in politics, and the irrational element in man"); Gallie, supra note 8, at 28–29 (for Kant, idea of human reason excludes use of war); see also Sullivan, supra note 1, at 235–241 (summarizing Kant's philosophy of history).

134. Gallie summarizes the Kantian tension between man's rational powers: Reason is "that tendency, in all human thought and conscious effort, towards, at one and the same time, ever greater unity, system and necessity, and *equally* towards ever sharper and more constant self-criticism and self-control." Gallie, supra note 8, at 14.

135. The question of the relationship between self-determination and human rights is a complex one. I discuss it in Chapter 5.

136. According to Kant, the state of nature exists when states are at war or a threat of war exists. See Kant, *Perpetual Peace*, supra note 1, at 111. Yet, the establishment of the liberal alliance, while a dramatic improvement, will still harbor dangers of war *against nonmembers*, i.e., despotic states. See infra text accompanying notes 146–167. Perpetual peace will be finally achieved when all nations become democratic and join the alliance.

137. See authors cited, supra note 116.

138. See, e.g., European Convention for the Protection of Human Rights and Fundamental Freedoms, article 6, 213 *United Nations Treaty Series* 221, 228 (1955).

139. See Tesón, *Humanitarian Intervention*, supra note 3, at 111–123 (arguing that intervention is appropriate only if (1) force is used to thwart human rights violations, (2) nonhumanitarian motives do not detract from paramount human rights objective, (3) means used is rights-inspired, and (4) victims welcome intervention).

140. Kant, *Perpetual Peace*, supra note 1, at 110.

141. Id. Kant concludes that a war of extermination, which extinguishes all rights, is absolutely prohibited because it would achieve perpetual peace only "in the vast graveyard of humanity as a whole." Id.

142. Kant reiterates this point in his commentary to the Second Definitive Article. See id. at 116–117.

143. See id. at 120–125.

144. In his commentary to the Third Preliminary Article, Kant seems to justify war in cases of self-defense. See id. at 108 (distinguishing between "paying men to kill or be killed," which Kant deems "inconsistent with the rights of humanity," and "the *voluntary*, periodic military training of citizens so that they can secure their homeland against external attack") (emphasis added); see also Gallie, supra note 8, at 24 (discussing Kant's advocacy of a confederation of common defense against aggression).

145. See, e.g., Doyle, *Liberal Legacies, Part II*, supra note 85, at 343–349.

146. United Nations Charter article 51 ("Nothing in the present Charter shall impair the inherent right of individual or collective self-defence [sic] if an armed attack occurs against a Member of the United Nations, until the Security Council has taken measures necessary to maintain international peace and security").

147. See Kant, *Perpetual Peace*, supra note 1, at 108; cf. Michael Walzer, *Just and Unjust Wars* 21–32 (1977) (war is crime because it forces people to fight for their rights).

148. Kant, *Perpetual Peace*, supra note 1, at 109.

149. Id.

150. See, e.g., id. at 115 ("Each nation can and should demand that the others enter into a contract resembling the civil one and guaranteeing the rights of each").

151. See Doyle, *Liberal Legacies, Part I*, supra note 73, at 213.

152. The nonintervention principle seems to us a permanent feature of international law, and so it might seem peculiar to see it included by Kant among the Preliminary Articles. Unlike Woodrow Wilson, for example, Kant was indeed a noninterventionist liberal, but what commentators have failed to emphasize is that his being liberal is a precondition of his being noninterventionist. See Waltz, supra note 43, at 339–340.

153. Even Hinsley, who repeatedly underscores the importance of state sovereignty, writes: "Just as [Kant] derived the right to freedom of the individual from the dictates of a moral law, so he derived the right to freedom of the state—*the route to and the guarantee of the freedom of the individual*—from the same moral law." Hinsley, supra note 57, at 63 (emphasis added). The moral law mandates freedom of the individual and freedom of the state as but a means to that end. See Kant, *Universal History*, supra note 1, at 34 (problem of just civic constitution cannot be solved without solving international problem).

154. See, e.g., Tesón, *Humanitarian Intervention*, supra note 3, at 86–87; Charles R. Beitz, *Political Theory and International Relations* 80–83 (1979).

155. See Tesón, *Humanitarian Intervention*, supra note 3, at 111–123.

156. Kant's view here is also inconsistent with his own rejection of the right to revolution. For it is often the case that the only way for a tyranny to become a liberal democracy, and thus qualify for the alliance, is for citizens violently to overthrow the tyrant. Of course, I have rejected Kant's views on revolution; someone may still salvage Kant's views on the nonintervention issue by disagreeing with him on the revolution issue. My own position is that the right of humanitarian intervention in appropriate cases is an extension of the right to revolution.

157. There is yet another case: the use of force by a nonliberal state against another nonliberal state. The justice of that will depend on whose rights are being violated. Even an illegitimate government may defend citizens against aggression by foreigners. However, despotic governments do not have any right to defend themselves against external force used to remove them from power, provided that such foreign help is welcomed by the victims themselves. See Tesón, *Humanitarian Intervention*, supra note 3, at 119–123.

158. See references supra note 1.

159. See Gallie, supra note 8, at 8–13.

160. In the words of Waltz, Kant's mode of analysis is "rigorous and yet subtle, his style difficult but clear, his writing crabbed and still, as Goethe said, sometimes slyly ironic and even eloquent." Kenneth Waltz, "Kant, Liberalism, and War," 56 *American Political Science Review* 331 (1962).

161. See Gallie, supra note 8, at 11; see also Armstrong, supra note 8, at 197–198.

162. See "Gorbachev Skips Nobel Award," *Chicago Tribune*, Dec. 11, 1990, at M4.

163. Kant, *Perpetual Peace*, supra note 1, at 107–118 (emphasis in original).

164. Here and in the next chapter, I prefer to use the word "law" rather than Humphrey's "right." The word "Recht" used in the original is ambiguous (as are the words "derecho" in Spanish and "droit" in French) and it may be translated as "law" or as "right," depending on the context. It is clear from the context in *Perpetual Peace* that Kant is referring to the objective international order, the law, and not to "right" in the subjective sense. The German word "Volkerrecht" is ordinarily translated as "international law," not "international right." Cf. the better translation is offered by Carl J. Friedrich in Immanuel Kant, *The Philosophy of Kant* 441 (Carl J. Friedrich ed., 1949) ("law of nations").

165. Kant, *Perpetual Peace*, supra note 1, at 125–126. Cf. Waltz, supra note 43, at 339–340 (Kant was not engaged in the puerile task of telling men of affairs to stop behaving badly).

166. See Hinsley, supra note 57, at 66.

167. See Gallie, supra note 8, at 9. This ambiguity is quite distinct from differences of interpretation about the essay's substantive content, discussed below.

168. See Karl Jaspers, *Philosophy And The World* 113–117 (E.B. Ashton trans., 1963) (Kant sets forth principles underlying international law, not political program). But see

Waltz, supra note 43, at 334 (Kant does set forth "shoulds" and "oughts" in international relations).

169. See Gallie, supra note 8, at 10; Hinsley, supra note 57, at 69.

170. See Hinsley, supra note 57, at 69.

171. This is clear in the work of Hinsley, for whom the preliminary articles are part of the solution and not a statement of the preliminary progress that must be made. Hinsley also flatly rejects the first definitive article (the requirement of democracy and human rights) by observing that "it is impossible to overlook the lameness of this conclusion [that free states are more likely to be peaceful]." Hinsley, supra note 57, at 71. His views are characteristic of the discomfort felt toward Kant's revolutionary humanism by those who cling to a statist world view and as a result adopt a statist reading of Kant.

172. See Schwarz, supra note 7, at 75; Carson, supra note 57, at 174; Doyle, *Liberal Legacies, Part I*, supra note 73, at 225.

173. See Gallie, supra note 8, at 10.

174. Kant, *Perpetual Peace*, supra note 1, at 111 (footnotes omitted; emphasis in the original).

175. The interpretation suggested by Gallie and Hinsley is not consistent with the meaning of the words "preliminary" and "definitive." See Webster's Third New International Dictionary 592, 1789 (1981). Hinsley tries to meet this objection by suggesting that the word "preliminary" is used in the sense of the law of treaties. Hinsley, supra note 57, at 69. Even if this is true, that does not provide nor explain the contextual meaning of the word "definitive."

176. See Hinsley, supra note 57, at 69; Gallie, supra note 8, at 9–10.

177. Article 4 of the United Nations Charter reads: "Membership in the United Nations is open to all other peace-loving states which accept the obligations contained in the present Charter and, in the judgment of the Organizations, are able and willing to carry out these obligations." United Nations Charter article 4, paragraph 1. While article 4 may conceivably be read as requiring respect for human rights from prospective members, the main organs of the United Nations have not interpreted it so. For a summary of the practice, see Guy Feuer, "Article 4," in *La Charte Des Nations Unies* 171–172, 177–179 (Jean-Pierre Cot & Alain Pellet eds., 1985).

178. See, e.g., article 7 of the Vienna Convention on the Law of Treaties, in which the only requirement for considering a person as representing a state for the purposes of expressing the consent to be bound by a treaty is that such person produce appropriate full powers." Vienna Convention on the Law of Treaties, article 7, *United Nations Document* A/Conf. 39/27, 5, 8 *International Legal Materials* 683 (1969).

179. Articles 2, 4 and 7 of the Vienna Convention on Diplomatic Relations give almost unlimited discretion to sending and receiving states, so in theory it allows for the receiving state either to refuse to establish diplomatic relations with a tyrannical government, or to deny *agrément* to representatives of illegitimate governments. Vienna Convention on Diplomatic Relations, April 18, 1961, articles 2, 4, 7, 23 *United States Treaties* 3227, 500 *United Nations Treaty Series* 95. There is a difference between denying *agrément* to the individual because of his or her past or other circumstances, and denying the *agrément* because the envoy is not representative of the sending state. The practice of states, however, has not shown much concern for true representativeness, with one exception: South Africa. The General Assembly recommended members to sever diplomatic relations with South Africa as early as 1962. See Ludwick Dembinski, *The Modern Law of Diplomacy* 92 (1988). South Africa is a clear case of *internal* illegitimacy for lack of representativeness and serious

human rights deprivations. The principle governing that case should be extended to other cases of tyranny.

180. See Wilson's famous Mobile statement, 7 *American Journal of International Law* 331 (1913) (discussing United States' desire only to deal with just governments in Central and South America).

181. See Namibia Opinion, 1971 *International Court of Justice* 16, 58, paragraph 133 (June 21) (obligation by states not to recognize South Africa's illegal occupation of Namibia because of South Africa's human rights violations in Namibia).

182. Recall the warnings of former Soviet Foreign Minister Shevardnadze, who resigned in protest of Gorbachev's courtship of the hardliners which he felt would lead toward the reestablishment of totalitarianism in the Soviet Union, Tom Wicker, "An Ominous Warning," *New York Times*, December 23, 1990, at O11. These warnings proved to be accurate: in the last week in August 1991, a coup d'état in the Soviet Union succeeded in reestablishing a dictatorship for a couple of days. Freedom and democracy, however, reemerged with renewed force after the restoration of the legitimate government. The adherence to the liberal alliance by the nations that succeeded the now extinct Soviet Union will be perhaps the most encouraging event of the century.

2

Sovereignty and Intervention

Introduction: A Challenge to Statism

The Kantian thesis challenges the widely held view that states, not individuals, are the basic subjects of international law and relations and that state sovereignty is the basis upon which international law properly rests. This view, *statism*, has several corollaries, but perhaps the two most important ones are the principle of nonintervention and the view that established governments necessarily represent the people over whom they rule. For statists, the state presents a united international front, as it were. The government of the state presents its foreign policy to the outside world, and outsiders treat it as the official policy of the state, regardless of whether the government really represents the people on whose behalf that policy is purportedly pursued. On this view, state sovereignty is an all-or-nothing concept that only collapses or changes radically, perhaps, when the target state is on the wrong side of a just war (e.g., the Axis powers or, more recently, Iraq).[1] In contrast, the principle of state sovereignty reigns supreme during peacetime. Any intervention that entails some degree of coercion or even intrusion, this argument concludes, is always prohibited in peacetime by the sovereignty principle.

Such is the gist of the doctrine of sovereignty in international law. The doctrine maintains that all states are equally legitimate for international purposes, provided that they have a population ruled by a government in a territory. Indeed, according to traditional doctrine, the state *is* a population ruled by a government in a territory.[2] When those three elements (territory, population, effective government) concur, the doctrine holds, we have a state in the international legal sense. States enjoys the rights that derive from sovereignty, just as individuals enjoy the rights that derive from personhood. Sovereignty, according to the traditional view, is not limited to protecting the state's territory against foreign invasions: more generally, sovereignty encompasses the right of a state "to freely determine, without external interference, their political status and to pursue their economic, social and cultural development."[3] Thus, the traditional, statist conception of sovereignty leaves states free to adopt any form of social organization; states are thus legally and morally protected against foreign interference aimed at criticizing or altering those internal social structures.

I believe that this proposition is conceptually and morally wrong in this traditional form and too extreme even in its more benign versions. The traditional view of sovereignty fails to make distinctions that are relevant to the moral justification of political institutions and international acts. More specifically, I wish to reject the twin premises that state sovereignty is an intrinsic value, that is, that sovereignty is a self-sustaining and autonomous moral principle, and that state sovereignty is an all-or-nothing concept, that is, that all states are equally sovereign by virtue of their statehood. I suggest instead two propositions that are the exact opposites of the ones just described: (1) sovereignty is an *instrumental* value supported by moral reasons linked to human rights and respect for individual autonomy,[4] and (2) sovereignty admits of *degrees,* in that the moral reasons supporting an act of intervention compete against the moral reasons that support sovereignty, and the result of that contest cannot be determined in advance. Put differently: only just states deserve to be fully protected by the shield of sovereignty. This view derives directly from the Kantian thesis defended in Chapter 1.

In addition, I pursue the distinction I drew in Chapter 1 between *horizontal* legitimacy and *vertical* legitimacy.[5] The former denotes the legitimacy of the social contract among the citizens that form the state, their political association. The second denotes the legitimacy of the agency contract between the subjects and the governed—the legitimacy of the government itself. Only states that are legitimate *in both senses* are fully protected by international law. But even where legitimacy in any of the senses is lacking, there are still very important moral constraints on outsiders: first, they may intervene *only* if they have a morally compelling reason to do so. Second, it makes an important difference whether the *state* or the *government* is morally blighted. If the state is legitimate but the government is not, then foreigners should proceed with caution: they should try not to violate the right of individuals to a life in common. And finally, there might be good consequentialist or prudential reasons not to intervene, especially if the contemplated action entails the use of force. My argument is that *if* intervention is otherwise justified, illegitimate states and governments are not protected by the principle of state sovereignty. It does not follow from this view that intervention is always justified against illegitimate states and governments. It might be that, all things considered, it is wrong to act against a particular illegitimate government. Put differently: I argue here that the illegitimacy of a government is a *necessary*, not a *sufficient* condition for intervention.

The Domestic Analogy

The classical version of statism relies on an analogy between states and individuals: *the domestic analogy.* Just as individual choices must be respected by other individuals in civil society, so states' choices must be respected by other states in the international society.[6] Thus, the principle of individual autonomy, the statist argues, is extended to justify state autonomy. National self-determination is a transposition of the principle of individual self-determination into international relations.[7] Statism views the state as a corporate being that holds rights (i.e., sovereignty) that can be analyzed in nonaggregative terms, that is, without reference to the rights, interests or preferences of the individuals that populate the state.

It is perhaps easy for philosophers to reject this anthropomorphic, organicist view of the state, but in fact it is the view adopted by most international lawyers and international courts. In international relations, it is almost undisputed that states are the acting units. Sometimes this thesis takes an extreme organicist form: the state is a moral being ontologically analogous to the individual, a being with a body, a mind, endowed with reason, and therefore holder of international rights.[8] Such a view (which has historically served as justification for atrocious forms of aggression and oppression) is today mercifully discredited. I will discuss instead three modern and more plausible versions of statism: the view that sovereignty is grounded in the nature of international relations; the view that national sovereignty, as the legal embodiment of self-determination, is a necessary condition for the realization of individual human rights; and the still more moderate view that, while states have to be minimally just to be legitimate, states are still *opaque* in the international arena.

State Sovereignty as a Consequence of International Anarchy

According to an influential current of thought, the principle of sovereignty derives directly from peculiar features of international society.[9] This view (called, somewhat misleadingly, Realism) claims that nation-states, not individuals, are the units of analysis in international relations because in a relatively anarchic international society they pursue their national interest regardless of the nature of domestic arrangements. Nations interact in a state of nature where they are forced, by that anarchic situation, to act according to a peculiar logic informed by the rationality of self-interest.[10] As Kenneth Walz put it, "the unity of a nation . . . is fed not only by indigenous factors but also by the antagonisms that frequently occur in international relations."[11] There is no escape from this situation, according to the Realist: all states, tyrannical or democratic, rich or poor, suffer the same fate. When they face one another they are just political units who are, as a matter of hard fact, unconstrained by any principle except rational prudence.

Now this is a theoretical, descriptive explanation of the behavior of states. How one can derive a *normative* principle of sovereignty from these premises is unclear. The argument could perhaps go as follows: in domestic social contract theory, human rights derive from what rational beings, acting in their self-interest, consent or would consent to. Similarly, states' rights (sovereignty), derive from the principles to which nation-states, *acting under the peculiar condition of international anarchy, consent or would consent*. And just as individuals will want to protect their freedoms as much as possible, so will states want to protect as much as possible their freedom of action—thus the principle of state sovereignty and its flip side, nonintervention.

The first objection to this view is simple: a state is not a person. To say that a person is free may mean many things, but a plausible meaning is this: a free person is one capable of choosing autonomously. Without discussing the complexities of the concept of autonomy, it is safe to say that for liberals freedom defined in this way is generally a good thing. But what does it mean to say that a *state* is free? It can only mean that the government of a state can make political decisions free of constraints from other governments. Whether or not this is a good thing in itself is open to question, but in any case the government's *freedom* cannot be a good thing *for the same reasons* an individual's freedom is a good thing. In particular, where a government's *freedom* consists in wielding (internally or externally) the coercive power of the state, that action has to be justified, like all exercise of political power, with the tools of political morality. In other words: while an individual's exercise of freedom is generally an intrinsic good, a government's exercise of sovereignty, that is, power over others, is not. Thus, the domestic analogy ("sovereignty is a good thing for the same reasons individual freedom is a good thing") fails.

Secondly, the proposition that there is a morality, logic, or rationality peculiar to international relations is dubious. As many writers have shown, we do and must make moral judgments about the international behavior of governments, judgments that are the natural extension of our everyday moral beliefs.[12] It is of course true that government officials face peculiar *conditions* in foreign policy. But that doesn't mean that they operate, or should operate, under a different logic, morality, or rationality. It means simply that because principles of morality apply in these special conditions, the results may be different than they would be under regular conditions. For example, the principles that underlie the social contract mandate that the government (say, the police) intervene to protect the life of someone who is threatened by a murderer. But *those same principles* may dictate that we not intervene to save victims of the Chinese regime if the result may be a nuclear war. Our morality, our rationality, and our logic have not changed: the factual conditions have.

Third, the statist's commitment to the *presumption of agency*, that is, to the view that the government of any state always represents the people internationally, cannot withstand scrutiny. States are groupings of individuals. When we say that the state acts, we mean that some individual acts on behalf of the state. But the notion of representation is normative. When we say that A represents B, we are presupposing a rule or system of rules that normatively defines representation. Not everyone who purports to represent a group actually represents that group. And which are the candidates for plausible rules of representation? The traditional view is that any individual who has succeeded in exacting obedience from the individuals that populate the state is deemed automatically to represent the state.

Kenneth Walz's view is typical: "The centripetal force of nationalism may itself explain why states can be thought of as units. . . . In the name of the state a policy is formulated and presented to other countries as though it were, to use Rousseau's terminology, the general will of the state."[13]

This is also the default position of governments and international lawyers. For them, with very few exceptions, a government is presumed to represent the state. Governments routinely send ambassadors to present their plenary powers to other governments, thus legitimizing their standing as representatives of their people, even in the face of clear evidence that the government does not represent anybody but is, say, a despotic dictator that acceded to power by brutal violence. The same is true with other areas of international law such as the law of treaties.[14] International lawyers take this ruthless reality of diplomacy as evidence for their statist thesis.[15] But the point of the Kantian thesis is precisely to show that the practice of treating morally objectionable rulers as legitimate governments is wrong. It follows that the legal theory that supports that practice (the "legalist" version of statism) is equally wrong.

For the statist, the only available rebuttal of this presumption of agency is to show that the individual who we thought had political control did not really have it. The person who we thought had subdued the people has not really succeeded in doing this. For example, he may be facing an armed rebellion, a forcible challenge to his authority.[16] Political power is the touchstone of international legitimacy, and the loss of political power likewise entails the loss of legitimacy. The legal incarnation of this doctrine is the *théorie de l'effectivité*, that is, the insistence that a government becomes internationally legitimate when it rules effectively over a territory.[17] This is not understood by lawyers simply as a necessary condition of legitimacy but as a necessary *and* sufficient condition.

Yet the theory of effective power, widespread as it is, cannot be defended under any plausible legal, moral, or political theory. Any theory of law has to distinguish between naked political power and legitimate authority, between purely physical coercion and justified coercion.[18] Lawyers and philosophers (at least in liberal democracies[19]) draw this distinction in all areas of the law, except in international law. International law thus becomes amoral, indifferent to principles of morality and legitimacy that most people consider essential in all other fields of law and politics. Again, it might well be that it is not right to intervene to alter an unjust political arrangement, but that will occur for independent reasons, not because the unjust arrangement is legitimate in some independent sense. There are two situations where foreign intervention should not be permissible. Either a state is sovereign because it is just (in the sense explained in Chapter 1), in which case intervention is precluded (deontologically) for that derivative reason; or outsiders should not intervene even when the domestic political arrangements are unjust for other (mostly consequentialist) reasons, in which case sovereignty as a deontological principle plays no role whatsoever. Sovereignty has no *independent* deontological sustenance.

State Sovereignty as a Guarantor of Communal Integrity

A more sophisticated defense of state sovereignty has been offered by Michael Walzer.[20] According to Walzer, the moral basis of sovereignty is the principle of self-determination. Communities have their own histories, hidden loyalties, and hatreds, and those communal bonds (and not some mystical view of the state as a moral person) are the bases for sovereignty. I have discussed Walzer's doctrine at length elsewhere,[21] and I will simply summarize that debate here. Walzer, following John Stuart Mill, claims that the autonomy of states (and its immediate consequence, the principle of nonintervention) derives from the imperative to preserve the *arena* in which people fight for their freedom. For Walzer, freedom and human rights are important and may very well be the ultimate foundation of the state. But this does not amount to a license to intervene for foreigners: they must respect the political process.[22]

This view, however, is paradoxical: in order to protect the political process, whose ultimate end is the recognition of freedom, we must protect the enemies of freedom, that is, illegitimate, dictatorial governments, even when doing so means helping in the denial of freedom. Walzer's argument points to moral reasons why foreigners must, other things being equal, respect the political processes in self-contained communities. But other things are often not equal, and what is delicately referred to as *the political process* is often an arena for denial of basic human rights. Why would one want to protect the contingent distribution of power and alignment of forces in a society regardless of how justified the powerholders are? In many (or maybe all) civil confrontations there are sides that are morally right and those that are morally wrong. For example, I would say that the revolutionaries in Romania were right and the forces of dictator Ceauşescu were wrong. Protecting the political process simply means refraining from helping the side that has a just cause or that is fighting for their survival. In some cases (e.g., governmental mass killings) it is a grotesque euphemism to call the event *the political process*. When human rights are seriously violated, sovereignty ought not prevail over the need to alleviate human suffering and counter evil and oppression. Put differently: the integrity of the political process is normatively dependent upon justice. There is nothing in the political process worth preserving that is independent of the reasons that justify or condemn the exercise of political power generally. Walzer's thesis can perhaps be formulated in harmless terms: if in the process of self-determination people's basic rights are generally observed, then foreigners must refrain from intervening. But Walzer would not accept this formulation: for him, politics prevail, normatively and conceptually, over morality. In truth, placing state sovereignty at the top of the international legal hierarchy amounts to exalting the state over the individual and to recognizing the prerogatives of rulers regardless of their methods of government and their legitimacy of origin. As I indicated in Chapter 1, the better view is that the protection of communal integrity depends upon the justice of the communal arrangements. Only morally defensible exercise of political power should benefit from the presumption of sovereignty provided by international law.

Qualified Statism

Lea Brilmayer has defended a mild version of statism that she calls *qualified statism*.[23] Brilmayer calls the view that I defend in this book (that state sovereignty is derivative of the rights of individuals) *derivative statism*.[24] While she sympathizes with liberalism, she finds the Kantian thesis (*derivative statism*) difficult to defend for a number of reasons. First, by giving priority to democratic legitimacy the Kantian thesis overlooks the problem of *externalities*, that is, the potential for one state's policies having effects within the territory of another. Second, the Kantian thesis overlooks the "tremendous moral significance of national membership in many people's lives."[25] The unrestrained liberal vision of the Kantian thesis would replace the communitarian notion of loyalty with a "thin and watery liberal facsimile."[26] Finally, the Kantian thesis insists that state autonomy deserves respect only when the state is legitimate, when the people have consented that the state act internationally on their behalf. But this view, Brilmayer believes, invalidates the consent of undemocratic nations, and this means invalidating most international norms.[27]

I do not find these objections to the Kantian thesis convincing. The first objection (that decisions within states cause negative externalities) is not an objection to the Kantian thesis at all. The Kantian thesis holds that only states that are morally legitimate are internationally legitimate. Brilmayer gives the following example: voters in one state harmed by the noxious fumes coming from another state cannot vote in the latter. She believes that this situation creates a problem for the Kantian thesis because those affected by the externality have no democratic control over the act in question (the emission of fumes). But those persons have democratic control in their own state, and *it* can then participate, say, in the creation of international norms regulating international pollution. Democratic theory does not mandate that all those who are affected by a decision of a legitimate authority must have the right to vote in the election of that authority.[28]

The second objection is part of a general attack that communitarianism makes against Kantian liberalism. According to communitarians, group membership, including national membership, has moral significance over and above the respect and pursuit of individual autonomy. The objection, however, will stand or fall with communitarianism. I am skeptical about communitarian arguments generally and am especially wary of the repressive policies that some of those arguments entail.[29] According to the Kantian thesis, group attachments (including national attachments) are vehicles for the pursuit of individual autonomy. Brilmayer's suggestion that this view is a *thin and watery facsimile* of nationalism may simply mean that nationalist rhetoric is more stirring than liberal rhetoric. I happily concede this and add that given the history of nationalism, perhaps this is a *virtue* rather than a drawback of the Kantian thesis. My arguments against communitarianism are developed in Chapter 6.

The strongest objection is the third one: according to the Kantian thesis state consent must be honored only if the state itself is legitimate. But because many states are illegitimate (the objection goes), the Kantian approach destroys the possibility of any workable international law. The Kantian thesis unduly disregards the consent by undemocratic states, and in doing soseriously devalues the participation of vast numbers of people in the creation of international norms. Whether the liberal likes it or not, a rational reconstruction of international law has to countenance the participation of undemocratic states.[30] Otherwise, vast numbers of people would be left without a voice in international relations. According to Brilmayer, the consent by an unrepresentative government is valid because there was no one else around to consent for that state.

The answer to this objection requires making distinctions about the available justifications for international acts. International acts may have deontological justifications or consequentialist justifications. From a principled standpoint, if A consents on behalf of B to create rights in favor of C, the consent is morally valid only if A legitimately represents B. Under the Kantian thesis, undemocratic governments are not valid consenting agents, come what may. However, Brilmayer is right that the Kantian then has to face a serious challenge in the normative analysis of international relations. Should we disallow as illegitimate the consent given in the past to a treaty by an unrepresentative government? The answer is this: many times democratic governments should honor past consent by illegitimate governments, not for deontological but for consequentialist reasons. Contrary to Brilmayer's thesis, honoring commitments entered into with illegitimate governments does not require treating them or their consent as morally valid. If the undemocratic government consented to a treaty, democratic governments will normally abide by the treaty for a number of reasons *unrelated to the validity of consent*. One reason may be the need to induce the illiberal government to do something that is morally desirable (e.g., nuclear disarmament). Thus the United States must arguably honor the recent agreement with North Korea, not because it believes that North Korean consent was validly given (it was not) but because so doing creates an incentive for the North Korean dictators to do something that is substantively desirable. Similarly, if the commitment is beneficial to the oppressed population rather than to the dictator, then honoring the commitment is the right thing to do, quite independently from the question of legitimate consent. The basis for honoring the commitment entered into with an illegitimate government is thus not *pacta sunt servanda*, since there has strictly been no *pactum*. The basis is instead a mix of prudential and moral reasons that are quite independent of the legitimacy of the unrepresentative government or the moral validity of its consent.

Brilmayer's rejoinder is not very convincing. The view that the agreements entered into with undemocratic governments must be honored only if they are substantively desirable (she argues) is inconsistent with international law, which gives special weight to the fact that the undemocratic government did consent. But this begs the question, for part of what we expect from a normative theory of international relations is to tell us what is wrong with the prevailing interpretations of international law. And, as I pointed out above, this is one of the things that is wrong with the prevailing international law views: that they improperly enfranchise undemocratic governments. International law must be conceived in a different way, one consistent with the precepts of justice. Here I believe Brilmayer falls into the Realist trap: we must validate the consent of dictators because this is the only pragmatically possible way to conduct foreign policy.

Brilmayer also believes that the *substantive desirability* argument is too paternalistic because it does not respect the autonomy of the people in undemocratic countries. But again, this move simply assumes state autonomy, which is the very notion challenged by the Kantian thesis. State consent is important (indeed dispositive in most cases) when the government validly consented, and this happens when the government genuinely represents the people. Brilmayer's objection assumes that victims of oppression have, in some important sense, delegated their right to consent to the undemocratic government. But if they have not, then it will not be correct to say that ignoring the consent of that government undervalues the autonomy of the citizens.[31] Liberal democracies must try their best to do the right thing, which includes respecting the interests of oppressed populations and the human rights of everyone and encouraging (and sometimes forcing) democratic reforms in those states.

Statism, then, prizes the sovereignty of states. But even after discarding statism, we should investigate when the infringement of sovereignty is justified from the standpoint of the Kantian thesis. Such actions may involve varying degrees of coercion,[32] but at the very least they involve the violation of a principle that is deemed central to the international legal system. In other words, an act of intervention impinges on the monopoly of coercive power that a government wields in its territory and is recognized by international law. In many cases, acts of intervention will involve actual violence to persons or damage to property. What aims can morally justify such actions? Can a government invoke the national interest, or national security, or self-defense, or expediency, or the need to punish criminals? Is something else required in the form of justification? Before we answer these questions, we must first examine the justification of international acts generally, and the justification of the principle of sovereignty itself.

The Justification of International Acts: The Realist Answer

Realists have long maintained that international behavior can be explained by postulating an overriding motivation, one that is the same for all states: the national interest. Realists see the task of the science of international relations as the study of the interactions of different national interests and the cooperative or confrontational situations those interactions generate.[33] Realism so defined attempts a *descriptive* explanation of international behavior. Whatever its merits as a thesis of political science (i.e., whether or not Realism adequately describes and explains international behavior), there is nothing in it that logically entails a *moral justification* of international behavior. The Realist can consistently claim that a state committed an action because it advanced its national interest but that on independent moral grounds the act was unjustified. The Realist need not claim that the national interest itself serves to justify international acts.

However, many descriptive Realists have imperceptibly slipped into *normative* Realism. Normative Realism is the view that national interest *justifies* international behavior.[34] Normative Realists have provided two kinds of argument. Some Realists have adopted a *state-of-nature* approach to international relations, that is, the Hobbesian position that nations are at (potential) war with each other.[35] According to this view, all is fair in war, and the only rule applicable to the state is one of prudential rationality. In a phrase, the state *should* act only to advance its national interest. According to this view, there is no such thing as justice or morality across borders. Realists are thus skeptical of any claims of morality in international policy.[36] Under this theory, a government errs when it does something it believes is in the national interest, but in reality is not; the leaders *should* have perceived the real national interest and acted on it but failed to do so.

The second path to normative Realism involves considerations of constitutional philosophy. Under liberal democratic theory, the government is the agent of the people. It is employed by the citizens of the state to serve *their* interests. A consequence of this agency relationship is that significant deviations from this purpose, such as when the government advances only its own interests, are grounds for criticism or, in the extreme, for declaring the illegitimacy of that government. Ultimately, betrayal of the democratic mandate may even justify overthrowing that government. These are the terms of the *vertical* social contract, the contract between people and government. This contract essentially specifies that the agent, that is, the government, is obliged to govern in the interest of the principal, that is, the governed.

Under this view, the duty of a government to serve the interests of its subjects is the paramount rule in international relations.[37] A government does not owe any duty to foreigners because they do not stand in any contractual relationship with it. As in the state-of-nature approach, prudence alone serves to limit foreign policy options. For example, a government seeking to advance its citizens' interests too aggressively may cause other states to retaliate, thereby *harming* those it sought to benefit. This view is appealing because it relies on democratic government *within* states to validate amoral behavior *among* states. Since governments are agents that represent their citizens, each government should attempt to further the interests of its citizens in unbridled competition with other governments. Any state should determine how to act internationally by analyzing its interests and the available options and rationally choosing the options expected to maximize those interests. There are no international principles of morality, unless morality itself is defined in terms of the rational choice just set forth. From the Realist standpoint, for example, American support for the ill-fated Bay of Pigs invasion was mistaken, not because it was morally wrong, as an instance of aggression or impermissible intervention, but because the United States government miscalculated the benefits that the invasion would bring to the United States.[38] Had the invasion succeeded and brought about the planned consequences, it would have been unobjectionable. The Realist may accuse a government of imprudence—an inability to foresee disaster—but not of immorality. Both the state-of-nature version of normative Realism and this latter version, based on the agency relationship between government and citizenry, conclude that national interest is the sole measure of international acts.

Extreme and Moderate Realism

According to normative Realism, international acts—including acts of intervention—are justified if they serve the national interest. We must, however, make a further distinction between *extreme* Realism and *moderate* Realism. According to extreme Realism, acts are justified whenever they advance the national interest. Extreme Realists thus regard the furthering of the national interest as a *sufficient* reason to carry out any operation. For example, the extreme Realist would say that when the U.S. government was deciding whether to abduct suspected criminal Alvarez-Machain from Mexico,[39] it should have balanced the expected national benefits in bringing him to justice with the potential adverse consequences of the operation. Benefits could include punishing an offender and deterring criminals from seeking shelter in other countries. Possible harms could spring from hostile Mexican responses, such as severing diplomatic relations or taking the case to an international organization like the United Nations. If, on balance, the benefits to the national interest outweighed the risks, then the abduction would have been justified on Realist grounds. That the operation might kill some innocent Mexicans or cause significant property damage in Mexico would not have weight except insofar as American interests would be affected thereby, since the extreme Realist believes the U.S. government owes no duty to Mexicans.

Moderate Realism, in contrast, contends that maximizing the national interest is a *necessary* but not a sufficient reason to justify an international act. International acts are justified when they further the national interest and *also* comply with moral principles and the requirements of necessity and proportionality applicable to all uses of force.[40] In our example, the moderate Realist might assert that the abduction of Alvarez-Machain could be morally justified only after all other means to persuade the Mexican government to render the suspects had failed, and then only if no Mexican lives were lost, since the American interest in preventing criminals from seeking safe haven in other countries arguably supersedes property considerations but not the loss of lives.

Utilitarian and Communitarian Realism

One preliminary question for the evaluation of Realism is what counts as national interest. Realists have two very different answers to this question. The first one is that national interest is the aggregate of present and future individual interests. The second answer is that national interest is an *enduring* interest held by the state or the nation over and above the interests of the individuals (present and future) that populate the state. There are goals that, if accomplished, would benefit most people in a country; for example, if American industry becomes more competitive, most American citizens will benefit since there would be more wealth and more jobs in the country. Therefore, diplomatic actions by the U.S. government that attempt to make American businesses more competitive, such as the establishment of conditions for open international trade, serve the national interest because most people in the country materially benefit from such actions. This approach defines national interest simply as the aggregate maximization of interests, or preferences, of the citizens of the state over time. What the national interest is depends upon empirical laws and theories that compute *actual* preferences and interests of the people. While such an empirical calculation may be highly complicated, there is nothing conceptually wrong with this method of defining the national interest. The definition does not refer to anything more than the actual interests of individuals; in that sense, the national interest is real, concrete, and measurable. I will call this definition, for want of a better name, the *utilitarian* conception of national interest. In its normative form, this thesis holds that the satisfaction of the net aggregate interests of present and future citizens of the state justifies international acts. An important consequence of utilitarian Realism is that the justification of international acts is sensitive to empirical claims about individual preferences. Some claims are simply empirically false, such as appeals to the national interest when the interest that is being served is that of a minority to the detriment of the population at large. The validity of claims that foreign policy serves the national interest is thus determined by empirical tests. In our example, the utilitarian Realist must consider possible consequences to the interests of citizens of the state in order to decide whether or not the international abduction is justified. An opinion poll that showed popular support for the abduction would count in favor of the abduction. Likewise, a poll showing opposition to the abduction would factor against executing the operation. The morally justified decision by the government would be the one that advanced the interests of the citizens of the state, and one way to measure these interests is to calculate their actual preferences at any given moment. (Of course, utilitarian calculations become even more complicated when one considers the interests of future citizens.)

Some Realists, however, have a different conception of the national interest. For them, national interest is *not* reducible to the aggregate interests of the citizens of the state. They reject the utilitarian claim that the national interest should be determined with reference to the current and future preferences of the people.

These Realists advance instead a holistic definition of national interest. National interest is ascribed to the state or nation as a whole. The national interest is *held by the nation or the state as a corporate entity that endures over time.*[41] This interest survives changes in internal sociopolitical arrangements and in governments. Instead of emphasizing actual preferences or interests, this view stresses communal considerations such as national glory or tradition, and ethnic or religious pride. I will call this version of Realism, for want of a better name, *communitarian* Realism.[42]

Of course, if majorities of the present and future population feels strongly about national glory or ethnic pride, their preferences will be maximized by an international act in pursuit of those goals. In this case, utilitarian and communitarian Realism will converge. The communitarian approach to national interest, however, is *not sensitive* to empirical falsification. Communitarians claim that communal values are to be found in the "intimations of the tradition" of a given society. If national interest is defined in this way, it will often be the case that the *actual* aggregate preferences of *present* citizens will not coincide with what is dictated by the "intimations of the tradition." On a communitarian justification of an international act, the fact that actual preferences do not coincide with the communitarian interest does not count against performing the act. This version of Realism is *deontological* in the sense that an appeal to the foundational principles *of the community* trumps the pursuit of the general welfare represented by actual popular preferences

Communitarian Realism has the virtue of rejecting the pure utilitarian approach to national interest described above. It recognizes that there may be higher principles that are not honored or appreciated by the majority of members of the community at a given historical moment. By refusing to base foreign policy on whatever the citizens of the state happen to prefer at a given time, or on their self-interest, communitarian Realism looks like an attempt to instill morality into international relations. In many instances the analysis will be intuitively appealing. For example, an argument against the C.I.A.'s involvement in the overthrow of former Chilean president Salvador Allende is that such action was incompatible with the principles embedded in the American tradition. For the United States to engage in that operation was inconsistent with the American tradition of respect for human rights and the will of the people. Since this tradition in turn defines national interest in foreign policy, it prevails over the possible short-term advantage of overthrowing a government perceived as unfriendly to the United States.[43]

Continuing with our example, the communitarian Realist has two possible arguments to support an international abduction of a suspected criminal. He can claim that the punishment of crimes, such as torture, that deeply offend American moral sensibilities, justifies the abduction especially since the crime was perpetrated against an American official. Alternatively, the communitarian Realist could simply contend that the abduction is justified as a way to advance the national interest of fighting the flow of illegal drugs into this country. These positions are not affected by either the public's support for, or its opposition to, the operation. Yet it is possible to supply a communitarian argument *against* the abduction. If the communitarian believes that respect for the international rule of law, embodied in commitments like treaties, serves important national interests and provides an incentive for other states to honor their legal commitments, then he may conclude that the abduction is unjustified. Here again, national interest is not coextensive with the mere short-term advancement of collective preferences.

It is worth noting, in passing, that for communitarians, too, there are good and bad communitarian arguments, just as there are good and bad utilitarian arguments—not all appeals to tradition will suffice. The debate over the morality of foreign policy is, for the communitarian Realist, always a debate about the correct interpretation of the national tradition.

A Critique of Realism

Much of the literature on nonforcible intervention (or low-intensity conflict) focuses on what strategies would best serve the national interest and is thus wedded to the normative Realist model just discussed. But is normative Realism a morally sound principle? I submit that it is not; advancing the national interest is neither a sufficient nor a necessary condition to justify international acts.

I will start with utilitarian Realism. This version of Realism, as suggested above, has considerable appeal because it is based on democratic principles. What could be more attractive than the suggestion that a government that we institute to defend our interests should do just that? Yet utilitarianism as a general moral theory has well-known fatal flaws. In the philosophical literature, the most important critique of utilitarianism comes from a deontological perspective.[44] International acts may serve the national interest in a utilitarian sense yet may be immoral. Just as an individual is expected to refrain from immoral acts even when they advance his self-interest, so in international relations governments must refrain from immoral acts even when they serve the national interest. The deontological critique thus disagrees with the often unstated premise of Realism that there is no international morality.

This flaw of utilitarian Realism can be clearly seen in a well-known problem of utilitarianism generally: its failure to take into account human rights. Surely someone committed to liberal principles would not accept the proposition that a government may blatantly violate the rights of persons in other countries, provided only that in doing so it advances the interests of its own citizens. For example, a government cannot justify killing or oppressing people in other countries simply in order to improve the economic condition of its citizens. The premise of utilitarian Realism is thus fatally incomplete: the role of government is not simply to maximize the interests of the citizens who appointed it but rather to maximize these interests *consistently with respect for human rights.* A morally justified democracy is a rights-constrained democracy, not a pure democracy where the majority does as it pleases.[45] It is correct to say government may have a *primary* duty to uphold *our* rights and *our* just institutions. But because human rights are international and universal[46] our government also has a duty to respect the rights of *all* people, foreigners included. Just as the majority may not oppress minorities within a state, so the majority may not legitimately direct its own government to ignore the rights of individuals in other states. Therefore a government's duty to maximize the preferences of its citizens cannot be a paramount international duty that excludes consideration of how people in foreign countries are treated. To be sure, utilitarian Realism has a role to play in the justification of foreign policy. When a government performs an international act (such as an act of intervention) that seriously *harms* the national interest even if the behavior serves worthy purposes, the citizens of the government's state have a claim against it for not doing its job properly.[47]

Communitarian Realism, unlike utilitarian Realism, shares with the Kantian thesis the view that valid principles trump actual interests and preferences. Yet despite its antiutilitarian, foundationalist approach, communitarian Realism is also untenable because it upholds a collective value and is, for that reason, also indifferent to human rights. Under communitarian Realism, an international act is justified when it is consonant with the tradition and the communal values of the state performing the act. Communitarian Realism does not take into account the resulting harms, including human rights violations, suffered by citizens and noncitizens alike. Because communitarian Realism favors the realization of a national interest that looms over and above the actual preferences of citizens, it is far more dangerous than utilitarian Realism, in spite of its current vogue. Indeed, communitarian Realism is too closely akin to the spurious and destructive themes of nationalism. Perhaps for that reason, communitarianism is also hopelessly relativistic. There is no internal principle to prevent the doctrine from being used to justify appalling regimes of oppression and frightful foreign policies, so long as those practices spring from the tradition of the society in question. In addition, communitarians lack the moral tools to come to the defense of *dissenters* from the tradition. For example, communitarians are bereft of arguments to defend the victims of the Tiananmen Square massacre, since arguably despotism has traditionally been part of the "intimation" of Chinese tradition. They also lack the moral tools to oppose the claim by the religious community[48] of Islamic fundamentalists to forcibly convert infidel nations, if that is part of the Islamic tradition. Communitarianism is incompatible with international human rights because the very premise of the theory rejects the notion of international justice or morality.

Unlike utilitarianism, communitarianism does not depend on principles of democratic representation. Communitarians have no reason to prefer a democratically elected government who fails to uphold that tradition to an undemocratic government who does. In the earlier example regarding the critique of the C.I.A.'s involvement in overthrowing Chilean president Salvador Allende, an appeal to community seemed acceptable because *the tradition it was based on was morally worthy on grounds other than the simple fact that it was a tradition*—it was a *liberal* tradition. In such a case, the communitarian Realist arrives at a morally desirable outcome but for the wrong reasons. One can of course argue that the C.I.A.'s help in ousting Allende was immoral because it was inconsistent with the American tradition of respect for human rights and the popular will. But what about the people most directly affected? It seems that the operation must be condemned for the effects it had on *Chileans,* not for the self-regarding reason that it was inconsistent with the tradition of the United States.[49]

A just tradition must be defended because it is just, not because it is a tradition; conversely, unjust traditions deserve no respect. A communitarian may reply that the relevant community should be defined as the *international* community. Because that community has agreed to an international law of human rights, international human rights are now part of the "intimations of the tradition" that determine the community interest.[50] This position, however, amounts to unconditional surrender, since it makes communitarian Realism true but trivial. If human rights are universal, then communitarianism is tantamount to liberalism. The communitarian can no longer identify a relevant community as legitimately denying human rights, since that community would also be part of the international community and therefore governed by the imperative to honor human rights.

Normative Realism, then, fails to supply a *sufficient* justification for international acts. Moreover, the pursuit of national interest, in either the utilitarian or communitarian versions, does not seem to be a *necessary* condition to justify international acts either. If we conclude that there is a duty to assist people in distress, or that there is a duty to transfer wealth to the needy under appropriate principles of distributive justice, international morality may mandate international aid by governments even when those acts do not advance the national interest. In conclusion, normative Realism is unappealing in any of its versions because of its indifference to universal principles of justice, human rights in particular. Utilitarian Realists are correct in seeking a liberal democratic foundation of national interest, but they lack deontological constraints on governmental behavior. Communitarian Realists, in contrast, are right to take a foundational approach, thereby rejecting the utilitarian determination of the national interest; however, they choose a faulty foundational principle—appeal to tradition. Both communitarian and utilitarian principles are insensitive to human rights.

The Kantian Justification of International Acts

The task then is to provide a theoretical basis for international morality and especially for legitimate intervention, one that avoids the pitfalls of Realism. Under the Kantian thesis, *an international act is in principle immoral when it violates human rights.* If we accept this suggestion we can see why the national interest alone cannot possibly justify acts of intervention that violate the rights of individuals in the target state. The reason is simply that *universal* human rights trump the pursuit of interest. A justified foreign policy, therefore, may be described as follows: *a government is entrusted by the citizens of the state with the conduct of foreign affairs so that the interests of the citizens will be served, provided that global human rights are respected.* The Kantian thesis is thus compatible with the pursuit of the national interest in the utilitarian sense, with human rights operating as a side-constraint to that pursuit.

The foremost interest of citizens in a democracy is to uphold and defend their just institutions; the government, therefore, has a duty to defend the state's just institutions. In a sense, this interest may seem to correspond to that offered by communitarian Realists, because the morality of defending just institutions does not depend on citizens actually wanting to defend them at any particular time. We praise a government that has the foresight to defend just institutions against the popular will.[51] As suggested above, the Kantian thesis differs from communitarian Realism, even though they may at times prescribe the same course of action. In those cases where an appeal to tradition is desirable, such as when the American tradition of defense of freedom and democracy is invoked, the communitarian interest is simply coincidentally in accord with the defense of just institutions. Liberals, however, will *already* have decided on independent grounds that freedom is worth defending. The government of a just state has a duty to defend its just institutions because they are *just* institutions, not because they are *its* institutions.

The second duty of a democratic government is to uphold and promote human rights and democracy *globally.* This tenet is supported by the two reasons discussed in Chapter 1.[52] The first reason is simply that human rights are universal, as indicated above. Human rights accrue to every human being, regardless of history, culture, or geographical circumstance. Every person has an equal claim to be treated with dignity and respect: this is the ethical foundation of international human rights. The second reason why governments must uphold human rights and democracy globally is that, as we saw, this is the only way to secure peace. By encouraging the creation and preservation of democratic societies abroad, the democratic government is building the liberal alliance, which alone can serve as the basis for a stable international community. Liberal democracies are far less prone to make war than illiberal regimes. The coexistence of democratic and undemocratic regimes is the main cause of conflict, because those two radically different political systems do not easily coexist.

We can now summarize the normative basis of foreign policy. A democratic government has a three-fold international duty: (1) to defend its own just institutions; (2) to respect the rights of all persons at home and abroad; and (3) to promote the preservation and expansion of human rights and democracy globally. These three ways of upholding human rights differ, however. The first duty of a government is to defend *its* just institutions; this duty is perhaps the only *absolute* duty that governments have. The second duty of a democratic government is to respect human rights, including protection of the rights of foreign persons when it conducts otherwise permissible acts of intervention. This duty is very strong although perhaps not always absolute.[53] The third duty of a democratic government, which is related to the second, is to defend and promote respect for human rights *by foreign governments.* This duty is strong yet constrained by moral and prudential considerations that relate to the rights of innocent people in the target state, as well as to the capabilities of the acting state, its resources, and the safety of its citizens.[54]

The corollary of the foregoing considerations is that *an act of intervention will be justified if, and only if, it is consistent with respect for international human rights.* A government may pursue the national interest, either in the utilitarian sense (defined as the satisfaction of the aggregate preferences or interests of the citizens of the state), or in the (putative) communitarian sense of defending just institutions, provided that in doing so it respects the rights of everybody. *This* version of moderate Realism is acceptable because the protection of human rights and the defense of just institutions operate as moral constraints on the pursuit of national interest.

The human rights approach helps us analyze many kinds of international acts. Take the case of insurgency and counterinsurgency. The Kantian thesis includes a theory of just war; it is the war waged in defense of human rights.[55] In most wars, international or civil, there is a side that is morally right. That side may be waging a war to defend itself from an aggressor, or to overthrow a tyrannical government (at home or abroad), or justly to secede from a parent state.[56] Insurgency operations by a democratic state designed to assist just revolutionaries are justified, provided that the help is welcome by the insurgents themselves. For example, a response to a request for assistance by Iraqi revolutionaries aimed at overthrowing Saddam Hussein would be morally justified. Similarly, counterinsurgency operations to assist legitimate, rights-respecting governments against illiberal uprisings are morally justified, provided that the government welcomes the assistance.[57]

Assistance to illegitimate governments, or illiberal groups in civil wars, on the grounds that they are friends of the legitimate government carrying out the operation, is forbidden in principle. A very important corollary of the human rights theory of international law and relations is that, normally, only legitimate governments may be supported.[58] The *liberal alliance* envisioned by Kant, and hopefully taking shape in the post–Cold War international society, is the only plausible foundation of international law, and illegitimate governments are excluded from its benefits. This point sharply brings out the contrast between Kantianism and Realism. Many Realists have maintained that, in foreign policy, we should support our "friends," even if they are despicable dictators.[59] Leaving aside for the moment the very plausible claim that in Realism's own terms such a policy is disastrous in the long run, the Kantian thesis condemns this view as profoundly immoral.[60]

The human rights–based justification of international acts is still very general, and at first blush many will find it unsatisfactory. One possible objection draws on principles of state sovereignty. An act of intervention may be conducted in such a surgical way that no one's rights are violated, yet the sovereignty of the target state would still have been punctured. That violation of sovereignty, it is argued, suffices to condemn all or most acts of intervention. In order to assess this objection, one must examine the ethical foundations of state sovereignty. So far I discussed the morality of foreign policy, that is, the moral considerations relative to the potential intervenor. I must now examine the morality of state sovereignty, that is, the moral considerations relative to the target state.

The Justification of State Sovereignty

I will now outline the principles I think underlie the concepts of state sovereignty and intervention. The twin principles of state sovereignty and nonintervention are among the best established principles of international law. A liberal conception of politics is one for which the justified civil society protects and recognizes basic human rights, of the type named in modern constitutions and pertinent international instruments.[61] A liberal conception of state sovereignty has to be congruent with the justification it offers for the legitimacy of the state generally. I suggest that a state is *sovereign* when it is *internally legitimate*.[62]

The best way to approach the question of the legitimacy of the state is to draw on the distinction between the horizontal social contract and the vertical social contract.[63] Citizens of the state are bound to one another by the principles of justice that underlie a just constitution—this is the *horizontal* social contract. Meaningful social cooperation requires the creation of government, that is, of institutions and offices to which political power is attached. These offices are occupied by persons who are democratically chosen by the citizens of the state. These persons enter, therefore, into an *agency* relationship with the people who have elected them. This agency relationship is the *vertical* social contract. In a democracy, the government is accountable to the people and has to remain faithful to the terms of the vertical contract.

It follows that illegitimacy may take place in two ways. First, the vertical contract may be breached, in which case the *government* is illegitimate. This occurs when the government is unrepresentative or, even if it was originally representative, it engages in serious and disrespectful human rights violations. The government has lost its standing since it no longer represents the citizens. Second, the horizontal social contract may break down, so that the *state* is illegitimate. This situation could result in anarchy, as in Somalia in the early 1990s, or in a fragmentation of the parent state into several independent states, as happened to the Soviet Union and Yugoslavia.

Sovereignty is the outward face of legitimacy. A government is legitimate when it genuinely represents the people and generally respects human rights. Such a government must be respected by foreigners, in particular foreign governments. A state is legitimate, and must be respected, when it is the result of a genuine horizontal social contract. In turn, a legitimate social contract, for instance a legitimate constitution, is one that, at the very least, protects the basic human rights of its citizens. Such a state must likewise be respected by foreigners, in particular foreign governments. A group of people residing in a territory, bound by a legitimate horizontal contract, may rescind the vertical contract as a result of a breach by their government. This may occur violently, as by revolution, or peacefully. The government in power becomes illegitimate; in other words, the vertical contract has collapsed. In these cases, citizens have not lost their rights. They have not forfeited their human rights or their civil society, which is the result of the social contract that protects such rights. The horizontal social contract, I emphasize, is derivative from individual rights. They have given up neither their individual rights nor their life in common, their commitment to social cooperation. The illegitimate *government*, however, is not morally protected. Foreigners, therefore, have a duty to respect human rights and a life in common in the state but do not owe a similar duty to the illegitimate government, because that government does not legitimately represent the state and its people anymore. In addition, an illegitimate government is not entitled to respect[64] because by hypothesis, if international law offered protection to this government, it could remain in power and oppress its people without fear of political pressure from the international community.[65]

It is possible, however, that the horizontal contract itself may collapse, causing civil society to disintegrate. There may be an illegitimate, spurious social contract—one that does not provide for respect for basic human rights. In these cases, the *state* is illegitimate. Of course, a fortiori the government will be illegitimate, since the vertical contract exists at the sufferance of the horizontal contract. In this case also, as in the case of collapse of the vertical contract, the former citizens—now stateless people, persons in the state of nature—maintain their individual rights.[66] Foreigners, and in particular foreign governments, must respect the human rights of the individuals that reside in that putative state, notwithstanding the collapse of the horizontal social contract. If the horizontal contract collapses, citizens do not have a claim to life in common anymore. Foreigners, therefore, are not under as stringent a duty to respect that "society" as in the case of collapse of the vertical contract. They must respect individual human rights, but there is no longer a social contract to respect. A group of individuals, not a state or a society, is all that is left.

In summary, a state is entitled to the complete protection of state sovereignty afforded by international law when it is founded upon a legitimate horizontal contract *and* a legitimate vertical contract. A state is entitled to less protection of its sovereignty when the *vertical* contract has collapsed. While human rights and the right to a life in common ought to be respected, the illegitimate government and its instrumentalities are not entitled to protection. Finally, when both the horizontal and vertical contract have collapsed, there is no sovereignty whatsoever, but the individuals that reside within the boundaries of the defunct state retain their rights, which foreigners should still respect.

We turn now to the application of the principles that support state sovereignty and how they can trump the behavior of foreign governments. I shall start with the somewhat easier question of the moral standing to intervene.

Who Can Intervene

Two conditions apply to the potential intervenor: its cause has to be just and its government has to be legitimate. We saw that the only legitimate aim of the intervenor is the protection of human rights. In some cases, as discussed above, there are moral reasons to make war, and, a fortiori, to perform less intrusive international acts. The overriding aim of a just war is the protection of human rights. A government's war to defend the rights of its citizens, when they are being violated by a foreign aggressor, is called self-defense. A government's war to defend the citizens of the target state from human rights violations by their own government is called humanitarian intervention. The second condition is that only a legitimate government has moral standing to carry out a legitimate operation (military or otherwise) *as a government.* Dictators may not validly perform acts of intervention. The reason is straightforward. The vertical contract is invalid and the agency relationship is spurious; consequently, the government cannot validly act on behalf of the citizens of the state. Its international acts, and in particular its coercive acts, such as war and acts of intervention, are invalid qua acts of the state.

At first blush, this conclusion seems counterintuitive. Why can't the illegitimate government of state A send a group of people to train and advise the combatants led by the legitimate government of state B in *its* fight against illiberal insurgents? Surely B will use all the help it can get. This, however, will not do—the government of A cannot validly order *citizens of* A to fight and perhaps risk their lives in another state, even for a just cause! Because A's is an illegitimate government, it lacks the moral standing to command. The citizens of A are not legitimately subordinate to the government and have no duty to obey. Of course, any individual has a right to join in a just war fought in another state when invited by the just warriors.[67] If people in A decide voluntarily, and are not deployed by A, to join the just counterinsurgency in B, they could do so in their private capacity. The illegitimate government may not engage the people and the collective resources of the state in any war or other coercive action.

The position defended here is in sharp contrast with Realism. Realists, especially communitarians, claim that every state has a national interest that is as legitimate and important as any other state's national interest against which it competes in the international arena. Realists do not seriously consider the possibility that a government carrying out an operation may simply be unrepresentative. There are many ways in which the Realist bypasses this inconvenient fact. For example, a Realist might argue that there are political or sociological reasons why the tyrant remains in power, or that tyranny is a natural phenomenon.[68] They might, more plausibly, distinguish between the dictator's domestic illegitimacy and his international standing to pursue the national interest. This justification ignores the fact that the international act performed by the dictator purports to engage the collective responsibility of the citizenry. Typically, the act may put the population at grave risk. Other governments may then legitimately challenge the authority of the dictator so to act, and this can be done only by resorting to some notion of domestic legitimacy.

When Intervention Is Justified

The question whether or not an act of intervention violates the target state's sovereignty is answered by applying the principles suggested in the foregoing discussion. First, I will make a terminological clarification. I use the word "intervention" in this chapter to denote any act that punctures the sovereignty of the target state. It includes military operations, but it is not restricted to them. The term includes nonforcible acts (whether or not they involve *some* degree of coercion on persons) performed in another state without the latter's consent. My aim is to explore to what extent such acts are morally precluded by the principle of state sovereignty. War is but an extreme case of coercion. Because war is subject to independent legal and moral constraints, it raises special problems. Yet I believe that intervention is governed by the same principles throughout the spectrum of coercion.

There are three possible cases relative to the target state. First, the target state is fully legitimate, meaning that both the state and the government are legitimate. Second, the target state rests on a valid horizontal contract, but the vertical contract is invalid, with the consequence that the government is illegitimate. Finally, the target "state" does not have a valid horizontal social contract—both the state and the government are illegitimate.

Intervention Against a Fully Legitimate State

Assuming the justice of the cause and conformity to the other moral constraints (i.e., proportionality and modus operandi), an act of intervention will violate the sovereignty of the target state when both the horizontal and the vertical contracts are legitimate.

The single exception, more apparent than real, to this principle arises when the legitimate government of the target state *authorizes* the operation, as is often the case with justified counterinsurgency. For example, whether U.S. efforts to help the government of El Salvador in the 1980s were barred by sovereignty considerations, other things being equal, depends on whether that government was legitimate. If the government was illegitimate, aid to that government was morally prohibited, come what may, because even express authorization by an illegitimate government is invalid. If the government was legitimate, the morality of the operation does not depend on sovereignty considerations, because of the authorization. Recall, however, that for the operation to be legitimate, the intervenor must fulfill other requirements, particularly the requirement of a just cause. A legitimate government may not always espouse a just cause, so the operation may be illegitimate on those grounds. In addition, the envisaged operation may be banned for being disproportionate, or intrinsically odious, or otherwise violative of human rights.

The Eichmann case may illustrate this point.[69] In 1960, Israeli agents located the infamous Nazi war criminal, Adolf Eichmann, living under a false name in Argentina. They abducted him in Argentina and took him to Israel, where he was tried, convicted, sentenced to death, and hanged. At the time, both the Israeli and the Argentine governments were legitimate.[70] Was the operation morally justified? This is a particularly instructive case, because punishing a war criminal is a worthy aim, especially for those, such as myself, who sympathize with retributivism. I believe, nevertheless, that the Israeli government was *not* justified in kidnapping Eichmann, as was recognized by the United Nations Security Council and the Israelis themselves, who apologized to Argentina.

First, it is necessary to examine the underlying aim of the operation. I have indicated that the main justification of international acts, and international coercion in particular, is the defense of human rights. The punishment of a war criminal, even one as evil as Eichmann, is a less compelling aim than a *direct* defense of human rights. The Israelis had two possible justifications for punishing Eichmann: retributive justice and deterrence. Retributive justice is an abstract idea of just desert that cannot easily be linked to the defense of human rights, even if one otherwise accepts the retributivist justification of punishment.[71] Deterrence is only *indirectly* linked to the defense of human rights. A deterrence argument would justify punishment of Eichmann in order to show potential war criminals and mass murderers that they will suffer should they violate human rights. Since the fear of punishment will prevent some war crimes, so the argument goes, the probability of rights violations will decrease.

Under either deterrence or retributivism, the goals pursued by the Israeli government, while morally worthy, are insufficient to outweigh a legitimate state's sovereignty. The Israelis should have requested authorization from the Argentine government before they abducted Eichmann. Even if the Argentines had refused to help the Israeli cause, and there is no evidence that they would have, I believe that the moral foundations that support the sovereignty of a fully legitimate state defeat legitimate retributive interests. Of course, given the horrific nature of Eichmann's crimes, the Argentine government would have acted immorally had it refused to surrender or, in the alternative, prosecute Eichmann. Even then, Israel could not justifiably seek a remedy that violated a legitimate state's sovereignty. Members of the liberal alliance have a duty to resort to rational methods of solving disputes. Abductions have no place *within* the alliance, no matter how noble the cause or how vile the target of the operation.[72]

What about the Alvarez-Machain case, mentioned above? Assuming the most favorable facts for the U.S. government, that is, that Alvarez-Machain was in fact guilty of complicity in acts of torture, the Alvarez-Machain case is indistinguishable from the Eichmann case. Mexico is a legitimate state, and the Mexican government a legitimate government. Mexico is a member of the liberal alliance;

therefore, its sovereignty must be respected. The United States has no right to intervene in Mexico; moreover, it had a solemn duty to resort to the agreed-upon methods of dealing with criminal fugitives, such as the extradition treaty in force between the two nations.[73] Had Mexico refused to extradite Alvarez-Machain, the United States would not have been justified in using coercion. Only diplomatic and judicial remedies, such as a case in the World Court, are available among liberal republics. It is unfortunate that the U.S. Supreme Court refused to give even the slightest consideration to this central question of international morality.

Intervention Against an Illegitimate Government

The second situation, in which the targeted state is legitimate but its government is not, is more complex. In such cases, assuming all other necessary conditions are met, acts of intervention are *legitimate only if they are directed against the government itself and its instrumentalities*. This means that the operations may not violate the human rights of the citizens or disrupt their life in common. The example of Iraq may serve to illustrate this point. I already indicated that a legitimate government's assistance to an insurgency of Iraqi citizens aimed at ousting the Iraqi dictator would be morally justified.[74] Suppose that the United States contemplates an operation to destroy the arsenal of Iraq, in particular all those facilities and materiel that may increase its nuclear capabilities. State sovereignty does not preclude this operation, because it is directed against the government and its instrumentalities and not against the citizens of Iraq.[75] In such cases, the citizens have not waived their human rights or their right to have a state or a life in common. Therefore, the operation must respect these rights and the local institutions that represent their freely chosen life in common. The intervention must be tailored as narrowly as possible as an action against the government, not the people. Some cases are relatively clear, as when a democratic government aids revolutionaries against a tyrannical ruler, or protects imminent victims of genocide, or rescues nationals in danger.

Even in these clear cases the citizens of the target state have not given up their state. The operation must respect the local institutions reflective of their life in common. One hypothetical example may help clarify this principle. Suppose the U.S. government has detected in Cuba a notorious drug lord suspected of very serious crimes in the United States. Is the United States morally justified in abducting this person from Cuba? The Cuban government, we shall assume, is illegitimate, but the Cuban *state* is not. In other words, Cubans have a right against foreigners that their life in common be respected. This may include institutions such as the judicial system. The answer to our question will depend on whether the courts in Cuba are independent or subservient to the Castro regime. If the former, the U.S. may not act and must instead utilize diplomatic channels, such as a request for extradition. If the latter, the courts are not an institution to administer justice to the Cuban people but rather a mere instrumentality of the illegitimate regime. In this case, I suggest that the United States may act, provided the operation satisfies the other requirements. Action is justifiable because the United States would be doing no more than capturing a suspected criminal from his hideout among a gang of outlaws of the international community. After all, illegitimate governments are no more than gangs of outlaws, usurpers.

Because the citizens in the target state retain their individual rights, acts of intervention are complicated by the very difficult and virtually unavoidable problem that some innocent people may be injured or killed during an otherwise justified operation. The most prominent doctrine to justify incidental killing of innocent people in a just military action is the doctrine of double effect, which is in part recognized by modern international law. According to this doctrine, incidental loss of lives in war is not prohibited if the *intent* of the just warrior is to obtain a military advantage, not to victimize innocents, even if he can *foresee* the deaths of innocent people.[76]

The doctrine of double effect, however, has been recently challenged by Judith J. Thomson. Her critique is skeptical of the moral relevance of the doctrine's crucial distinction between specific intent to kill bystanders and mere foresight that bystanders will die. In her view, if there is any justification for the incidental loss of lives of bystanders in a war, it must depend on the justice of the cause—on the larger purpose of the operation.[77] Thomson, however, bypasses this question as too complicated, *et pour cause:* justifying the loss of innocent lives is perhaps the major challenge faced by any nonutilitarian theory of just war.[78] Providing a satisfactory defense of the doctrine of double effect is beyond the scope of this discussion. I will, however, make three observations. First, unless we find *some* justification for the incidental killing of innocent people, no war or revolution could ever be justified. I am aware, of course, that this begs the larger question of the justification of war: maybe pacifists are right, and no violence is ever justified; or maybe utilitarians are right, and the only plausible thing to do is to weigh costs and benefits of war. But *if* one rejects utilitarianism, and *if* one accepts as a point of departure that sometimes fighting a war or a revolution is the morally right thing to do, then we must come up with some rights-based justification for the incidental killing of bystanders. Second, the justification for the incidental loss of innocent lives in a nonforcible act of intervention does not differ from the justification given for such loss in conventional war. Whether one chooses the doctrine of double effect or the larger cause doctrine to justify incidental loss of innocent lives in a just war, the same rationale is available for justified acts of nonforcible intervention. Recall that the other constraints, such as proportionality and modus operandi, always apply. Finally, there is an important difference in blameworthiness between the warrior fighting for a just cause who diligently tries to protect innocents and the just warrior who chooses to terrorize and victimize them in his pursuit of the just end. An operation against an illegitimate government, then, must not be *aimed* at innocent people, even if that is conducive to the demise of the tyrant. Moreover, the agents conducting the operation must design it with the protection of bystanders in mind.

Intervention Against an Illegitimate State

When a state is illegitimate the social contract has collapsed and sovereignty considerations no longer apply. In some instances when the horizontal contract has disintegrated, anarchy reigns and different groups may control different parts of the territory.[79] The intervention still has to have a just cause and, as always, the individual rights of the residents ought to be respected. All the considerations regarding innocent bystanders discussed in the previous section apply here as well. In these cases the people must be allowed to rebuild a legitimate state if they wish to do so. Humanitarian intervention must be accompanied by measures facilitating the political reorganization of local forces on the basis of free elections and respect for human rights. People who traditionally have lived in a region must be permitted freely to enter into a social contract.[80] These are not easy questions to answer, and the solutions will vary considerably depending on the facts.

Necessity, Proportionality, and Decency

The main purpose of this chapter has been to suggest principles with which to evaluate acts of intervention in light of state sovereignty. Two other conditions, however, further restrict the legitimacy of these acts. The first is the customary requirement of *necessity* and *proportionality*. Acts of intervention satisfy the requirement of necessity only if no less intrusive means are available to accomplish the same goal. Proportionality involves calculations of the costs and benefits of the operation in a way that is not solely dependent upon the national interest, however measured. The general rule is that the coercion used in the operation and the consequent harm done by it have to be proportionate to the importance of the interest that is being served, both in terms of the intrinsic moral weight of the goal and in terms of the extent to which that goal is served.

The second of these final conditions for a morally defensible act of intervention is that the modus operandi must not be so odious as to be corruptive of the virtues that people must exhibit in a liberal democracy. The operation should not be morally self-defeating.[81] This requirement rests upon an important moral insight: there are things we cannot do to others because of what *they* are (i.e., they hold rights), and there are things we cannot do to others because of what *we* are.[82] What are we? As individuals having inherent dignity and value, and as members of a just civil society—a liberal democracy—we must act in such a way as to cultivate our civic virtues and best character traits. This applies, a fortiori, to actions by the government, which is supposed to act for the *polis*. In part, the insistence on governmental virtue in the conduct of foreign policy derives from self-interest; we cannot expect our government to behave honorably with *us* if it goes around the world sending hit squads to assassinate and torture people, even for just causes.[83]

An example may help illustrate this proposition. Is it morally permissible to assassinate Saddam Hussein? I would think not. The proper course of action is to help the Iraqis overthrow him, capture him, and bring him to trial before Iraqi courts or an international court in accordance with internationally accepted norms of fair trial. Assassination is banned, not because the punishment is necessarily inappropriate in light of Hussein's crimes but rather because agents of a liberal democracy must conduct themselves in a way that honors the civic virtues for which they stand. Criminal punishment can only be imposed through the mechanisms allowed by liberal society. The same reasoning applies to other intrinsically contemptible modes of action, such as torture and terrorism, regardless of sovereignty considerations, just cause, or national interest.[84]

A Note on Neoliberalism and International Relations

In recent years an energetic school of thought has reacted against the predominant Realist model. This movement, which calls itself "neoliberalism," has challenged the Realist assumption that states ought to be considered as closed and self-contained units in international relations. In the words of a representative of this trend: "All governments represent some segment of domestic society, whose interests are reflected in state policy. . . . The behavior of states . . . reflects the nature and configuration of state preferences [i.e., as shaped by their domestic origin and configuration]."[85] Not all governments, therefore, are the same. Above all, the national interest is determined not by the anarchical nature of international relations, but by the domestic features of the state. This view is an important improvement over Realism. It removes the theoretical obstacle that obsessed Realists, namely the apparent united front presented by states in the international arena. Neoliberals correctly observe instead that the people who rule states are political actors and that therefore what they do and say internationally is intimately related to their domestic origin and role. Neoliberals thus attempt to puncture, in a descriptive sense, the barrier of sovereignty. For that they deserve ample credit.

Yet in spite of its name, this view is still far from the liberal view espoused in this book. Neoliberalism is quite close to Realism because it accepts the premise that states act out of interest alone. The only amendment to Realism, albeit an important one, is that domestic politics adetermine the national interest and consequently the foreign policy of the state interest. This seems to me correct yet insufficient on two grounds. First, the dynamics of the relationship between domestic politics and the national interest that projects itself outwards is quite complex, and it is not captured by the surprisingly neoMarxist assertion that the ruling elite transposes its domestic interests into the international arena. Second, and most important, this view fails to address the crucial dimension of *legitimacy*. While liberalism is compatible with several possible views of human nature, it is not a theory about the dynamics of politics, domestic or international. It is a theory about the *justification* of political power of any kind. It is a normative thesis about rights, obligations, and principles. So even though this new school of thought is an improvement over Realism because, in a descriptive sense, it pierces the veil of state sovereignty, it says nothing about legitimacy in the international system (or the domestic, for that matter). For that reason, the theory seems to be a misnomer:

the link between neoliberalism and liberalism in the tradition, say, of Kant, Locke, and Rawls, seems quite weak.

Defenders of the thesis, in response, make two points: first, the label "liberalism" emphasizes the importance of international institutions (or regimes) in facilitating cooperation among states.[86] Second, liberal states get along better with one another (the Kantian empirical argument described in Chapter 1). As to the first point, international institutions may or may not serve liberal values (as exemplified by the highly illiberal United Nations during the 1970s). As to the second point, one can ask what is the basis for preferring the liberal alliance over other arrangements. After all, liberal governments are also carriers of class or other interests. In order to privilege liberal states and governments, one has to say that they are morally legitimate while illiberal states and governments are not. The neoliberals reply, with Kant, that the liberal alliance should be privileged over their illiberal colleagues because liberal states do not go to war. But, as I discussed in Chapter 1, this reason for preferring the liberal alliance is precarious. If someone could show that an evil world empire is even *more* likely than a liberal alliance to maintain a *pax romana*, then these writers should prefer that arrangement. In short: there is no escape from normative theory, from the question of legitimacy. The liberal alliance that seems to be emerging from the Cold War is not to be praised only, or primarily, because it is more apt to maintain peace: it is to be preferred because it reflects morally just political arrangements.

Notes

1. For a discussion of the collective intervention in Iraq to protect the Kurds, see Fernando R. Tesón, *Humanitarian Intervention: An Inquiry Into Law and Morality* 234–241 (2d ed. 1997) [hereinafter Humanitarian Intervention]; and Sean D. Murphy, *Humanitarian Intervention: The United Nations in an Evolving World Order* 165–198 (1996).

2. The *Restatement of Foreign Relations Law* § 201, is typical of the traditional view. See also Montevideo Convention of 1933, article 1: "The state as a person of international law should possess the following qualifications: (a) a permanent population; (b) a defined territory; (c) government; (d) capacity to enter into relations with other states."

3. See, inter alia, Declaration On Principles of International Law Concerning Friendly Relations and Cooperations Among States in Accordance with the Charter of the United Nations, United Nations General Assembly Resolution 2625 (XXV), United Nations General Assembly, 25th Session, Supplement No. 28, at 121, *United Nations Document* A/8028.

4. To my knowledge, this view was first defended by Charles R. Beitz in his seminal work *Political Theory and International Relations* 69–83 (1979). I adopt it in Tesón, *Humanitarian Intervention*, supra note 1, Chapters 3 and 4.

5. See supra, Chapter 1.

6. This view benefits from the authority of Spinoza and Rousseau. For Spinoza, see Kenneth Waltz, *Man, the State, and War* 174 (1958). See also Jean-Jacques Rousseau, *Du Contrat Social* [1762] 185 (Seuil ed. 1977) ("a l'egard de l'etranger, il [i.e., the state] devient un etre simple, un individul").

7. For a full discussion of the principle of self-determination, see infra, Chapter 5.

8. I discuss the nationalist thesis in Chapter 5.

9. See references supra Chapter 1.

10. I discuss this assumption in Chapter 3.

11. Waltz, supra note 6, at 179.

12. The leading works in this regard are Michael Walzer, *Just and Unjust Wars* (1977); and Beitz, supra note 4. See also, Lea Brilmayer, *Justifying International Acts* (1989) and Marshall Cohen, "Moral Skepticism and International Relations," 13 *Philosophy and Public Affairs* 299 (1984).

13. Waltz, supra note 6, at 177–178.

14. See Vienna Convention on the Law of Treaties, May 23, 1969, article 7, *United Nations Document* A/Conf. 39/27.

15. Thus, Thomas Franck, for example, concedes that international law responds to the "priorities and sensibilities of rulers" and believes that that is evidence against considering justice as an essential component of international legitimacy. Thomas M. Franck, *The Power of Legitimacy among Nations* 226 (1990).

16. See, e.g., James Crawford, *The Creation of States in International Law* 269–270 (1979); and J.L. Taulbee, "Guerilla Insurgency and International Law" 12 *Indian Journal of International Law* 185–199 (1972).

17. See, inter alia, Charles De Visscher, *Theórie et Realité en Droit International Public* 255 (4th ed. 1970).

18. Even positivism as a general theory of law endorses the distinction between pure power and legal authority. See, e.g., H.L.A. Hart, *The Concept of Law* 82–91 (2d ed. 1994).

19. In some legal systems, courts use the so-called "de facto" doctrine (*doctrina de facto*) to validate legislation enacted by dictators. In Argentina, for example, the courts invoked the doctrine of effective political power *in international law* to legitimize unconstitutional usurpations of power. See the superb treatment of this infamous piece of legal history in Carlos S. Nino, *Un País al Margen de la Ley* (1992). I believe this practice illustrates my point that traditional international law *favors* oppression.

20. See Michael Walzer, "The Moral Standing of States: A Response to Critics," 9 *Philosophy and Public Affairs* 209 (1978–79).

21. See Tesón, *Humanitarian Intervention*, supra note 1, at 92–99.

22. See Walzer, supra note 12, at 89.

23. See Lea Brilmayer, *American Hegemony: Political Morality in a One-Superpower World* 175–192 (1994).

24. Id. at 181.

25. Id. at 184.

26. Id.

27. Id. at 185.

28. Thus, the fact that people in California produce noxious fumes into Arizona might give me the right to request (say, to courts or administrative agencies) that the fumes stop. But this is very different from having the right to vote in California.

29. See the discussion infra, Chapter 5. The best reply to communitarianism is, in my view, Will Kymlicka, *Liberalism, Community, and Culture* 47–99 (1989).

30. This approach is quite similar to the one John Rawls has taken. I discuss it fully in Chapter 4.

31. As an example, consider this counterfactual: people in my native Argentina would be better off, I believe, if foreigners (both governments and corporations, like banks) would have refused to consider the Junta's consent as valid.

32. See Sam C. Sarkesian, "The American Response to Low-Intensity Conflict: The Formative Period," in *Armies in Low-Intensity Conflict: A Comparative Analysis* 19, 21 (David A. Charters & Maurice Tugwell eds., 1989) (showing a continuum of coercion in different types of conflict).

33. Seminal works in the Realist tradition include Hans J. Morgenthau, *Politics Among Nations* (1959); Waltz, supra note 6; and Hedley Bull, *The Anarchical Society* (1977). I realize, of course, that I am oversimplifying Realism. The doctrine has many variations, yet I deal in the text with the central and, as far as I know, uniform methodology of national-interest analysis.

34. See, e.g., George F. Kennan, "Morality and Foreign Policy," 64 *Foreign Affairs* 205, 205–208, 217 (1985–86).

35. 2 Thomas Hobbes, "On Dominion" in *The English Works of Thomas Hobbes of Malmesbury*, 63, 169 (Sir William Molesworth ed., 1841) ("For the state of commonwealths considered in themselves, is natural that is to say, hostile"). See generally *Hobbes: War Among Nations* (Timo Airaksinen & Martin A. Bertman eds., 1989). For a modern version of this view, see Terry Nardin, *Law, Morality, and the Relations of States* (1983).

36. For a convincing response to the Realists' moral skepticism, see Cohen, supra note 12.

37. See id.

38. Why not calculate the benefit of the international act to the world in outright utilitarian fashion? By privileging self-interest (national interest), normative Realism is closer to ethical egoism than to utilitarianism.

39. See United States v. Alvarez-Machain, 112 S.Ct. 2188 (1992).

40. For a discussion of necessity and proportionality, see infra text accompanying notes 86–89.

41. I have called this idea "the Hegelian Myth." See Tesón, *Humanitarian Intervention*, supra note 1, Chapter 3.

42. Communitarians have confined themselves to domestic political philosophy. For representative communitarian views, see Michael J. Sandel, *Liberalism and the Limits of Justice* (1982), and Michael Walzer, "The Communitarian Critique of Liberalism," 18 *Political Theory* 6 (1990). To my knowledge, no one has applied communitarian philosophy to international law and relations. Walzer is a curious case. Even though he is usually seen as a communitarian philosopher, his views on war are predominately liberal. Liberal writers have their own critiques of communitarianism. See Kymlicka, supra note 29; Amy Gutmann, "Communitarian Critics of Liberalism," 14 *Philosophy and Public Affairs* 308 (1985); Carlos Nino, "The Communitarian Challenge to Liberal Rights," 8 *Law and Philosophy* 37 (1989).

43. For a defense of this view, see Kennan, supra note 34, at 214.

44. The seminal works in this regard are John Rawls, *A Theory of Justice* (1971) and Ronald Dworkin, *Taking Rights Seriously* (1978).

45. See Immanuel Kant, "To Perpetual Peace: A Philosophical Sketch" [1795], in *Perpetual Peace and Other Essays* 107, 114 (Ted Humphrey trans., 1983); see also supra Chapter 1.

46. The concept of the universality of human rights has been persistently challenged over the years (especially by governments who wish to violate them), but I believe that such universality holds both as a matter of morality and as a matter of positive international law. More recently, the otherwise quite deficient Vienna Declaration has reaffirmed the principle of universality. See Vienna Declaration and Programme of Action, 25 June 1993 (copy

furnished to the author by the U.S. Department of State), part II, paragraph 1 ("The universal nature of [human] rights is beyond question").

47. When an agent, such as a lawyer, fails to serve the interests of his client, the client has a claim against the lawyer, even though the lawyer be motivated by the noblest of concerns.

48. While community may often be seen as defined by national borders, community may or may not coincide with nations—witness religious communities, or the moral community of Europe defined by the European Convention on Human Rights.

49. The coup opened the door to years of oppressive military government.

50. I take this to be the thrust of the New Haven school, with its emphasis on clarification of global community policies. See Myres S. McDougal et al., "The World Constitutive Process of Authoritative Decision," in *International Law Essays* 191 (Myres S. McDougal & W. Michael Reisman eds., 1981). For my critique, see Tesón, *Humanitarian Intervention*, supra note 1, at 17–21.

51. An example of this is the refusal of the French government in exile to accept the surrender of the French people to the Nazi occupiers during World War II.

52. See supra, Chapter 1.

53. There are a number of reasons to support the view that states legitimately have lesser duties vis-à-vis foreigners. These are analogous to the reasons that individuals have a greater duty toward their family members than to others. Yet even these subordinate duties are absolute within their proper compass: the fact that we normally do more things for the people that are close to us does not mean that we can violate the rights of others.

54. Notice that I am talking here about duties, not rights. I take for granted, at this stage of development of international law, that democratic governments have a *right* to demand human rights compliance from other governments and, in some extreme cases, even to intervene by force to help victims of serious oppression. See generally Tesón, *Humanitarian Intervention*, supra note 1.

55. See id. at 121–122; see also David Luban, "Just War and Human Rights," 9 *Philosophy and Public Affairs* 60 (1980).

56. See generally Allen Buchanan, *Secession: the Morality of Political Divorce From Fort Sumter to Lithuania and Quebec* (1991) (advocating various arguments as moral grounds for the right to secede). I discuss secession in detail in Chapter 6.

57. This proviso derives from considerations of autonomy, which apply to acts in defense of others. See Judith J. Thomson, "Self-Defense," 20 *Philosophy and Public Affairs* 283, 305–306 (1991). But self-defense of the state is always, in effect, defense of others. In repelling an aggressor, the government assists citizens who are being victimized by aggression, and individuals fight in defense of fellow citizens. It follows that, as I have tried to show elsewhere, the rationale for self-defense does not differ in substance from the rationale for humanitarian intervention. See Tesón, *Humanitarian Intervention*, supra note 1, at 119–120; see also Fernando R. Tesón, "International Obligation and the Theory of Hypothetical Consent," 15 *Yale Journal of International Law* 84, 117 (1990).

58. I say "in principle" and "normally" because one can imagine a situation where the only way to avoid a moral catastrophe is to temporarily support an illegitimate government. An interesting case arises when two tyrants are fighting each other. Here the liberal democracy must refrain from helping either, except in very extreme situations, such as when one tyrant, if victorious, will drop a nuclear bomb or cause a similar catastrophe. But it is never morally right to support a tyrant against a democracy, or a tyrant against democratic forces resisting him, or illiberal rebels against a democratic government.

59. Even in the midst of the current global democratic revolution, we can see the endurance of this ruthless approach: Western governments befriend the Syrian dictator Hafez al-Assad and the current Chinese leadership, on account of spurious *national interest*.

60. We do not even need a very deep theory of morality to condemn the Realist's advocacy of help to *friendly* dictators. Whether one relies on the universality of human rights (as I do), or on an American or Western communitarian tradition, or on pure compassion, the result is the same.

61. See, e.g., Universal Declaration of Human Rights, General Assembly Resolution 217A (III), 3 United Nations General Assembly (Resolutions, part 1) at 71, *United Nations Document* A/810 (1948).

62. I made this point in Tesón, *Humanitarian Intervention*, supra note 1, at 77–79, 81–99, 117–121. See also Beitz, supra note 4.

63. The distinction between the two kinds of social contracts was suggested by Hannah Arendt, "Civil Disobedience," in *Crises of the Republic* 49, 85–87 (1969). I elaborate the idea here in more detail.

64. I realize that this is not the thrust of international law, which tends to protect any government that has succeeded in subduing the population. See Tesón, *Humanitarian Intervention*, supra note 1, Chapter 4.

65. This is not to say that foreigners may do *anything* with regard to an illegitimate government. In particular, they may not overthrow it without the consent of the citizens of the state. Id. at 126–129.

66. Imagine that in an unexplored area of the globe we discover individuals who do not have any political or social organization, who just wander in the region. Human rights, I believe, would pertain to them, although I will not attempt to prove this point.

67. I believe that people have a *duty* to assist, to the extent possible, their fellow citizens (i.e. citizens of the same state) against an unjust aggression; this is the only possible justification of conscription enforced by legitimate governments. I will not, however, attempt to demonstrate this difficult point here.

68. Cf. Michael Walzer, "The Moral Standing of States: A Response to Four Critics," in *International Ethics* 217, 229 (Charles R. Beitz et al., eds., 1985).

69. Attorney-General of the Government of Israel v. Eichmann, 36 *International Legal Reports* 5 (District Court of Jerusalem 1961), reprinted in D.J. Harris, *Cases and Materials on International Law* 266–274 (4th ed. 1990).

70. This was one of the brief periods of civilian government in Argentina.

71. See Jeffrie G. Murphy, "Retributivism, Moral Education, and the Liberal State," *Criminal Justice Ethics*, Winter–Spring 1985, at 3. Kant's reason for rejecting deterrence and adopting retribution is unsatisfactory. See Immanuel Kant, *Metaphysical Elements of Justice* 99–106 (John Ladd trans., 1965) (criminals must be punished because if we don't, we share in their blood guilt).

72. Of course, the situation changes radically when we change the dateline. Suppose Eichmann is residing in Buenos Aires in 1978, sheltered by the fascist military régime. The considerations against abducting him do not apply here and Israel would have had a strong moral case for conducting the operation. The requirement that the operation be as surgical as possible still applies.

73. See Extradition Treaty, May 4, 1978, United States–Mexico, 31 *United States Treaties* 5059.

74. See supra text accompanying note 62.

75. Recall that the other conditions must obtain. In this case, the aim—prevention of aggression by a tyrannical government—is justified.

76. An updated version of the doctrine is offered in Warren S. Quinn, "Actions, Intentions, and Consequences: The Doctrine of Double Effect," 18 *Philosophy and Public Affairs* 334, 334–336 (1989).

77. See Thomson, supra note 57, at 292–296.

78. In *Humanitarian Intervention*, I adopted Daniel Montaldi's suggestion that incidental loss of lives in an otherwise justified war can sometimes be justified by reference to the nature of the evil that the just warriors are attempting to suppress. I suggested that the suppression of serious and disrespectful human rights violations was an interest compelling enough to outweigh, sometimes, the bystanders' right to life. Tesón, *Humanitarian Intervention*, supra note 1, 103–108. Although I think I was on the right track, this view (which is consistent with Thomson's "larger cause" suggestion) needs to be elaborated further.

79. Lebanon in the 1970s and Somalia and Yugoslavia in the early 1990s may be examples of this situation.

80. By "freely," I refer to *individual freedom*.

81. Virtue theory is usually traced back to Aristotle. See generally Nancy Sherman, *The Fabric of Character: Aristotle's Theory of Virtue* (1989). For a contemporary account, see Alasdair C. MacIntyre, *After Virtue: A Study in Moral Theory* (2d ed. 1984). The effect of adding virtue considerations to rights considerations is that the scope of morality is enlarged. In that sense, virtue theory provides important insights and supplements to liberal rights theory. However, contrary to virtue theorists, I regard civic virtues as parasitic on the values that underlie a liberal democracy, not the other way round.

82. See Robert A. Nozick, *Philosophical Explanations* 400–402 (1981).

83. See generally Thomas Nagel, "Ruthlessness in Public Life," in *Public and Private Morality* 75, 78–79 (Stuart Hampshire ed., 1978) (discussing whether public morality can be derived from public morality).

84. Of course, Saddam Hussein may die at the hands of agents sent to arrest him if he chooses to resist, and the action will not thereby become illegitimate.

85. Anne-Marie Slaughter Burley, "International Law and International Relations Theory: A Dual Agenda" 87 *American Journal of International Law* 205, 228 (1993) (citing Andrew Moravcsik, "Liberalism and International Relations Theory" (working paper, Center for International Affairs, Harvard University, 1992)). This article contains further references on neoliberalism and its debate with Realism.

86. A representative author is Robert O. Keohane, *After Hegemony* (1989).

3

International Law, Game Theory, and Morality

Introduction

International law writers since Grotius have claimed that the consent of states is the foundation of international law.[1] According to this theory, positivism, the two standard forms of state consent, custom and treaty, alone create international law.[2] Custom is aggregate consent over time, or acquiescence to mutual behavior by most or some of the states (universal or regional custom); a treaty is consent expressly given in one act. There are several versions of positivism, but the most popular claims that states consent from *interest*.[3] In this view, states create international law in two steps: first they identify matters of common interest, and then they consent to those norms that best serve those interests. States agree to treaties and customary practices in an effort to implement cooperation, if their interests converge, or reach acceptable compromises, if their interests diverge. States consent to international law from self-interest, and their consent in turn creates legal obligations. So positivism rests on two pillars: national interest and state consent. Nations are motivated by self-interest when they confront one another, and they create norms to regulate matters of common interest. According to positivists, then, international law emerges as a normative solution to the clash of national interests in the relations among states.

In this chapter I argue that this breed of positivism is untenable for three reasons. First, the simultaneous appeal that positivists make to national interest and state consent prevents them from adequately explaining international obligation. Second, nations may consent to immoral things. Third, consent by a government to a norm does not automatically entail consent by the people of that state to that norm. While challenging positivism as a thesis of international jurisprudence, I nonetheless defend the international lawyer's normative account of international obligation against the prudential account favored by international relations scholars. In the next section I present some problems raised by the application of the familiar Prisoner's Dilemma to international relations. In the third section I explain why game theory fails to explain moral choice. In the fourth section I first analyze the concept of treaty and conclude that game theory cannot explain the obligation to observe treaties. I then propose a game-theoretical analysis of the concept of custom and conclude that game theory, while useful to predict the emergence of custom, cannot explain why customary norms are binding. In the fifth section I suggest that *pacta sunt servanda* and *opinio juris* are best understood as moral condemnations of self-interested deviation from international norms created to solve Prisoner's dilemmas. In the sixth I argue that state consent cannot be the basis of obligation if one accepts that governments may consent to immoral things, that is, if one accepts, as lawyers do, the concept of *ius cogens*. Finally, in the last section I reformulate in game-theoretical terms my long-standing critique of statism. The Appendix illustrates the logic of the Prisoner's Dilemma with an example.

National Interest and Game Theory

Positivism gives a simple answer to the oldest question in international jurisprudence: Why should states obey international law? The question, however, is ambiguous. Someone who poses the question may be asking any of the following:

1. What *in fact* motivates states to obey international law?
2. Is there a *prudential* reason for states to obey international law?
3. Is there a *moral* reason for states to obey international law?

International lawyers and political scientists have mostly focused on the first question.[4] The answer requires an investigation into state motivation and will consist of a descriptive, sociological study of why governments behave the way they do. An answer to the second question requires a more complex analysis: one would have to determine how nations should behave if they properly understood their national interest. The third question, finally, is normative and requires an appeal to a moral-political theory of international law. In Chapters 1 and 2 I described such a theory: governments should abide by an international legal system that is itself just, that is, when it is construed in accordance with liberal principles of justice.

The appeal to national interest, however, connects positivism with a different tradition in international theory, Realism.[5] This tradition focuses, not on the third question above (the moral reasons to obey international law) but on the first and second questions. The states' international behavior, Realists claim, is determined by the nature of the international system, from the structure of incentives faced by governments of sovereign states in their relations with one another. The Realist analysis of state behavior focuses on *strategic* incentives—those faced by rational self-interested governments in light of the expected behavior of others. The Realist explanation of international behavior relies on a perceived structure of costs and benefits, or payoffs, generated by strategic interaction. The tool that writers have used for this analysis is game theory.[6] Game theory is particularly well suited to international relations because the lack of higher authority places international actors in a situation of pure strategic interaction, where they are solely concerned about the limits that the behavior of others places in their pursuit of self-interest. When states refuse to cooperate with one another one cannot recommend government intervention (as one would routinely do when individuals refuse to cooperate) for the good reason that there is no world government. Unlike what happens in domestic law, in most international situations the expected payoffs to states are not altered by the threat of sanctions, because sanctions are weak or nonexistent.[7] Pure strategic incentives are, therefore, central to the conduct of foreign policy.

Game theory teaches that international cooperation is difficult, even when it is desirable, because many international situations take the form of the Prisoner's Dilemma (PD). (The reader unfamiliar with the logic of the Prisoner's Dilemma might now want to consult the Appendix to this chapter.) This analysis of international relations explains why states, who operate in a semi-anarchical situation and would be better off cooperating, nevertheless often refuse to do so: mutual cooperation is not automatic even if it is preferable to mutual defection. States often refuse to cooperate because they are afraid of being exploited by other states. The dominant strategy is for each to defect; and because all states reason in the same way, the frequent result is mutual defection.[8] With no higher power to curb defections, nations are thus caught in the corrosive logic of the Prisoner's Dilemma.

This analysis, however, calls for a number of cautionary observations. First, not all international situations take a PD form; nations may face each other in many different kinds of situations.[9] They may encounter situations of conflict or situations of cooperation; more often, they may relate to one another on relatively broad issues that include both.[10] A situation involves conflict when it is true that anytime a change in outcome makes some player better off it makes some other player worse off. A situation of pure conflict is one in which *every* change in outcome leaves one player better off and the other worse off. A game involves cooperation if some change that makes one player better off makes another player better off as well. A game is pure cooperation if in it *every* change that makes one player better off makes all players better off. If two nations fully converge in their interests, their rational behavior is always to cooperate. They do not need to bargain or communicate because they are guided by an invisible hand, as it were. International relations scholars call this matrix Harmony.[11] States do not need to cooperate because the self-interested behavior of each will converge with the equally self-interested behavior of the other: there are no gains from defection. Self-interested behavior converges in spontaneous harmony and there is nothing to cooperate or coordinate about. Conversely, sometimes states will never achieve mutual benefit from cooperation because there are no mutual interests. This is the game of Deadlock.[12] States do not have any interest in common: each state can gain nothing by cooperating even if the other state cooperates. In both these situations each nation lacks an incentive to take into account the behavior of the other. They are better off ignoring one another.

Hopeful observers may confuse Harmony or Deadlock with genuine PD cases. If two neighboring states are arming, this may occur either because each country is fearful of being exploited if it disarms (PD), or because there is no advantage whatsoever in disarming, regardless of what the other country does (Deadlock). Similarly, if two states disarm, it may be either because they cooperated to avoid the dangers of cheating, for instance by providing for adequate monitoring or reprisals (a solution to the PD), or because disarming is in the best interest of each regardless of what the other does (Harmony). Kenneth Oye puts it well: "When you observe conflict, think Deadlock—the absence of mutual interest—before puzzling over why a mutual interest was not realized. When you observe cooperation, think Harmony—the absence of gains from defection—before puzzling over how states were able to transcend the temptations of defection."[13]

International situations may also take the form of the Coordination Dilemma.[14] In this matrix cooperation is the preferred outcome, but there are several cooperating options and the parties cannot easily identify which one the other parties will choose. Take the case of makers of compact discs (CDs) and CD players. Both industries are interested in cooperating to sell their products to consumers. In order for that to happen, however, it is crucial for them to agree on one standard size for the CD. It doesn't matter much which size, but they have to settle on one to be successful. After the size has been agreed to, it is irrational for any individual producer to depart from the norm, for example by making CDs or CD players of a different size: there are now no gains from defection. They know they are better off if they all choose one size, but they do not know in advance which, and if they do not coordinate their action there will be no cooperation. In these situations, then, mutual cooperation arises when one party identifies a cooperating alternative and signals its intent to the other parties to behave accordingly. The cooperating choice becomes the *salient* feature of the interaction, and it becomes more so with repeated play.[15] The outcome is stable because no party has an interest in defecting. For example, states parties to a multilateral treaty have an interest in knowing what reservations other parties make, and when and how they can object to those reservations. The Vienna Convention on the Law of Treaties provides some procedural rules for making and objecting to reservations.[16] Governments presumably don't really care about what those procedural rules should be, for example, whether the deadline to object to a reservation should be twelve or eighteen months, but they do want all states to agree to one of those alternatives. While in the Coordination matrix states face initial obstacles to cooperation caused by their uncertainty about the moves of others, the matrix is different from the PD matrix and chances for mutual cooperation are greater.

A second observation is also standard: when the PD is repeated, cooperation can emerge as a long-term strategy. Players may depart from the dominant strategy of mutual defection and decide to cooperate when they have an expectation to interact again—this is called *iteration*.[17] As Robert Axelrod has shown, if the actors have an expectation of interacting frequently in the future, their best long-term strategy may be to cooperate.[18] The motivation is the prudential realization that one has to interact with the same players in the future. One example of iteration occurs when the community has social cohesiveness. Game theory treats states as anomic self-interested actors, unable to make reciprocal promises.[19] But if there is high social cohesiveness in the international community, defection is expensive: the defector will be punished in future interactions with the same players. Here the matrix will reflect the new payoffs, altered by the long-term consequences of defection. Whether the international community or a subset of it is sufficiently cohesive to reduce the number of defections is, of course, an empirical matter. Take the case of the Kantian liberal alliance discussed in Chapter 1. A game-theoretical analysis of the alliance may see it as a relatively cohesive community in which sister democracies tend to cooperate with one another on many issues. They cooperate, on this view, because they have expectations of mutual interactions and are not prepared to pay the cost of punishment for defection. I suggest, however, that this description of the liberal alliance is incomplete at best. Its shortcoming stems from a weakness in game theory: its difficulty to explain moral choice. In the next section I explore this problem.

The Difficulty of Game Theory to Explain Moral Behavior

A central claim of the Kantian thesis is that persons are ethical agents, that they are able to act ethically and that sometimes they do so. How does game theory account for the behavior of ethical agents? Suppose a democratic government is trying to isolate a tyrannical regime by imposing commercial sanctions against the country. Other governments, however, refuse to join because they want to take advantage of the boycott by trading with the regime and thus occupy the place left in the market by the boycotting country. The ethical government will still do what it believes to be right, even when it thereby becomes vulnerable to exploitation. Some writers call such behavior irrational or extrarational.[20] Others, however, explain moral choices in a different way. According to Robert Keohane, an agent has an ethical preference when he prefers to be exploited than act unethically.[21] The matrix will look as follows:

	Cooperate	Defect
Cooperate	4\2	3\4
Defect	2\1	1\3

Here the Row player is ethical while the Column player is not. Let us take a possible interpretation of the current situation in Cuba. Row (the United States) has decided to apply trade sanctions to the Castro regime on account of Castro's serious human rights violations.[22] In doing this, the United States suffers an economic loss, because Column (say, the European Union) refuses to join the boycott and trades instead with the Cuban regime. The U.S. government, let us assume, believes that the boycott is the right thing to do given the importance of getting governments to respect human rights and thus chooses to impose sanctions even though there are associated costs. Under Keohane's analysis, this means that the United States prefers to be ethical regardless of what the European Union does. The matrix, therefore, is no longer a PD structure, as shown above. The first preference of the United States is to impose the boycott and have the European Union join as well (mutual cooperation). Its second preference is to boycott even when the European Union defects and trades with Cuba (unrequited cooperation). On this view, ethical behavior *means* cooperating behavior that the agent chooses even when he knows that others will take advantage of him. The ethical agent prefers to be exploited than to act unethically.

In a similar vein, Robert Cooter explains internalization of a norm as the situation where the agent experiences a "guilt penalty" to its violation, thus altering the psychological payoffs.[23] We can say (following Cooter *mutatis mutandi*) that the international community includes both cooperators and defectors. In turn, some cooperators act out of respect for international law (principled players) and some for convenience (adventitious players). Cooter defines a principled agent as one who cooperates even if the objective payoff for cooperating is slightly lower than for defecting.[24] These agents have internalized the norm. Adventitious players are those that will cooperate only if the payoff for cooperation is at least as high as for defection: they have not internalized the norm. So governments that act out of respect for international law are willing to sacrifice their interests slightly, whereas those that comply with international law just for prudential reasons are unwilling to give up even that slight amount of benefit. In our example of Cuba, the European Union might perhaps be willing to join in the sanctions against the island if it is at no cost to them. At the moment when condemning the Castro regime causes the European Union an economic loss greater that the benefits of the condemnation, it will defect. Thus, on Cooter's analysis, the European Union would be either a defector or, at best, an adventitious cooperator. It would not have internalized the moral norm that mandates condemnation of despotic regimes. The United States is, in contrast, a principled cooperator because it is willing to undergo small losses for its moral behavior. Yet when the losses are high (as they presumably would be if the United States decided to condemn China for its human rights abuses, for example) the United States will relent and defect also. On this view, the U.S. government will still be a principled agent, because it is willing to incur *some* cost for compliance. This view seems to imply that when the cost of virtue is high principled behavior is irrational.

Illuminating as these explanations may be on many aspects of human behavior, their account of ethical behavior is unsatisfactory. The game-theoretical explanation does not account for the difference in the *kind* of choice between mere preference and moral choice.[25] If an agent chooses ethically, he is not simply preferring one course of action to another because of a calculation of expected payoffs to the agent's interest. He makes the moral choice simply because he thinks the choice is correct. If the choice is his moral duty, it overrides other alternatives regardless of payoffs to self-interest (at least, perhaps, until the point where the cost to the agent becomes prohibitive). A moral agent does not do his duty *because* it increases his payoffs; in fact, he often does his duty in exactly the opposite situation: the ethical agent chooses *against* his inclinations, against his preferences. In international relations, the genuine moral actor is not simply weighing the alternatives in terms of expected payoffs to national interest, as Keohane's and Cooter's approaches seem to suggest. What is distinctive about doing our duty is that we are obligated to do it especially when it is costly to us, when doing it frustrates some preference or interest that we have. That is why moral choice cannot be captured by strategic analysis.

As Kant noted, the view that ethical choice is just another preference trades on the ambiguity of the word "good."[26] The word can mean something that is good in itself, or something that is good only relatively to something else: the act of complying with a moral principle, without reference to an ulterior end, falls into the first category and so it is *essentially* different from the act of pursuing our interest, our happiness.[27] This confusion results in a second ambiguity: that of the word "preference." It is of course tautologically true that if an agent chooses to do X rather than Y (for whatever reason, including a moral reason) then he prefers X to Y.[28] Rational choice theorists treat this tautology as an insight, as evidence to support their view that all agents make preferences, whatever moralists may call them. But if X is the agent's moral duty and he acts from duty, then X is not a preference for that agent in the more narrow sense in which the term is used by economists and rational choice theorists: the sense of preferring X because the agent perceives X to maximize his self-interest more than Y. If the agent has a deontological reason to do X, then his doing X is not just another relative preference. As Jeffrie Murphy put it: the conflict between duty and inclination is not a conflict *within* my empirical self but *with* my empirical self.[29] The upshot of the objection is this: sometimes governments will act ethically, from duty, and this is not reducible in a straightforward way to an attempt to advance the national interest. This conclusion does not support the view that ethical behavior is irrational or extrarational. Of course, moral behavior is irrational in the trivial sense that it is not strategic, but there is no reason to confine rational behavior to strategic behavior. Ethical behavior is the result of the one motivation that rational choice theorists by definition cannot recognize: moral motivation. Game theorists only need to know *that* the agent did X; and this knowledge is enough for them to postulate, without more, that the choice was strategic. Kantians need to know *why* the agent did X before determining the nature of the choice.

The explanation of why the liberal alliance cooperates illustrates the differences between Kantians and Realists. For Realists, as we saw, sister democracies cooperate because they find themselves in an iterated PD situation. Defection is too costly because governments expect to interact with one another and defectors face punishment in future interactions. The Kantian, without of course denying the importance of prudential motivations, suggests that the inclination of democratic governments to cooperate with one another stems, at least sometimes, from their principled adherence to the liberal values of democracy and respect for human rights. It may well be that sister democracies have prudential reasons to behave well, but I do not believe this tells the whole story. People in democratic countries (and the governments that represent them) may *believe* that democracy and respect for human rights are morally right and be inclined to cooperate with fellow liberal societies precisely for that reason, which is independent of calculation of interest. Of course, democracies often have opposing interests (witness the trade differences between the United States, the European Union, and Japan), and thus they are sometimes tempted to defect. Yet we may assume that often they cooperate because they believe that cooperation is the right thing to do, regardless of future payoffs. As we shall see in the following sections, this shortcoming of game theory has serious implications for the view that interest plus consent generates legal obligation.

International Law and Game Theory

How can game theory explain international law? We saw that on the traditional view states create customary or conventional rules to advance their interests. Some of those rules are generated by Harmony matrices, others by cooperation in PD situations, still others by cooperation in Coordination-type situations. From a game-theoretical perspective, the binding force of international law is merely the expectation that other nations will abide by the rules out of self interest. Positivists, however, claim that norms are created by consent. Governments interact in a variety of situations and they voluntarily create rules to govern their mutual behavior. This of course they do moved by interest, but their consent creates binding rules. The question that interests me now is this: Does game theory (which, when applied to international relations, is a model for analysis of the pursuit of national interest) support positivism? Would self-interested actors feel bound by norms to which they consent? Is it possible, in short, to have at the same time national interest and consent as the founding pillars of international law?

To the extent that game theory is an analytical tool to predict where national interest will lead when meshed with other national interests, it should be able to tell a story about international law. The general idea is that international norms, including international law and international regimes, emerge as a result of states' interaction over time. This claim sounds trivial enough, but there are three nontrivial claims associated with it. The first is that the kind of interaction that generates international norms is strategic interaction, in the sense described above. The second is that international norms (treaties and custom) emerge as a way to solve problems of cooperation, such as Coordination and PD situations. The third is that states abide by international law because it is in their interest to do so, when that interest is properly construed. Let us examine, then, treaty and custom from this perspective.

Treaty

A treaty is an international agreement concluded between two states in written form and governed by international law.[30] A treaty is, therefore, an explicit agreement between states (and international organizations). The conventional account of how treaties emerge is as follows. Two or more governments find that they share a matter of common interest (potential cooperation) or that they have a dispute that they wish to settle (potential conflict). They thus initiate negotiations until they reach a point of understanding. That point may have been reached by persuasion, mutual concessions, more or less veiled threats, or any combination thereof. At that point each party believes that it cannot possibly gain more and the treaty is then adopted. When the treaty enters into force it becomes legally binding by virtue of a norm of customary international law that mandates compliance with treaties: *pacta sunt servanda.*[31] Treaties are rendered obligatory, therefore, by a rule of customary law. There are also rules governing termination of treaties by breach of the other party, by faulty consent (fraud, error, coercion), or by fundamental change of circumstances.[32] In principle, states may adopt proportionate countermeasures for breach of treaty, but under article 2(4) of the United Nations Charter they may not generally exact compliance by force.

How does a treaty emerge? Why do states feel that they need a treaty to address a matter of common concern? Under game theory, a treaty can be defined as a *norm* that emerges as a *solution* to problems posed by certain problems of strategic interaction faced by self-interested governments in their relations with one another.[33] Several situations are possible. Let us assume first that the matrix is Harmony. In this case the parties simply do not need a treaty, because their spontaneous behavior leads to the satisfaction of their interests (the invisible hand). Their behavior is spontaneously coordinated, as it were, and there is no incentive to formalize cooperation as long as the common interest persists. For example, the United States allows its citizens freedom of information and people in Canada receive, as a result, books and newspapers, which in turn are freely allowed in Canada. The spontaneous behavior of the U.S. and Canadian governments leads to a Pareto improvement for both nations. There is no agreement between these two governments, and they do not need one as long as the invisible hand does its job.[34]

The second possibility is for the parties to be placed in a Coordination dilemma. If so, they will need a treaty as a means to fix on the cooperation points. They adopt the treaty to *signal* to each other which of the available means of cooperation they will adopt: they coordinate their actions.[35] Because the parties have a mutual interest in cooperating, a strategy of cooperation is dominant with respect to a strategy of defection. However, there is more than one way to cooperate, more than one equilibrium point. Which one an agent will choose will depend on which one the other agents will choose, so sometimes lack of trust or of communication will prevent them from reaching a mutually desirable solution. Negotiating a treaty is a good way to help overcome the problems of distrust and miscommunication.[36] When governments communicate through negotiation they become aware of the mutual advantages of reaching a solution and thus agree to the treaty. The treaty, an explicit agreement, identifies the point of equilibrium and becomes "the firmest rallier of the participants' expectations regarding each other's actions."[37] The agreement, moreover, is self-enforcing: both parties have incentives to comply because the solution reached by the treaty is an equilibrium point. For example, Argentina and the European Union have a mutual interest in trading. Argentina can sell foodstuffs to Europe and Europe can sell industrial products to Argentina. Both parties, let us assume, experience a Pareto improvement as a result of this exchange. However, there are many possible procedures to implement trade, all of them equally plausible a priori. Cooperation might be frustrated if the parties don't know how to approach one another, how to make payments, and so on. A trade treaty, by stipulating definite mechanisms of exchange (among, perhaps, several possible) resolves these problems and clears the way for the parties to engage in mutually beneficial behavior.[38]

It is instructive to distinguish the Coordination matrix from the Harmony matrix described above. Both in Harmony and in Coordination the parties' interests converge. But unlike what happens in Harmony, in Coordination the behavior of each is affected by the actual or expected behavior of the other. They can achieve their mutually beneficial result only if they coordinate their actions; thus the need to communicate. In Harmony, the independent pursuit of self-interest by each leads spontaneously to the optimal result for both. There is no need to coordinate anything and consequently Harmony, unlike Coordination, is not a dilemma.

Let us suppose, however, that the parties are caught in a PD matrix. Here the situation is altogether different. Each state will have an incentive to defect to take advantage of the other party even when mutual cooperation would be more beneficial to both than mutual defection. In a PD structure, parties will need the treaty to deter potential violators and free riders tempted to take advantage of those who comply. For example, let us assume that the nuclear powers want to negotiate a treaty for the gradual elimination of nuclear weapons.[39] The nuclear powers are collectively better off by eliminating all nuclear weapons than by all keeping them. However, each is better off having the other countries eliminate their nuclear weapons while preserving its own; therefore, this is a PD situation. Many writers have already noted that this situation is significantly different from the previous problem of Coordination.[40] In the case of Coordination everyone stands to lose by deviating from the treaty because it represents a stable point of equilibrium. In the PD situation, however, the optimal collective result is *unstable*: parties are always tempted to defect, and it is rational for a player to do so if it can get away with it.

What is the normative status of the treaty in a PD situation? The PD structure of incentives creates a serious problem for positivism (the view that international obligation is based on consent derived from interest). The problem here is that if the parties are motivated by interest, they can hardly have a reason to honor the treaty when doing so is not in their interest. Even if the parties enter into an agreement in order to reach the collective optimal solution (mutual cooperation), there is no incentive for a party to comply with the agreement after the treaty has entered into force if that party can exploit the other with impunity. It may be rational for one of the parties treacherously to violate the treaty if breach is in that party's interest. And the treaty itself cannot create an obligation, because game theory's assumption is that parties act out of interest, not out of a sense of duty. If, however, what we mean by the assertion that the treaty is *binding* is that it is rational for the state to comply with it,[41] then the treaty is not binding on the potential successful defector.

Of course, my criticism (that there can be neither an obligation nor a rational incentive for a state to comply with a treaty in a PD situation) seems too quick. There are several responses to the criticism, and while they do not entirely succeed, they help refine it. First, one can respond that in PD situations the parties to a treaty can attach sanctions for breach in order to deter defectors.[42] A treaty is not binding unless it is backed by such sanctions, because otherwise the treaty cannot solve the PD situation satisfactorily. When sanctions are stipulated in the treaty (or their possibility is otherwise known to the parties), the payoffs change and the situation is no longer a PD matrix. Would-be defectors are deterred by the sanctions and it is now in their interest to comply with the treaty.[43] In our example, if the treaty on elimination of nuclear weapons authorizes the parties, individually or through the United Nations Security Council, to enforce its terms (for example, by destroying the hidden weapons of the offender) then the situation will no longer be a PD structure. The enforceable treaty makes it rational for the would-be defector to renounce its intentions. Yet here again, if the would-be defector thinks it can cover its tracks and avoid the sanctions (for example, by concealing its nuclear weapons in a remote area), then it will not have a rational motivation to comply. And if the claim that a treaty is binding is equivalent to the claim that it is rational to comply with its terms, then the treaty will not be binding on the would-be defector.

A second response draws from the idea of iteration discussed above. We saw that if the PD situation is repeated with the same players, would-be defectors will have a long-term interest to comply, because they run the risk that their present defection will be punished in the future. According to Axelrod, cooperation in a PD can be achieved if the agents are aware that they face "the shadow of the future"—repeated interactions with the same players. The game-theoretical calculations here are quite complex, but the central idea is clear: a *tit-for-tat* strategy may suffice to deter potential offenders in the long run because they face retaliation (*tit-for-tat* in an iterated PD is the strategy of doing what the other does, but never being the first to defect).[44] So in our example of the treaty on elimination of nuclear weapons, the would-be defector, while it may gain short term advantages from defection, may be nonetheless deterred from keeping its weapons because it will otherwise be punished in the next situation in which it interacts with the same parties. For example, it will be denied trade or other benefits. The incentive to cooperate in an iterated PD requires, however, two conditions: the agents should not discount the future too much, and they should be able to observe each other's moves.[45] If the government does not really care about future interactions with the parties against which it is planning its defection, that is, if all it really cares about is the preservation of its nuclear weapons, then it has no reason to comply with the treaty.

More centrally, as in the previous cases, iteration does not create an *obligation* to obey the treaty. The would-be offender refrains from violating the treaty for prudential reasons, so *pacta sunt servanda* plays no role whatsoever. If iteration is the true reason why states should abide by treaties, then the rule should be formulated very differently. The rule should read: "A state should honor treaties if and only if doing it is in the state's long-term interests." It may well be that this rule is all international lawyers need to explain treaty obligations, but it is certainly very far from *pacta sunt servanda*. Iteration does not create an obligation to comply; it only warns states to be careful in the calculations of their long-term interest. In other words: traditional international law treats *pacta sunt servanda* as a deontological principle not subject, generally, to calculations of national interest. In contrast, the game-theoretical explanation treats *pacta sunt servanda* simply as a generalization of the prudential rule that it is generally in the best long-term interest of states to honor treaties and thus as a rule that *is* subject to calculations of national interest. These two versions are very different, and their difference, as I said in the preceding section, lies in the logical structure that each of them possesses. Game theory cannot explain obligation, come what may.

Another response is suggested by Phillip Pettit: agents are motivated by the esteem (affection, respect) that they receive from others. In his words:

> The key to the attitude-based strategy of derivation [of norms] is the recognition that there is a cost-benefit structure operative in social life which rational choice theory has generally neglected: the structure associated with people thinking ill or well of

an agent—or being thought to think ill or well—whether they actually censure or praise.[46]

On this view, the claim that only severe sanctions create incentives for agents to comply with agreements is an exaggeration. The desire for esteem, respect, or affection may be enough to induce them to honor their agreements. This approach can be nicely applied to international law: a state will abide by a treaty in a PD situation not only when it can expect to be physically punished if it defects but also when the desire for *national prestige* is intense enough to deter defection. In our example, a state tempted to keep its nuclear weapons might nonetheless want others to regard it as an honorable, law-abiding nation, and so it might want to honor the agreement for that reason.[47] Of course, it is always an empirical matter whether the offending nation's chances of covering its tracks are great enough to outweigh its desire for prestige. The desire for prestige is, in other words, an additional factor in the computation of national interest.

If the desire for prestige is great enough, the situation is no longer a PD. The difference with the previous view (that sanctions change the payoffs) is simply a difference about what motivates governments: nations are moved in part by a concern that other nations not think badly of them.[48] The desire for prestige, not the fear of sanctions, changes the payoffs. But the reason to comply with the treaty is still self-interested: increasing the nation's prestige is part of the national interest that the government attempts to advance by complying. Here again, if the government does not believe that compliance will increase prestige, or if the advantages from breach are great enough, the government will breach the treaty. And, once again, if the binding force of the treaty depends on interest, then the treaty will not be binding on that state.

The upshot of the game-theoretical analysis of treaties is this: states do not have an incentive to perform an international act or omission unless doing so is in their self-interest. This situation does not change when a state agrees to a treaty, because a state always has a rational incentive to violate the treaty when doing so is in its interest. Even where states are sufficiently motivated to comply (for iteration, or fear of sanction, or loss of prestige), the motivation will always be prudential. Under the assumptions of game theory, consent does not do *any normative work* in the explanation of international behavior. A treaty performs instead two nonnormative functions: it signals the salient point of cooperation in Coordination situations, and it signals the possibility of retaliation and criticism in PD situations. In short: under the game-theoretical approach, consent cannot possibly generate an obligation to comply with the treaty.

Custom

Unlike treaty, custom is concordant practice repeated over time that eventually becomes backed by a general opinion that criticizes deviation, praises compliance, or both.[49] According to the traditional view, custom consists of two elements: state practice and *opinio juris*. The practice of states is diplomatic behavior; *opinio juris* is the belief that such behavior is legally required or permitted.[50] Here I am interested in the view that customary law, too, is the result of the intersection of states' interests. Custom creates law, on this view, when states spontaneously behave in a way that others accept and correspond. Custom, unlike treaty, is spontaneous. Nations then continue behaving the same way and start criticizing those who deviate. When criticism for deviation is strongest we speak, following Hart, of norms of obligation. When criticism is weak, we speak of norms of courtesy.[51] On a first approach, *opinio juris* can then be defined as strong criticism for deviation.

A game-theoretical analysis of customary law might run along the following lines: states spontaneously identify certain salient features of a situation as those that might be appropriate for a point of equilibrium. We saw that a point of equilibrium is one of Pareto optimality that is also stable, that is, from which it is irrational to depart once it has been reached. Because there is more than one such point, states must coordinate behavior. Custom is the way in which states, through their behavior, identify one equilibrium point among several possible, just as a treaty does. If other states follow suit, then the point of equilibrium has been reached and a customary norm emerges. If this analysis is correct, it follows that a customary norm arises initially to solve a Coordination matrix. In a coordination problem, as we saw, the question is to coordinate our behavior so that we will both improve. Each agent has to choose among several alternative actions, where the outcome of any action depends upon the action chosen by each of the others. A norm emerges and persists if it efficiently resolves this dilemma. The nature of the problem is such that the agents either win or lose together.[52] A customary norm, as a regularity of behavior, is in the interest of all involved, and so deviation is irrational. We all improve by following the norm. In the words of Edna Ullman-Margalit, "the reward for conformity to a regularity in these circumstances . . . consists in the very act of conforming, since it guarantees what is desired by all: the achievement of a coordination equilibrium."[53]

But how can regularity of behavior turn into a *binding* norm? This is the question that international lawyers ask: When does *opinio juris* emerge? A plausible answer is this: a repeated pattern of behavior becomes a norm when the participants in the practice wish to channel the behavior of newcomers.[54] This is the situation of new states in the international community. With the arrival of new states, the identity of the agents engaged in the practice changes, and it is by no means guaranteed that the newcomers will want to join in the specific equilibrium point chosen by the original participants in the practice. By describing the regularity now to newcomers as a *binding customary norm*, the incumbents attempt to secure the cooperation of new states. This is the phenomenon that traditional scholars try to describe when they assert that new states are bound *ipso facto* by international law.[55]

The analysis can be further extended to the change of *governments*. When the government of a state changes there is also a change in the identity of the participants in a practice. International law, of course, proclaims the principle of the identity of the state, but this is just a fiction aimed at holding new governments to the international commitments entered into by previous governments.[56] The behavior required by international law is behavior required of the government. If the government changes, then the legal requirement is addressed to a different person, to a newcomer. Incumbent governments, those who have participated in the practice, want to make sure that the new government will follow the practice in question; that is why the practice is described to the newcomer as binding. The new government cannot simply object that the practice is not in *its* interest. *Opinio juris* emerges, therefore, when the original participants in a spontaneous regularity of behavior start treating that behavior as legally required in order to secure the adherence of new states and governments.

When this happens, however, the matrix changes. It is not longer a Coordination problem but a PD problem and not just for newcomers but for incumbents as well, provided that we maintain the assumption that compliance was strategic in the first place. The possibility of exploitation destroys the automaticity of cooperation for everyone. The original participants in the practice now have to guard against exploitation, and this creates an incentive for everyone to defect. The (previous) point of Pareto improvement is no longer stable. The *normativity* that is now superimposed to the practice (*opinio juris*) is aimed at deterring potential violators by altering their payoffs for deviation. If the violation of customary law carries sanctions, we are in a situation almost identical to that of a treaty that contemplates sanctions, discussed above. The original state practice, which was initially a Coordination matrix, has now mutated into a PD matrix. This explains the emergence of *opinio juris*. (As we shall see a full explanation of *opinio juris* requires a normative component as well.)

When a customary international norm arises to solve a PD matrix (which, as we saw, is a mutation from an initial Coordination matrix) we have, plausibly, a *mixed equilibrium*.[57] A mixed equilibrium is one where most nations cooperate and some defect (if most defect there is no customary norm). Those states that follow the norm expect modest payoffs in a high proportion of interactions, whereas the defecting states expect high payoffs in a low proportion of rounds. In a mixed equilibrium these two strategies have the same expected value.[58] Thus, for example, customary international law requires that governments secure authorization by coastal states before fishing in their Exclusive Economic Zone (EEZ).[59] A state that decides to ignore the norm and harvest in someone else's EEZ expects that the beneficial consequences of this act (the value of the harvest) will compensate the harmful consequences of retaliation. Moreover, in a mixed equilibrium some states comply with customary norms for "principled" reasons,[60] others follow the norm for prudential reasons, and still others defect (the mixed equilibrium always includes both cooperators and defectors). Game theorists define the principled actor, as we saw above, as the one that cooperates even if the objective payoff for cooperating is slightly lower than for defecting. The government that follows the norm for prudential reasons (the "adventitious" player) will do so only when the objective payoff for cooperation is at least as high as for defection.[61]

If the preceding analysis is correct, it is unlikely that a customary norm will emerge *initially* to solve a PD problem, because a state caught in the dilemma will rationally defect if in that way it will maximize its interest. The so-called *instant custom* will only be possible in a Coordination structure of incentives and not in a PD structure.[62] In a PD, a state that foresees gains from defection has no incentive to observe the regularity that is being proposed by other nations that are trying to get the practice started. Under the assumptions of game theory, it seems unlikely that a regularity of behavior will emerge spontaneously in a PD situation. By definition, cooperation by a state in a PD situation is irrational if it does not further the state's interests. In a PD, spontaneous cooperation is difficult, and thus custom will not easily emerge: states will defect at the first opportunity. In other words: Custom is not likely to emerge if defection is the dominant strategy, as it is in a PD. Binding customary law is the result of an initial Coordination matrix that later mutates into a PD matrix by the arrival of new states or governments. The *emergence* of custom requires a Coordination matrix; the *endurance* of custom requires that the participants find a solution to a PD matrix.

We can now summarize the game-theoretical explanation of customary international law. Customary norms emerge in the following situations:

1. Governments facing a Coordination matrix where they need to identify a point of cooperation;
2. Situations of iterated PDs where governments perceive the potential future interaction as sufficiently important. Because nations expect to confront each other again many times, it is important for them to allow the "shadow of the future" to count in the calculation of national interest; and
3. Situations where the self-enforcing regularity in a coordination situation becomes a PD situation by the arrival of new states and changes of government in old states. When that happens, the customary norm is no longer self-enforcing, because it is no longer in the interest of the parties to follow the practice in all situations. States need additional motivation (sanctions or their equivalent) that are external to the situation itself. This situation can be described as a mixed equilibrium.

The criticism I made to the game-theoretical analysis of treaties applies equally to the game-theoretical analysis of custom. Game theory can explain why states follow practices but cannot explain why they *ought* to follow practices. The international lawyer claims that when a customary norm has arisen it is binding, not that it is in the state's interest to follow the norm. Game theory cannot reconstruct this claim: it explains it away. If the norm has emerged to solve a Coordination matrix, then it is always rational for states to comply with the norm. Neither consent nor *opinio juris* do any work here. If, however, the norm emerges to solve a (formerly Coordination matrix mutated into) PD matrix, then the standard PD analysis holds: states will be motivated to comply if violation is costly, but they will defect if violation is cheap. Here too, the concept of obligation is out of place. Interest does not and cannot generate obligation.

Pacta Sunt Servanda and *Opinio Juris*

As I mentioned before, the traditional view of treaties is that states negotiate and make treaties in order to address matters of common interest. If one asks why a treaty in force is binding, the answer is that there is a rule of customary law according to which treaties must be honored—*pacta sunt servanda*, as we saw.[63] Yet I showed that if one believes in the model of rational, self-interested nations, *pacta sunt servanda* will not predictably emerge as a customary rule. Rather, the behavior that the rational actors imagined by game theorists will observe will be something like this: "I will comply with treaties that solve coordination problems, since it would be harmful for me to depart from the equilibrium point. I will also comply with treaties that solve PD problems, unless it is in my interest to defect, that is, if I can defect and get away with it, all things considered (including iteration)." So, in a world of self-interested states, *pacta sunt servanda* cannot possibly be a customary norm, because governments will not support the rule that treaties must be honored regardless of cost.[64]

So what is the status of *pacta sunt servanda*? I suggest that *pacta sunt servanda* is a *moral* rule, not a customary rule. It stems from two related moral intuitions. The first is that, other things being equal, keeping one's word is the right thing to do, regardless of interest and especially when it is against interest. The second is that, other things being equal, it is morally wrong to *exploit* those who in good faith rely on our promised behavior. But game theory cannot rest on these moral premises, for the good reason that there are no moral premises in game theory. On a rational interest model, the behavior of states cannot support *pacta sunt servanda*, because self-interested states will rationally support (and seem to have historically supported) a rule that allows for opportunistic breach. It is true that governments have always publicly supported *pacta sunt servanda*, even though it is a rule that is not in their interest to support. The reason for this lip service is, I suggest, quite straightforward: everyone with a normal moral sense knows that, other things being equal, the right things to do are to honor treaties and to refrain from exploiting others, but when the time for action comes, self-interest often gets in the way. That is why the practice of states shows an abundance of opportunistic breaches, with the resulting gap between words and deeds. Why do international lawyers ignore this practice and continue to say that *pacta sunt servanda* is a customary norm? I suggest that they have the right moral instinct coupled with the wrong theory of custom. It is morally clear that states must honor their treaties (other things being equal), even against their interest. Indeed, a possible definition of a moral agent is "one who, in a PD chooses the cooperative action on the assumption that the other is also going to make the same choice, and who, moreover, does not deviate from this choice even if he be certain that the other cannot . . . punish him later by deviating too."[65]

While, as I shall argue below, this definition misses crucial features of morality, it helps us understand the concept of *pacta sunt servanda* in the law of treaties. We say that *pacta sunt servanda* is a binding rule of international law, not because we have inferred the rule from a supposedly objective examination of state practice (it could not be that way anyway, since, as we saw, diplomatic history abounds in opportunistic breaches). We assert the obligation to honor treaties because we realize that the contrary rule (that states may make promises with the reservation that they may breach them opportunistically) is morally intolerable.[66]

A similar analysis applies to the concept of *opinio juris* in customary international law. To claim that there is a binding customary norm is morally to condemn defection from a practice. In the law of treaties, the purpose of *pacta sunt servanda* is to underscore the moral force of promises and to condemn opportunistic behavior. Similarly, international customary law cannot be simply inferred from state practice.[67] To say that X is a customary rule is to condemn, for moral reasons, self-interested deviation. The inductive approach to custom fails, therefore, to tell the whole story. To be sure, citing the practice of past condemnation counts as support for a customary rule, but lawyers will often defend a rule in the face of inconsistent practice because it is the right, fair, or best rule.[68] The principle that states must observe international human rights provides an interesting illustration. How can that principle be binding customary law, given that many governments persistently violate human rights? Game-theoretical explanations do not work, because it is always rational for governments to violate human rights if oppression is in their interest (for example, if they want to suppress bothersome dissent). But lawyers rightly describe the obligation to respect human rights as a moral imperative subject neither to confirmation by state practice nor to the possibility for governments to balance that obligation (in most cases) against their other national interests. Violators are those who deviate from the ideal norm. In other words: when human rights advocates vindicate respect for human rights as a customary norm they are saying that cooperation (respect for human rights) is the right outcome, that it is right for governments to cooperate and wrong to defect. But this norm cannot be possibly supported by state practice, because the practice includes the deviators. So our rights-loving lawyer interprets history as an interaction between cooperators and deviators in a mixed equilibrium and chooses cooperation as the right norm, the right outcome. She chooses the norm because she regards it as the best norm, not (as the traditional theory would have it) because it is inductively inferred from state practice.

A brief examination of some of the cases where the World Court applied rules of customary law supports my contention that the ascertainment of custom does not involve any serious inductive analysis. One even gets the impression that the Court purposely avoids *using* the terms "custom" or "customary law."[69] The Court uses instead vague expressions such as "usages generally accepted as expressing principles of law";[70] "general rules of international law";[71] "the practice of certain states";[72] "generally accepted practice";[73] "the actual practice"; and "*opinio juris* by states."[74] Whatever the language, the crucial point is this: *in none of in these cases did the Court engage in an examination of state practice.* This remarkable omission is all the more surprising given the Court's professed positivist creed that custom must be tested "by induction based on the analysis of a sufficiently extensive and convincing practice, and not by deduction from preconceived ideas."[75] Far from doing this, the Court just picks a rule (perhaps the one that it thinks fairest or most efficient, perhaps one that is the middle ground between the parties' claims) and then proclaims that the rule is supported by "general practice." An extreme instance of this approach was the Nicaragua case, where the Court determined the content of the customary principles of nonuse of force and nonintervention without consulting, even perfunctorily, the practice of states.[76] Conversely, the Court will *disregard* the inductive evidence if the Court believes that it will not lead to the best result.[77] One can understand why the Court is reluctant to abandon the positivist illusion: it is important to pretend that the law does not come from nowhere, that real men and women, governments, have somehow created the law; otherwise, the Court might be accused of arbitrariness, of making up rules. That commendable purpose, however, should not obscure what is really going on: the adjudication of cases reveals, rather than an interest in finding patterns of state behavior, an impulse to decide cases correctly by applying the best, just, fair, or efficient rules.[78]

The discussion of treaty and custom has shown that game theory has trouble explaining the status of players who are trying to act ethically, to do the right thing. As a result, game theory can never explain obligation; it can only explain prudential motivation. Positivism tries to harness interest to consent, but this enterprise is, I think, doomed: positivists cannot at the same time claim that national interest and state consent generate obligation. They may claim that in many cases parties to agreements have an interest to comply. They may claim that in many cases agreements create obligation. Or they may in many cases claim both, that parties have an interest and an obligation to comply. *But they may not claim that obligation derives from interest.* A state may simply lack an incentive to comply with an agreement, and it is hard to see how the positivist can persist in the view that the state must nonetheless comply.

At this point, the positivist has one last move: he may concede that national interest cannot go all the way toward explaining obligation. He may say that national interest is the initial motivator, but when the parties agree to a norm, that act of consent creates obligations, so now national interest is out of the picture. He must shift grounds, as it were: self-interest generates the agreement, but once the agreement is in place, it (and not self-interest) is the basis of obligation. This description is in a sense correct: obligation arises (other things being equal and subject to the qualifications of the next two sections) when legitimate governments agree to a treaty and participate in custom. However, the positivist pays a high price: he must give up consent as the foundation of international law. If my descriptions of treaty and custom are correct, then in order to explain obligation we need to postulate a *moral* norm that condemns deviation. Put differently: positivism rests on the naturalistic fallacy[79] and cannot therefore survive unless it adds a normative (moral) premise, which by definition cannot be consensual. To concede the necessity of a moral norm to explain international obligation is to concede that positivism is false, because the whole point of positivism is to rely only on state consent, and thus to reject reliance on moral norms. I now turn to the other two objections to the positivist account of international law.

Immoral Consent and *Ius Cogens*

The game-theoretical view is that norms emerge to solve problems of cooperation: in the case of a coordination problem, the norm identifies the point of equilibrium. In a PD problem the norm attaches consequences to deviation and thus alters the matrix, making it rational for parties to comply. International lawyers explain this phenomenon by positing consent as the basis of obligation. States consent to treaty or custom and these norms are then binding; consent creates obligation. We saw that this view cannot possibly be defended under the pure prudential model suggested by game theory.

Yet the view that consent is the basis of international obligation is implausible for an entirely different reason: states may conclude immoral agreements and participate in immoral customs. When Molotov and von Ribbentrop agreed to partition Poland, no one in his right mind would have claimed that the agreement was binding.[80] If it was not, then consent alone cannot be the basis of obligation. Here the answer by game theorists and international lawyers differ. Let us first address the game theorists' approach.

We saw that game theorists define the moral person as one that chooses cooperation even when he risks being exploited. But, as commentators have pointed out, this definition overlooks the fact that bad people also cooperate.[81] Cooperation might be good for those who cooperate, but it is not necessarily good for everyone, and it is certainly not necessarily morally right. The Molotov–Ribbentrop Pact was (so they thought) good for Nazi Germany and the USSR but not for the world, even less for Poland; far from being morally defensible, it was morally abject.

To respond to this objection, some writers have suggested an amendment to the definition of moral behavior: choosing a cooperative behavior in a PD situation counts as moral behavior only if it involves no disadvantage to anyone extraneous to the situation.[82] Another way of putting this condition is that in order to count as moral behavior cooperation in a PD matrix should not cause negative externalities. The Molotov–Ribbentrop Pact had obviously horrendous effects on the Poles and the rest of the world. Therefore, the argument goes, it did not count as moral behavior even though it was an act of cooperation: it was cooperation among criminals. This move will not do, however. There are many treaties and customary rules that cause harm (negative externalities) to third parties, but the international community rightly does not consider them unlawful or immoral. When European nations decided to form a common market, they surely caused negative externalities. Many decisions of states to cooperate harm third parties, yet we do not consider them wrong, and they are not internationally unlawful.

International lawyers are, of course, well aware of the problem of immoral consent. International law invalidates international agreements when they conflict with a peremptory norm, a norm of *ius cogens*. What is a norm of *ius cogens*? According to the Vienna Convention on the Law of Treaties, it is "a norm accepted and recognized by the international community of states as a whole as a norm from which no derogation is permitted."[83] Without more, this definition is of course tautological: a norm that does not admit derogation is just that—a norm that does not admit derogation. How do we know when an international norm does not admit derogation? One looks in vain in the specialized literature for substantive criteria for *ius cogens*.[84] Writers have largely accepted instead a positivist "pedigree" test for *ius cogens*, suggested by the language of article 53: peremptory norms are those that are accepted as such by the large majority of governments.[85] But that test cannot be right, for one would assume that *ius cogens* obligations apply to the act of accepting and recognizing a new norm *of ius cogens* as well. In other words: the obligation not to contract out of peremptory norms must lie outside the will of states, because the very purpose of those norms is to put certain matters *outside* the realm of state consent. While neither the Vienna Convention nor the specialists offer a substantive criterion, a theory of peremptory norms, writers are more or less agreed on a list of such norms.[86] Nobody knows why these norms are peremptory, but everyone seems to know them when they "see" them. I showed in the previous section why these norms cannot be inferred inductively, as the positivists think. On the contrary, even a quick examination of the proposed lists of preemptory norms shows that they embody fundamental moral principles. I suggest, then, that *ius cogens* norms, too, are best understood as *moral* norms.[87] International lawyers who treat *ius cogens* norms as customary norms have, once again, the right instinct coupled with the wrong legal theory. They rightly realize that immoral consent should not create obligations, yet they wrongly cling to the view that only consent can determine what is immoral. To them, the only relevant feature of, say, the prohibition of murdering prisoners of war is that it has been agreed to by the large majority of states. If the large majority of states had agreed instead to *permit* murdering prisoners of war, then that would be fine, too. This is another instance where positivism leads not to a conception of law but of antilaw. The question-begging solution of the Vienna Convention is typical of the poverty of positivist thinking: states may not agree to outrageous things, but what is outrageous is determined by agreement of states.[88]

The solution to this puzzle is to take some distance from both positivism and game theory and to appeal instead to moral-political philosophy. Agreements and other forms of cooperation are objectionable not when they merely cause negative externalities or visit disadvantages on third parties but rather when they cause *injustices* to persons. Not just any harm is immoral, only unjust harm. And in order to decide which negative externalities states can inflict by their consent and which they cannot, we need a moral-political theory, a theory of justice. *Ius cogens* simply embodies the view that while the fact that a state has consented to future behavior provides *a moral reason* for performing that behavior, sometimes other moral reasons must prevail. Performance of agreements or customary practices[89] may visit great injustices to persons, either to the populations of the states concerned or to persons in other countries.

The Confusion of Government with People

International law automatically treats the behavior of governments as the behavior of nations. I criticized this assumption, statism, in Chapter 2; I have elsewhere called it The Hegelian Myth;[90] some authors call it the domestic analogy; still others refer to it as the opacity of the state.[91] My critique of statism can be now reformulated using game theory. When international relations specialists use game theory to explain state behavior, they assume that the government's international behavior *is* the state's international behavior. National interest is what the government determines it to be. The government acts and the payoffs in the matrix are assumed to be the payoffs for the state, that is, for the whole state, its citizens, present and future.

Yet this analysis fails to describe what really happens. Governments have their own interests. We need not be as cynical as public choice scholars to realize that governments have, at best, mixed interests. For the sake of simplicity, let us reduce government motivation to four categories: (1) incumbency, the desire to remain in power; (2) the desire to acquire prestige and recognition for itself; (3) the desire to advance the interests of its citizens; and (4) the desire do the right thing. Be that mix as it may (and I suspect that the first two components are the stronger ones), almost by definition the result will not be the behavior that responds to the interest of the citizens. Governments have their own agendas, and consequently they *reap payoffs of foreign policy that are different from the payoffs of the governed almost all of the time*. This means that an international PD situation is more complex that a PD situation among individuals: *for every international act there are two different payoff boxes and consequently two parallel matrices*. One is the payoff for the government and the other for "the nation" (meaning by this, perhaps, the aggregate interests of its citizens). In my earlier example of nuclear disarmament, whether a given country will keep or destroy its weapons will depend not just on how much the country's *citizens* expect to gain from each alternative but on how much the *government* expects to gain, for example, by increasing its chances of reelection.[92] Game theory could explain international behavior accurately, in the sense of predicting rational state behavior, only if the two matrices were identical. As it is, game theory can at best predict rational government behavior. Because of its statist assumption, positivism cheats persons out of their autonomy to consent in foreign relations.

The same objection holds in a Coordination situation. The statist approach can explain the identification of an equilibrium point (out of several possible) for the governments. This equilibrium point may not be the same for the citizens, and that's why we see challenges to international law with changes in government. For example, in the case of the Right of Passage through Indian Territory the issue was whether or not there was a bilateral custom between Great Britain (as colonial administrator of India) and Portugal (as colonial administrator of Goa, an enclave in Indian territory).[93] The Court found that there was such custom. But the unanswered question was why should India abide by the custom that arose between the colonial rulers.[94] The point of equilibrium (the regularity achieved with the customary right of passage) was in the interests of the colonial powers Britain and Portugal but not necessarily in the interests of the people of Goa and India that the Indian government now claimed to represent. There were two matrices of payoffs, but one of them had been ignored. This is true everywhere. It holds for all governments, democratic or not, although the payoff matrix of a democratic government is presumably closer to the payoff matrix of its people, if only because the government's survival depends on the people's electoral choices. The analysis holds for all international acts, including norm-creating acts such as treaty and custom. Game theory, therefore, must drop the assumption of the opacity of the state, because otherwise the matrices will not be describing the consequences of foreign policy for the state (understood as people plus territory plus government) but only for the rulers.

The Kantian thesis is a promising way of approaching international law and relations because it provides tools to explain what positivism leaves unexplained. Political legitimacy is a normative concept that does not depend on the complete overlap of the government's and the people's interests. Such an overlap is almost impossible: the interest of the government is virtually never coextensive with the interest of the people. But it is possible to reduce the harms caused by this crude reality. One way to explain the point of democratic institutions as defined in this book (respect for human rights plus true representative government) is to see them as attempts to place limits on the government's pursuit of its own interests at the expense of the people's interest, to bring the two matrices together. By forbidding the government to violate human rights, we place limits on the ways in which the government might want to pursue its interests (for example, by suppressing dissent in order to survive in power). By requiring periodic democratic elections, we can get rid of bad governments, for example, those that pursue their own interests (with means other than rights violations) at the expense of the governed. Game-theoretical analysis thus may provide an additional argument for democracy. Typically, a government is relatively more democratic when its payoff matrix comes closer to the payoff matrix that represents the aggregate interests of the population. While the two matrices will almost never coincide, they will be farther apart in nondemocratic systems. Perhaps this is one way of interpreting Kant's argument, discussed in Chapter 1, that enduring peace requires democracy because nondemocratic governments do not incur great costs when they send people to war. In a democratic society the structure of costs and benefits of the government comes closer to the structure of costs and benefits of the people. The people have more control over governmental decisions, and thus they will be slow to fight wars the burden of which they know they will shoulder.

I conclude that the standard theory of the sources of international law rests on a mistake. The mistake is created by positivism's uncritical adherence to the view that only the acts of governments create international law. Because of their refusal to understand moral motivation, positivists are led to defend an incoherent theory of international obligation. They claim that national interest is the engine of international relations, yet they insist that obligation is based on consent, even when it is against interest. I showed that this view can only be defended by appealing to moral principles outside consent. However, there is more than meets the eye in the positivist view. At first blush, positivists seem to reject the role of values and purposes in legal interpretation, but I do not believe that this is their true position. Notwithstanding their protestations to the contrary, positivists do not really reject moral norms. They rely, like natural lawyers, on a nonpositive moral norm: one that mandates preservation of existing states and strong deference to incumbent governments. But (with notable exceptions such as Michael Walzer) they pretend that their view is "objective," simply the result of dispassionate lawyers trying to say what the law is without allowing their biases to interfere. This is a false and disingenuous position, and the world of ideas would greatly benefit if they tried to support with arguments their normative assumption—statism. Positivists like to point out that their view (that law is created exclusively by states) is respectful of state sovereignty (which they see as the legal incarnation of national difference) and thus more legitimate than natural law alternatives. But the positivists' emphasis on governmental will is not a vindication of legitimate national differences, but rather an only slightly qualified deference to people in power.

As positivists formulate their theory, then, it is incoherent. But my critique leaves open the possibility that Realism is coherent. Perhaps it is possible to explain without incoherence the social world as the exclusive result of persons acting as rational maximizers of self-interest and of states acting as rational maximizers of national interest. Perhaps the idea of obligation is an illusion, and moral motivation can always be reduced to rational-choice explanations. But I think that such a worldview would be extraordinarily impoverished, that most of what is human in us would be lost if we adopted the rational choice paradigm where all our actions, from the vilest to the most sublime, could be translated into attempts to maximize our interest. If moral motivation is an illusion, maybe it is one that is worth preserving after all.

Appendix: An Illustration of the Prisoner's Dilemma in International Relations

To illustrate a typical international PD, let us assume that two states (call them Argentina and Brazil) are considering whether to increase military spending, to arm themselves. Both countries, let us assume, are competing for hegemony in South America. Let us also assume that there are no other actors who can influence the decision of these two players (for example, there is no pressure from the United States to get either or both to disarm). Each of the governments has only to consider the behavior of the other. The following matrix shows a possible structure of payoffs in such a situation:

Argentina

		A	D
	A	2/2	4/1
Brazil			
	D	1/4	3/3

The symbols in this matrix are as follows. One player, Argentina, is represented in the column; the other player, Brazil, is represented in the row. The letter *A* stands for arm; the letter *D* stands for disarm. Each player can choose to arm or to disarm; this generates four possibilities for those two individual choices combined. The numbers stand for the payoff for each combination, ranked by the size of the benefit (thus, for each actor: 4>3>2>1). The number to the right conventionally represents the payoff of the column player; the number to the left that of the row player. In this matrix, Argentina's best outcome (4) is to arm and to get Brazil to disarm, because in that way it will achieve hemispheric hegemony. Argentina's worst outcome (1) is the reverse, that is, to disarm unilaterally and thus become vulnerable to armed Brazil's hegemonic power. Argentina's second best outcome (3) occurs if both countries disarm; its third best outcome (2) occurs if both countries arm. This is worse than mutual disarmament (because of the danger of war plus the costs entailed) but better than being dominated. The same analysis holds for Brazil: to take advantage of the other party's naïveté is the best outcome; mutual cooperation (disarmament) is the second best outcome; mutual defection (arms race) is the third best outcome; and unrequited cooperation (unilateral disarmament) is the worst outcome.

The dominant strategy for each country caught in this dilemma (sometimes also called the Security Dilemma) is *not* to cooperate, that is, to arm. By arming, each country takes an insurance against its worst possible outcome (political subjugation) and even has a chance, on a lucky day, to achieve its best outcome, if the adversary is naive enough to disarm unilaterally. Because both governments reason in a similar way, both will arm, thus reaching the upper left square (2/2, mutual defection) in the matrix above. The interesting and counterintuitive consequence is that the *collective* result of this mutual defection, which is the rational choice for each country considered individually, is Pareto-inferior to mutual cooperation. Each is better off if both disarm than if both arm. But because disarming exposes each to being exploited by the other, the dominant strategy is to arm.

Notes

1. A complete list of positivist authors in international law would be too long to include here. A representative sample includes: Louis Henkin, *How Nations Behave* (1979); Thomas M. Franck, *The Power of Legitimacy Among Nations* (1990); Ian Brownlie, *Principles of International Law* 1–31 (1990); George Schwarzenberg, *The Inductive Approach to International Law* 4–7 (1965); Lassa Oppenheim, *International Law* 15–19 (H. Lauterpacht ed., 8th ed. 1955). Hans Kelsen, perhaps the greatest positivist, raises special problems because he expressly rejects consensualism. See Hans Kelsen, *Principles of International Law* 152–155; 311–317 (1952). I have elsewhere shown why I nonetheless believe that Kelsen is a consensualist. See Fernando R. Tesón, "International Obligation and the Theory of Hypothetical Consent," 15 *Yale Journal of International Law* 84, 98–99 (1990). Positivism as a theory of international jurisprudence is a subspecies of positivism as a theory of general jurisprudence, but they are not necessarily coextensive. Both reject appeals to morality or natural law. But while international positivism relies on state consent, general positivism simply believes that the truth of legal propositions depends solely on the truth of certain nonmoral facts, consensual or not, (e.g., a vote in the legislature) that have occurred in the past.

2. I do not consider here "the general principles of law recognized by civilized nations," (article 36(c) of the International Court of Justice Statute) in part because they are far less important in practice, and in part because most writers give a positivist reading of them: they are those principles of law recognized in the internal laws of states. See, e.g. Walter Friedmann, "The Uses of 'General Principles' in the Development of International Law," 57 *American Journal of International Law* 279, 282–283 (1963).

3. See, e.g., Henkin, supra note 1, at 32–37.

4. See, e.g., Harold Koh, "Why Do Nations Obey International Law?" 106 *Yale Law Journal* 2599 (1997) (book review).

5. See references in Chapter 2 at note 33.

6. For a general survey of the use of game theory in international relations, see Duncan Snidal, "The Game Theory of International Politics," in *Cooperation Under Anarchy* 25 (Kenneth A. Oye ed., 1986).

7. For a study on game theory in domestic law, see Douglas C. Baird et al., *Game Theory and the Law* (1994).

8. For a definition of dominant strategy, see id. at 306.

9. See Kenneth A. Oye, "Explaining Cooperation Under Anarchy: Hypotheses and Strategies," in *Cooperation Under Anarchy* 1, 6 (Kenneth A. Oye ed., 1986).

10. I adopt the definitions that follow from Russell Hardin, *Morality Within the Limits of Reason* 32–33 (1988).

11. See Oye, supra note 9, at 6–7; see also Robert O. Keohane, *After Hegemony* 51–55 (1984).

12. See Oye, supra note 9, at 6–7. Keohane calls it Discord. Keohane, supra note 11, at 51–54.

13. Oye, supra note 9, at 7.

14. See Edna Ullman-Margalit, *The Emergence of Norms* 77–83 (1977).

15. See Martin Hollis, *The Cunning of Reason* 32 (1987).

16. See Vienna Convention on the Law of Treaties, May 23, 1969, articles 19–23, *United Nations Document* A/Conf. 39/27 [hereinafter Vienna Convention]. Of course, state interaction may take many other forms: the game of chicken, the bargaining game, the stag's hunt, the assurance game, etc. See generally, Ullman-Margalit, supra note 14.

17. The classic work is Robert Axelrod, *The Evolution of Cooperation* (1984).

18. Id. at 12–24; see also Keohane, supra note 11, at 75–78.

19. See Keohane, supra note 11, at 73–74.

20. See, e.g., Russell Hardin, *Collective Action* 117–122 (1982).

21. See Keohane, supra note 11, at 74.

22. For the human rights situation in Cuba, see 1997 *Amnesty International Report* 132.

23. See Robert D. Cooter, "Decentralized Law for a Complex Economy: The Structural Approach to Adjudicating the New Law Merchant," 144 *University of Pennsylvania Law Review* 1643, 1662–1663 (1996). Cooter is aware that Kantians disagree with this characterization of moral motivation. Id. at 1663.

24. See id. at 1667. Cooter's discussion of customary law includes other topics much relevant to international law which I cannot pursue here, such as the analysis of the costs of horizontal enforcement of the law.

25. See Immanuel Kant, "On the Common Saying: 'This May be True in Theory, But It Does Not Apply in Practice,'" in *Kant's Political Writings* 61, 67–68 (Heiss ed., 1991). Here I follow the interpretation of Kant's essay by Jeffrie G. Murphy in his splendid piece, "Kant On Theory and Practice," 37 *Nomos* 47 (1995).

26. See Kant, supra note 25, at 67.

27. See id.

28. See Murphy, supra note 25, at 60–61.

29. Id. at 57.

30. Vienna Convention, supra note 16, article 1(a). The Convention entered into force on January 27, 1980. As of mid–1994, 74 states were parties to the Convention.

31. See, e.g., Mark W. Janis, *An Introduction to International Law* 10–11 (2d ed. 1993). But see id. at 65 (*pacta sunt servanda* is best seen as neither a customary nor a conventional rule, but rather as a rule of *ius cogens*). The rule can also be found in the Vienna Convention, supra note 16, article 26.

32. See Vienna Convention, supra note 16, articles 42–64.

33. See Ullman-Margalit, supra note 14, at 9.

34. International lawyers would probably not describe this pattern as a customary norm, even though there are countless of instances of spontaneously coordinated behavior of this kind. The reason is, I think, that they reserve this term for cases where there are obstacles to cooperation, where it would be rational for some states to defect, such as PD and Coordination matrices.

35. Here I draw from Ullman-Margalit, supra note 14, especially Chapter 3.

36. For a classic analysis of how treaties and other cooperation regimes help overcome distrust and other transaction costs, see Keohane, supra note 11, at 85–109.

37. Ullman-Margalit, supra note 14, at 116.

38. I am not suggesting that all trade situations are Coordination matrices. They might be Harmony matrices, Coordination matrices, or PD matrices. Cf. Keohane, supra note 11, at 54–55 (one should not posit rigid rational-choice models for trade relations).

39. For a survey of the problems raised by the Treaty on the Non-Proliferation of Nuclear Weapons, see *Beyond 1995: The Future of the NPT Regime* (Joseph F. Pilat & Robert E. Pendley eds., 1990).

40. See, inter alia, Ullman-Margalit, supra note 14, at 102–103.

41. This is Ullman-Margalit's view. See id. at 22, 38, 89.

42. See id. at 117.

43. For an explanation of how sanctions alter the payoffs, see Baird, et al., supra note 7, at 14–19.

44. See Axelrod, supra note 17, at 27–69.

45. See Cooter, supra note 23, at 1658–1659.

46. Phillip Pettit, "*Virtue Normativa*: Rational Choice Perspectives," 100 *Ethics* 725, 742 (1989).

47. There is an interesting dynamic here. It may well be that the nation in question has a chance secretly to keep its nuclear weapons and get away with it, that is, avoid the physical enforcement visited by the other parties. But in that case, the government will not be able to reap the benefits of national prestige, because it will not be in a position publicly to display the destruction of the country's weapons.

48. See Pettit, supra note 46, at 745.

49. The classic definition is found in article 38(1)(C) of the International Court of Justice Statute. For a traditional account, see Karol Wolfke, *Custom in Present International Law* (2d ed. 1993).

50. Anthony D'Amato has shown why this traditional explanation of custom is inadequate. See Anthony A. D'Amato, *The Concept of Custom* 47–72 (1971).

51. H.L.A. Hart, *The Concept of Law* 9–12, 85–87 (2d ed. 1994).

52. See Ullman-Margalit, supra note 14, at 78, 84.

53. See id. at 85 (emphasis in the original).

54. Id. at 85–86. She also mentions as a reason for codifying a practice the higher degree of articulation associated with a norm, as opposed to a mere regularity of behavior.

55. See, e.g. Mark Villiger, *Customary International Law and Treaties* 17–18 (1985); Jonathan Charney, "Universal International Law" 87 *American Journal of International Law* 529, 538, 541 (1993). In its leading case on custom, the World Court said that customary law cannot be subject to "any right of unilateral exclusion exercisable at will." North Sea Continental Shelf (Germany v. Denmark and Netherlands), 1969 *International Court of Justice* 3, 38–39 (Feb. 20). The matter is controversial, however: other positivists, perhaps taking the positivist view to its logical consequences, believe that new states can, upon birth, pick and choose among the existing rules of international law. See, e.g., R.P. Anand, *New States and International Law* 62 (1972).

56. On the principle of identity of the state, see James Crawford, *The Creation of States* 400–420 (1979); Brownlie, supra note 1, at 82–85. See also the Tinoco Arbitration (United Kingdom v. Costa Rica) 1923 Taft Arbitration, RIAA (i) at 369.

57. Here I follow, *mutatis mutandi*, the analysis of customary law by Cooter, supra note 23, at 1660–1675.

58. See id. at 1660.

59. It is generally agreed that the provisions of the United Nations Convention on the Law of the Sea regarding the Exclusive Economic Zone have become customary law *en dehors* the Convention.

60. In Cooter's sense of principled behavior. See supra text accompanying notes 23 and 24.

61. Id. at 1667.

62. The World Court seemed to recognize the possibility of instant custom. See North Sea Continental Shelf (Germany v. Denmark and Netherlands), 1969 *International Court of Justice* 3, 42 (Feb. 20). For a critical view of instant custom, see Prosper Weil, "Toward Relative Normativity in International Law?" 77 *American Journal of International Law* 413, 435 (1983).

63. *Pacta sunt servanda* is also a treaty rule. See Vienna Convention, supra note 16, article 28. But the Vienna Convention is itself a treaty, so *it* can only be binding under a superior norm, a nonconsensual *pacta sunt servanda* rule.

64. If this is correct, maybe the reason why (as Louis Henkin has famously written) most of the states comply with most of international law most of the time, is because first, there are many Harmony matrices; and second, all nascent customary rules and many treaty rules are solutions to Coordination problems, not to PD problems.

65. See Ullman-Margalit, supra note 14, at 41.

66. Kant thought that lying promises (promises made with the secret reservation that the promisers may violate them opportunistically) were self-contradictory and thus in violation of the categorical imperative. See Immanuel Kant, *Grounding for the Metaphysics of Morals* [1785] 14–15 (J.W. Ellington trans., 1980).

67. I made the same point in Fernando R. Tesón, *Humanitarian Intervention: An Inquiry Into Law and Morality* 11–15 (2d ed. 1997).

68. See some examples in the following paragraph.

69. See Wolfke, supra note 49, at 9.

70. Lotus Case, 1927 *Permanent Court of International Justice* (ser. A) No. 10, at 18 (Sept. 7).

71. Fisheries Case (United Kingdom v. Norway), 1951 *International Court of Justice* 116, 133 (Dec. 18).

72. Nottebohm Case (Liechtenstein v. Guatemala), 1955 *International Court of Justice* 4, 22 (Apr. 6).

73. Judgments of the Administrative Tribunal of the International Labor Organization, Advisory Opinion, 1956 *International Court of Justice* 85.

74. Continental Shelf (Libya v. Malta), 1985 *International Court of Justice* 13, 29–30 (June 3).

75. Delimitation of the Maritime Boundary of the Gulf of Maine Area (Canada v. United States), 1984 *International Court of Justice* 246, 299 (Oct. 12).

76. Military and Paramilitary In and Against Nicaragua (Nicaragua v. United States), 1986 *International Court of Justice* 14, 100–101 (June 27). The Court simply relied on non binding declarations of the United Nations General Assembly.

77. See North Sea Continental Shelf (Germany v. Denmark and Netherlands), 1969 *International Court of Justice* 3 (Feb. 20).

78. Of course, this interpretation does not imply that the Court always *does* apply noninductively the best rule, only that that is what it attempts to do.

79. It is interesting that this is precisely the charge that positivists have leveled against natural law theorists. See Kelsen, supra note 1, 149–150, 241.

80. See generally, Izidors J. Vizulis, *The Molotov–Ribbentrop Pact of 1939* (1990).

81. Ullman-Margalit, supra note 14, at 42.

82. Id.

83. Vienna Convention, supra note 16, article 53.

84. There is also great confusion in the literature between the obligations generated by *ius cogens* and the obligations to obey international law generally. For example, in a book devoted to the subject, Lauri Hannikainen rightly proclaims that *all acts* (not just treaties) contrary to peremptory norms are invalid. See Lauri Hannikainen, *Peremptory Norms [Ius Cogens] in International Law: Historical Development, Criteria, Present Status* 6 (1988). But this is true of *jus dispositivum* (nonperemptory law) as well. The distinction between both kinds of international law is perhaps best formulated in counterfactual terms. A prohibition of *ius cogens* would run as follows: "A state may not violate this norm, and it could not validly agree to depart from it by regular law-creating processes such as treaty or custom." A regular (*jus dispositivum*) prohibition would be formulated differently: "A state may not violate this norm, although it could validly agree to depart from it by regular law-creating processes such as treaty and custom." I cannot, however, pursue the matter here.

85. See id. at 210–215.

86. See, e.g., id. at Part III.

87. To my knowledge, the view that what international law prohibits are immoral treaties (or customs) was pioneered by Alfred von Verdross, "Forbidden Treaties in International Law," 31 *American Journal of International Law* 571 (1937). Maybe this is what the Vienna Convention means when it requires the international community "as a whole" to accept a peremptory norm. Maybe the idea behind the Convention is that these norms are indeed moral imperatives, but that the only way to ascertain whether or not a moral imperative exists is to consult what the large majority of states think. I don't need to take a position on this question of metaethics. Suffice it to say that *ius cogens* is higher law that trumps consent in any of its forms.

88. Weisbrud also notes this confusion, and his response is to suggest the dismantling of *ius cogens* altogether. His suggestion makes sense, of course, if one wants to cling (as he does) to the dogma that states have undisputed and unlimited discretion to determine the rules of international law. See A. Mark Weisbrud, "The Emptiness of *Ius Cogens*, as Illustrated by the War in Bosnia–Herzegovina," 17 *Michigan Journal of International Law* 1, 24–40 (1995). My approach is perhaps close to what Weisbrud calls natural law (which he rejects, unconvincingly in my view, at 30–31). The view that states may not agree to immoral behavior requires abandoning both positivism and moral relativism.

89. Interestingly, lawyers do not apply *ius cogens* to trump objectionable customs. The ancient right of conquest might be an example of immoral custom.

90. See Tesón, supra note 67, Chapters 3 and 4.

91. See discussion and references supra Chapter 2.

92. I don't mean only egregious instances of governmental self-interest such as tyrannical use of power, bribery, or corruption, but, for example, the desire to "make the history books," or, more modestly, to increase one's chances of winning reelection.

93. See Oye, supra note 9, at 1, 6.

94. India argued the legitimacy issue, but in a peculiar way. She contested the jurisdiction of the Court because the dispute concerned exclusively Indian territory (that is, she treated Goa, the enclave administered by Portugal, as really Indian territory). See India's Fifth Preliminary Objection, Right of Passage Over Indian Territory (Portugal v. India), 1960 *International Court of Justice Pleadings*, vol. I., at 122–185. The Court rejected this

argument also in a peculiar way. The very fact that India contested the sovereignty made the dispute "international," and thus within the terms of the optional clause. Right of Passage Over Indian Territory (Portugal v. India), 1960 *International Court of Justice* 6, 32–33 (Apr. 12).

4

The Rawlsian Theory
of International Law

Introduction

The Kantian thesis defended in this book can be reformulated using modern social contract theory. Certainly the most illustrious representative of modern deontological liberalism is John Rawls.[1] In his early work, Rawls discussed international law only briefly.[2] In a recent article, however, Rawls has extended his acclaimed political theory to cover international relations.[3] Substantively, Rawls's theory of international law moves in the direction suggested in this book, because it assigns a role, albeit a modest one, to human rights and political legitimacy. However, to the extent that Rawls's effort purports to be a rational reconstruction of the international law for our new era (as he certainly intends it to be),[4] it fails to capture central moral features of the international order. His proposal is still too forgiving of serious forms of oppression in the name of liberal tolerance. Because of that, the theory falls short of matching the considered judgments prevailing today in the international community and thus fails Rawls's own test of epistemic adequacy.

A Summary of Rawls's International Theory

Rawls addresses a central problem of liberal theories of international ethics: What is the moral status of nonliberal states and governments?[5] Rawls's answer to this question is quite original. For Rawls, there are three kinds of regimes, defined by the extent to which they allow individual freedom: liberal, hierarchical, and tyrannical. A workable international society includes, as members in good standing, regimes of the first two kinds but not regimes of the third kind. Tyrannical regimes are outlaws.[6] But Rawls believes that both liberal and hierarchical states can agree on the same principles of international ethics. In particular, they can agree on a set of limitations to internal sovereignty and on the prohibition of war.

Rawls's arguments in support of this conclusion merit some examination. Some Rawls commentators have suggested that the correct approach is to have a global social contract of individuals.[7] We imagine individuals who, under a veil of ignorance, agree on international principles of justice. They do not know what society they will belong to. They do not know their conception of the good, their histories and traditions. The idea, which for many Rawlsians was a mandatory element of *A Theory of Justice,* is that the parties would rationally choose to maximize certain primary goods. These are defined as goods that free rational agents would want to procure *regardless* of what else they would want: rights and liberties, opportunities and power, income and wealth.[8] In his international theory, however, Rawls himself refuses to follow this procedure. In the international contract he abandons the assumption of moral equality and freedom for all the parties in the original position.[9] Yet paradoxically, the principles of international justice must be agreed upon from the liberal society outward. In the first part of the article Rawls sketches the international principles that obtain among *liberal* states.[10] There Rawls follows Kant and other liberal internationalists. Liberal states are guided by liberal conceptions of morality and by similar assumptions about equal citizenship and moral agency.[11] The international law governing the liberal alliance is therefore not a surprise. War is prohibited except in self-defense; peoples are equal parties to their own agreements; intervention is prohibited; treaties are to be observed; the laws of war apply (when they act in self-defense); and human rights in the rich, liberal sense (such as the ones recognized in the European Convention on Human Rights) are honored.[12] These principles are almost identical to those defended by Kant in *Perpetual Peace.*[13] Nonintervention, however, is qualified: if a liberal society degenerates into tyranny (that is, in one of the situations of partial compliance addressed by nonideal theory) the right to independence cannot shield the abusive regime from condemnation, "nor even in grave cases from coercive intervention by other states."[14] Such condemnation and coercive action may be authorized by a body such as the United Nations.[15] Rawls then sets forth the conditions for *nonideal* theory for a society of liberal states, and, following the findings by Doyle discussed in Chapter 1, concludes that the liberal alliance fulfills the condition of stability, because the historical evidence shows that liberal states do not go to war against one another.[16]

The second step in Rawls's reasoning is to extend the contractarian justification of international law beyond liberal societies in order to reach what Rawls calls "hierarchical" societies. What are "hierarchical societies" in Rawls's system? Crucial to Rawls's argument is the existence of divergent, yet reasonable, possible kinds of moral-political intuitions. Citizens in liberal democracies start with the assumption that all persons are equal and free and proceed from there under the veil of ignorance to agree on the principles of justice suited to a liberal democracy. In contrast, citizens in what Rawls calls hierarchical societies start with very different moral intuitions, namely those that obtain when the assumption is *not* freedom and equality of all *individuals* but rather the Hegelian idea that the primary moral unit is the community (or communities).[17] In these societies, whatever rights individuals have derive from their membership in groups. As such, rights are merely *enabling* rights, that is, those that enable individuals to perform their *duties* as members of the relevant community.[18] In hierarchical societies, rights are not attributes of persons inherently endowed with reason and dignity. Rather, rights are (1) derivative of membership in a group that sustains a common conception of the good (such as a religious worldview); and (2) merely instrumental to the performance of social duties. For Rawls, the social contract is a "device for representation,"[19] the aim of which is to formulate principles of international law that all well-ordered peoples would agree to. Hierarchical societies are, then, those informed by nonliberal yet not unreasonable[20] conceptions of the good. The crucial point in Rawls's international original position is that members of hierarchical societies *would not be free and equal agents*. By extension, *representatives* of those societies would not incorporate that assumption into their hypothetical reasoning leading to the law of peoples.

According to Rawls, for a hierarchical society to earn its rightful place in the family of nations it must fulfill three conditions. First, the regime must be peaceful, not aggressive, that is, even though the society in question is defined by a comprehensive conception of the common good, it does not try to impose that conception on others, especially on liberal societies. Second, in contrast to the liberal state, the hierarchical society is informed by a conception of the common good that is deemed privileged over others (e.g., a state religion). Rawls, following Philip Soper, argues that a legal system founded on such basis is apt to create *moral* duties on citizens.[21] How does this happen, given the fact that some, perhaps many, people are bound to dissent from the official conception of the good? Rawls insists that such a society is well-ordered if the officials sincerely take into account the interests of all citizens *within* the conception of the good. This means that the government does not arbitrarily privilege some over others.[22] The system is not democratic (people do not elect the government), but officials treat dissent seriously *at some point* in the political system of consultation. Once a political decision has been made, however, there is no right to dissent or right to free speech generally.[23] Courts believe sincerely in this conception of justice and apply it fairly in the sense of formal justice (e.g., like cases are treated alike). This hierarchical society does not recognize freedom of religion in the liberal sense but does not persecute other religions.[24] Also, there is no right to equal citizenship, since the official conception of the good may assign different groups to different political roles in ways that are incompatible with liberal notions of equality.[25]

The third criterion derives logically from the second: a nonliberal hierarchical society observes what Rawls calls "basic human rights." These are defined by Rawls as the right to life, the right to a modicum of liberty (Rawls mentions only freedom from slavery and forced labor, but he means other freedoms as well, such as the freedom from torture[26]); the right to (personal) property, the right to formal justice, but, crucially, not the right to free expression.[27] In a footnote, Rawls discusses the Universal Declaration of Human Rights. For him, article 3 to 18 embody "human rights proper." *A contrario sensu*, the rest of the rights listed in the Declaration are "liberal aspirations."[28] These "aspirations" include, inter alia, freedom of opinion and expression (article 20), the right to peaceful assembly and association (article 21), and the right to political participation (article 22). Rawls does not believe, therefore, that the law of nations must guarantee these three rights. This redefinition of "basic human rights" proposed by Rawls is intimately connected to his belief that *liberal* human rights are culturally and historically contingent. Human rights in the liberal sense are the product of the peculiar history of the West, in particular of the wars of religion.[29] Liberal human rights, therefore, do not have universal validity. It follows that in order to formulate principles of international justice that all rational *representatives* in the world can agree to, Rawls has to rely on a weaker and more general concept of rationality—one that avoids making the assumption of individual autonomy.[30]

Such a regime, for Rawls, is not tyrannical. Its legal order is "decent,"[31] and for that reason the society is in full compliance with the law of nations. Rawls believes that if the three conditions previously described are fulfilled, the regime will be fully legitimate, mainly because the regime is legitimate in the eyes of its own people. As a consequence, a hierarchical society is entitled to the protection afforded by the principle of nonintervention,[32] although of course criticism in liberal societies is always possible in the light of the freedom of speech that obtains there.[33] If the hierarchical regime degenerates into tyranny it loses its status as a member in good standing in the community of nations and it becomes vulnerable to intervention, at least in serious cases of human rights violations (recall that the same is true for liberal societies that go wrong).[34]

Rawls also departs from *A Theory of Justice* on the thorny question of international distributive justice. In sharp contrast to other contractarians like Charles Beitz and Brian Barry,[35] Rawls does not believe that the difference principle[36] holds globally. If the difference principle were universally valid, then the international economic system should be arranged in a way that improves the situation of the poorest nations. This would require, of course, much more than mere duties of assistance: it would require massive transfers of wealth from rich to poor countries. But Rawls does not believe that there are prima facie duties of international transfers aimed at changing the global distribution of resources into a "Rawls-superior" pattern.[37] The most important reason for this conclusion is that well-ordered societies are a varied lot, and "not all of them can reasonably be expected to accept any particular liberal principle of distributive justice."[38] In his view, the best way to secure international distributive justice is to get all societies to maintain "decent political and social institutions."[39] This means, for Rawls, that the probabilities of economic prosperity will be greatly enhanced if societies fulfill the conditions of legitimacy: fair treatment according to the comprehensive conception of justice and observance of "basic human rights." In that way, one of the main obstacles to prosperity, government corruption, would be eliminated. Relying on the research by Amartya Sen on famines,[40] Rawls concludes that more progress will be made, especially in developing countries, if political legitimacy and stability are achieved before any scheme of global redistribution could work.

The duty of assistance, therefore, is not a liberal principle of justice; rather it stems from the conception of the society of peoples "as consisting of well-ordered peoples," where, again, "basic" human rights are observed and "basic human needs are to be met."[41]

Rawls's vision of the international community can thus be summarized as follows. Liberal societies are founded on assumptions about persons being free, equal, reasonable, and rational moral agents.[42] The political morality, the public conception of justice in liberal societies, is derivative of such assumptions, as developed most recently in *Political Liberalism*. Hierarchical societies are founded instead on Hegelian assumptions about human nature and the political morality derived from them. International law, if it is going to work and be truly universal, must accommodate both kinds of assumptions on a plane of (international) equality. All well-ordered states are internationally legitimate. Both liberal and hierarchical states (which comprise the class of well-ordered states) are therefore sovereign from the standpoint of international ethics ("the law of peoples"); consequently coercion (Rawls mentions economic sanctions and war) cannot be used against them. In particular, liberal states are not morally justified in coercing hierarchical societies into changing their ways, much as those ways may offend liberal sensitivities.[43]

A Critique

Rawls's effort contains valuable insights on a number of important points. First, Rawls rightly rejects traditional statism as the foundation of international law and ethics and substitutes instead a modicum of human rights and political legitimacy.[44] *The Law of Peoples* is not statist because it rejects the view, common among international lawyers, that all states are equally legitimate provided they have an effective government. Rawls, following Kant, makes distinctions *among* states based on applicable principles of political legitimacy. Second, he correctly endorses a right of humanitarian intervention in cases of serious violations of human rights. And third, Rawls's case for refusing to extend his principles of distributive justice to cover the world seems to me convincing (although I will not address this difficult issue here). Yet his theory fails on the crucial issue of human rights on both ends of the construction of the theory. Faithful to the methodology he first developed in *A Theory of Justice*, Rawls constructs his international theory starting from what he believes to be plausible assumptions for the subject to be addressed—in this case, the law of nations. In addition, by reflective equilibrium, the theory must match our considered moral intuitions about international law. The attempt, however, fails on both counts: the assumptions of the international social contract are so weak as to be trivial or implausible (although they cannot be strictly questioned since they are *ad hoc*). Most important, the result falls short of matching the considered moral intuitions that have been accepted by the international community for quite some time now. The upshot is that Rawls's "law of peoples" is too tolerant of governments that, both on elementary notions of justice and on well-established principles of international human rights, do not deserve such a high degree of deference. To be sure, Rawls is correct that *force* ought not be used against hierarchical regimes (since by definition they do not engage in the most extreme forms of human rights violations), but that position can be defended on independent grounds: it does not necessitate the endorsement of such regimes as reasonable or legitimate.

The Abandonment of Liberalism

In his international theory Rawls, as indicated above, abandons the individualist assumptions about human nature. In *A Theory of Justice* he wrote:

> The essential idea is that we want to account for the social values, for the intrinsic good of institutional, community, and associative activities, by a conception of justice that in its theoretical basis is individualistic. For reasons of clarity among others, we do not want to rely on an undefined concept of community, or to suppose that society is an organic whole with a life of its own distinct from and superior to that of all its members in their relations with one another.[45]

In contrast, in *The Law of Peoples*, Rawls indicates that this individualist assumption is biased in favor of liberalism. The law of nations must, therefore, make room for nonindividualistic (i.e., communitarian) normative conceptions. One wonders, however, if this innovation is anything more than an *ad hoc* hypothesis. Rawls believes that the abandonment of the individualist premises of liberal theory is the only device that can yield the results that he has *in advance* decided are the most plausible for the law of nations: that as long as states are not clearly tyrannical, they ought to respect one another's values. Yet I do not think that a political theory can survive if one keeps amending its assumptions at every turn to reach results that do not seem to match the theory in its original form. This is simply a way of *immunizing* a political theory against (moral) falsification. The threat of falsification of liberal theory is, of course, the sense that other cultures do not value freedom, human rights, and democracy, as the West does. So in constructing an international ethical theory either one abandons the assumption that all rational persons, given the constraints of social cooperation, would rather be more than less free, or one incorporates that assumption into the international contract as well, with the result that states (and the cultures that they represent) that do not respect autonomy are out of compliance with the principles of international justice. This book chooses the latter; Rawls, the former.

Rawls rejects a global contract among individuals (as opposed to representatives of states) because "in this case it might be said that we are treating all persons, regardless of their society and culture, as individuals who are free and equal, and as reasonable and rational, and so according to liberal conceptions."[46] This, Rawls believes, makes the basis of the law of peoples too narrow.[47] The central question here is one of the definition of the self: what is a person, a human being? Is it possible to defend *any* moral theory without presupposing some degree of sameness among all persons? This is a much debated question in philosophy today, and I will not address it here. Yet the greatness of *A Theory of Justice* was, in my opinion, its persuasive (and very Kantian) attempt to capture our essential *humanity* regardless of other contingent interests or preferences that people may have in this or that tradition or culture (what Kant calls "anthropological" traits).[48] This is precisely the greatness of the international human rights movement, too.

If one chooses this approach, then all persons, and therefore all parties to the social contract, *possess some common characteristic* that does not depend on culture or history. We have to assume, for example, that all of them are free and equal rational agents, or that all of them are, as David Gauthier has suggested, constrained preference maximizers,[49] or that all of them are beings graced by God and whose main purpose is to serve Him. These assumptions are incompatible with each other, but if any one holds, it holds for every person. Human nature, whatever it is, is constant for all human beings; the only alternative is the position that moral personality is socially determined (or constructed) in its entirety. Rawls's move is to assume in the international contract that some parties in the original position are free and equal moral agents while some others are instead constituted by a comprehensive conception of the good that, say, excludes moral equality. This weakens, perhaps irreparably, the usefulness of the contractarian devise. If instead Rawls's original assumptions in *A Theory of Justice* are retained, the global social contract will yield principles that are universal and valid for all societies and peoples. If the parties in the original position agree on a list of human rights (as they must), those rights are, in one sense or another and without prejudging the question of enforcement, morally valid across borders. Instead, the weaker, more general conception of rationality that Rawls proposes for international law in *The Law of Peoples* is the predisposition to sincerely uphold a comprehensive view of the good, *whatever that view might be.* The only rationality (or reasonableness) that representatives of liberal and hierarchical societies have in common is the prudential rationality of doing their best to advance their conception of the good while respecting inconsistent conceptions of the good by others.

Rawls believes that representatives of hierarchical societies are rational (notwithstanding the nonliberal social arrangements they advocate), in two ways: first, they "care about the good of the society they represent and so about its security." Hence, they would rationally agree on laws against aggression.[50] They also care about the benefits of trade and assistance in time of need, which, Rawls believes, help protect human rights. Second, they do not try to extend their influence to other societies; they accept fair terms of cooperation between them and other societies.[51] These reasons, however, are so weak as to amount to nothing beyond, perhaps, old-fashioned Realism. A notable feature of Realism is the postulate that nation-states, through their governments, should always act in what they perceive to be their national interest. The Realist model is a world in which the law of nations amounts to a simple compromise between different kinds of societies with irreconcilable interests and values.[52] Rawls's "law of peoples" does not differ much from this model, because the *moral* assumptions about human nature are gone. All that remains are the prudential reasons that Realists have long insisted are the only ones that matter. The appealing postulates about human nature present in Rawls's previous work (free reason and the moral inviolability of the person) have been reduced to squalid concerns about (universalizable) nonintervention. All the parties agree to are: the prohibition of war, (qualified) nonintervention, and "basic" human rights, the minimum necessary to enable everybody to play some political role under otherwise quite oppressive political conditions. (One could as plausibly suggest that representatives of hierarchical societies, not being democratically elected, are interested in *incumbency*, and that is why they would, quite rationally, support a strong principle of nonintervention.) Yet it must be conceded that Rawls has positioned himself in such a way that the international contract is not internally assailable. If one abandons the assumption that all rational persons would seek freedom as a primary good, then obviously the resulting principles of international ethics would not give very high priority to freedom. The only freedoms that the new international ethics will countenance are those freedoms that are minimally required to pursue *any* conception of justice that is sincerely held.

Especially troubling is Rawls's endorsement of the concept of *enabling* rights. These, it will be recalled, are the rights that hierarchical societies recognize and are defined as those rights that enable individuals to perform their social duties. For Rawls, observance of "basic" human rights in hierarchical societies "does not require the liberal idea that persons are first citizens and as such free and equal members of society who have those basic rights as rights of citizens. Rather, it requires that persons be *responsible and cooperating members of society who can recognize and act in accordance with their moral duties and obligations.*"[53]

Yet it is surely a peculiar definition of "right" one that is entirely dependent on the right-holder being *obligated* to perform the behavior that is supposed to be authorized by the right. A right defined as the behavior that the public authority merely *permits* because it is also the content of an obligation is at best a tautology (that which is prescribed is also permitted) and at worst an authoritarian distortion of the original meaning of human rights as the legal expression of human freedom. (The notion of enabling rights is reminiscent of Bertrand Russell's observation about Hegel's definition of freedom: the "freedom" to obey the police.) On this issue, Rawls's defense of hierarchical societies suffers from the same infirmities as its source—Philip Soper's theory of law.[54] Rawls, following Soper, makes obedience to the law depend on the good faith and sincerity of the rulers. But this (as opposed to the moral content of the law, or the democratic credentials of the rulers) is a highly implausible foundation of legal obligation. As Joseph Raz observed: "The divergence of opinion about morality between me and a Nazi government or between me and a fundamentalist Muslim government is so great that I would deny that just because they believe in the rightness of their action there is some joint pursuit in which we are partners."[55]

The problem with Rawls's hierarchical societies is, however, more general. A close examination of his main claim about hierarchical societies uncovers a serious case of "group thinking." For what does it mean to say that a *society* has a comprehensive view of the good that, say, excludes free speech? It cannot merely mean that *the government* thinks so or that the official interpreters of the "worldview" think so. That would merely amount to unconditional surrender to authoritarianism, and certainly Rawls would require more than that. Does it mean then that *a majority* of the people believe that there shouldn't be freedom of speech? This cannot possibly do, because the very meaning of a right (one convincingly championed by Rawls in *A Theory of Justice*) is that it trumps majoritarian preferences. In other words, Rawls's "basic human rights" cannot be just those rights that hold as long as a majority of the population doesn't decide to eliminate them. So the only possibility left is some form of conservative communitarianism: we say that there is a comprehensive conception of the good that validly denies free speech (to continue with that example) when historically the people (both rulers and citizens) in that particular culture have sincerely thought such conception to be legitimate. In short, we look to tradition and history; they, and not the government or the majority, establish the limits to freedom.

Even leaving aside some obvious problems with such a doctrine (What reading of the tradition? Which tradition if the society has many?), it is worth noting its extreme conservatism: there is hardly any room for reform, for innovation. Democratic dissidents and human rights reformers in hierarchical societies are just out of luck, since they are, on the communitarian view, political misfits who battle mindlessly (and unjustifiedly) against tradition. People in hierarchical societies who believe in autonomy as the central moral value (e.g., the democratic dissenters in China) can be validly frustrated by whatever collectivist idea is embodied in the tradition (e.g., the Chinese authoritarian worldview). The proposition (central to Rawls's thesis) that a society's political legitimacy is grounded on a comprehensive conception of the good held by the society conceived as some form of organic being is either conceptually indefensible or morally implausible. And in case of doubt, we should always err on the side of freedom, because *governments* will, more often than not, defend their political space where they can exercise a maximum of power, with the consequent restriction of individual freedoms. We should not accept at face value the representation by some government that "their society" doesn't recognize this or that human right. Such statement is made by the very individuals in power who wish to deny the right and who happen to be the historical culprits of the world's worst evils—aggression and oppression. Their representation of the societies' "worldview" is always suspect when that "worldview" purports to deny freedom, and it should be subject to a searching scrutiny.[56]

Rawls's international law principles do not even authorize representatives of liberal societies publicly (that is, in an international forum such as the United

Nations) *to criticize* the nonliberal practices (e.g., suppression of speech) in hierarchical societies. To be sure, Rawls concedes that citizens in liberal societies can freely criticize nonliberal societies within their own liberal political fora, given liberal freedom of speech.[57] But can a liberal government put forth, say, a diplomatic protest *to the illiberal government* for the silencing of dissidents? Rawls postulates the existence of a forum, such as the United Nations, where representatives of both liberal and hierarchical societies would vent their "common opinions" and "policy towards the other (i.e. dictatorial) regimes."[58] But if representatives of liberal societies in the United Nations criticized what they regarded as violations of *liberal* human rights (say, denial of freedom of speech) in hierarchical societies, under *The Law of Peoples* this would be an unjustified criticism. For in Rawls's international system liberals would have no argument derived *from international law* to make such criticism. They could do so only if the hierarchical societies violated what Rawls calls "basic" human rights, such as if they arbitrarily killed or tortured people or if public officials behaved arbitrarily within their conception of justice. But they have no arguments, for example, if the hierarchical regime cracks down on dissidents, as long as those dissidents already had their say at some point in the political process. On this as on other points, I do not believe that Rawls intended to limit "international speech" in this way. But I believe that by weakening the grounds on which representatives of liberal and nonliberal societies can press claims against each other, *The Law of Peoples* inflicts a serious blow to human rights activism.

In his defense of hierarchical societies, Rawls relies on the liberal commitment to tolerance: just as we must tolerate different conceptions of the good held by fellow citizens in a democratic society, so we must tolerate other *societies* informed by different conceptions of the good.[59] Tolerance of hierarchical societies is simply the natural extension of tolerance of persons with different views about the good life. However, this view is unconvincing because it is unduly anthropomorphic. Tolerance of illiberal views is indeed mandated by liberal principles, but this does not mean that we ought to tolerate illiberal *governmental behavior*, especially if such behavior takes the form of coercion against people who dissent. Nor does liberal tolerance of illiberal views mean that those views are in some sense justified or even reasonable. Instead, I suspect that liberals are committed to tolerance of illiberal views because of a mix of Kantian concerns for individual autonomy (even when the autonomous person chooses wrongly); utilitarian concerns, well supported by experience, about the dangers of state censorship; and epistemological concerns related to the provisional nature of knowledge.[60] Although these concerns explain toleration of all kinds of speech in a democratic society, they do not justify toleration of illiberal governmental coercion.

Consider also Rawls's requirement that hierarchical societies (indeed, that all societies) allow for emigration.[61] The justification of that right in Rawls's hierarchical societies, however, is problematic. From the standpoint of the receiving (liberal) society, immigrants from hierarchical societies should be held to a stringent standard, such as the one provided by current law (well-founded fear of persecution), because under Rawls's law of nations the regime of origin is legitimate. In other words, if the asylum officers in the liberal society follow Rawls's prescriptions, they will conclude that someone who simply feels oppressed in the hierarchical society (the liberal dissenter) and who would like, understandably, to live in freedom does not have an argument based on international law to ground this desire. He can, therefore, be denied asylum. But if this is so, then the right to emigrate from hierarchical societies does not mean much, since liberal dissenters who wish to emigrate do not have a corresponding right to be admitted in liberal societies. Perhaps Rawls would disagree with this line of reasoning and advocate a broad right of asylum (or immigration). But then such immigration policy must be based on some suspicion that hierarchical societies are not so legitimate after all. Otherwise, why would liberal societies be willing to admit dissenters of hierarchical societies? Rawls might answer: "Because they have freely chosen to live in a liberal system." Yet in Rawls's own view, such choices are unavailable to the liberal dissenters, because, as we saw, *citizens in hierarchical societies are not supposed to be free moral agents*. Their rights derive from their nonvoluntary membership in the (hierarchical) group; they cannot validly choose to live in a liberal system. Put differently: Rawls is willing to honor the free choices *to emigrate* by dissenters who are being silenced (legitimately, he would say) by the hierarchical regime. He is not willing, however, to honor the dissenters' choices *within* their own societies because their conception of the good allows for suppression of dissent. While defending hierarchical societies as legitimate he allows liberal dissenters through the back door of immigration. Such a view can only be based on a universal respect for autonomy, that is, the right of individuals, regardless of history, culture, or tradition, to choose the society in which they want to live. This view is, I believe, entirely correct; it is also inconsistent with Rawls's claim that respect for autonomy is culturally bound. If there is a right of individuals to emigrate and be admitted in states of their choice, then respect for autonomy cannot be simply an assumption biased in favor of the West.[62]

The Inconsistency with the International Law of Human Rights

This leads me to a decisive objection against Rawls's system of international ethics: it falls considerably short of matching the considered moral judgments of the international community. The range and kind of human rights that are now recognized by international law considerably exceeds the modest requirements of legitimacy proposed by Rawls. For the sake of simplicity, I will discuss three topics: democratic governance, gender equality, and the rights of political dissenters.

Democratic Governance. The case for the existence of an international legal right to democratic governance seems very strong and is supported by modern international practice.[63] This would not be a dispositive argument for those committed to an *ideal* normative liberal theory of international relations, since on that view, if positive international law does not recognize democratic governance, too bad for international law. But it should be very important for Rawls, because he wants his "law of peoples" to match the considered moral intuitions that reasonable representatives of diverse cultures share. In my view, the international law of human rights can plausibly be said to describe those intuitions.[64] So if Rawls's theory can be shown to fall short of even the modest requirements of international human rights law, then Rawls would have to amend the theory.

Even if one disregards positive international law, however, there are many a priori reasons why reasonable people would agree to a norm mandating some form of democratic governance. The first reason is related to the question of *agency*. If international law is largely created by nation-states, then the international community needs some criterion to determine when some official actually *represents* the state. Traditional international law has proposed the criterion of *effectiveness*. A government internationally represents a people living in a territory if that government has effective political control over that people (what the French call *le principe d'effectivité*).[65] Such view, however, is suspect, and Rawls does well in not adopting it. If the international system is going to be the result of what the "peoples of the United Nations" want it to be,[66] then it makes sense to require that governments who participate in the creation of international law be not just those in power but the real representatives of the people who reside within the boundaries of the state. A rule requiring democratic legitimacy in the form of free adult universal suffrage seems the best approximation to actual political consent and true representativeness. Rawls can of course argue that hierarchical societies simply have a different rule of state agency. On that view, governments of hierarchical societies are legitimate because they are the ones designated by whatever traditional rule of representation applies there (e.g., birth). But one cannot define representativeness as simply whatever rule a society happens to favor. Either someone represents someone else or he doesn't. Perhaps Western electoral systems are not the only answer. But surely the proposition, repeatedly endorsed by the United Nations, that "the will of the people shall be the basis of the authority of government"[67] is far more generous than the criteria of representation that Rawls would allow in his system.

Second, there are strong grounds for believing that democratic rule is a necessary condition for enjoying other human rights. While it is always possible to imagine a society where human rights are respected by an enlightened despot, this has never occurred in practice. This is why the right to political participation is included in the major human rights conventions.[68] The right to participate in government is a very important human right in itself; it is also crucially instrumental to the enjoyment of other rights. Its violation should therefore trigger appropriate international scrutiny.

The third and decisive reason for requiring democratic rule is found in the arguments examined already in detail in Chapter 1 of this book: liberal democracies are more peaceful, and therefore a rule requiring democratic rule is consonant with the ideal of a lasting world peace, in a way that the rule of effectiveness or pure political power, which countenances tyrannies, is not. This is so because nonliberal regimes tend to be more aggressive *and* because the difference in regimes is a major cause of conflict. Democracies have built-in mechanisms that cause them to avoid war with one another altogether. The reason why democracies are sometimes belligerent is that they often perceive threats by illiberal regimes to their democratic institutions. These threats are sometimes real and sometimes imaginary, which is why democracies also get involved in unjustified wars. But these wars are always against nonliberal regimes: as Rawls, following Kant and Doyle, readily recognizes, democracies *do not* make war against one another. So if the aim of international law is to secure a lasting peace where the benefits of international cooperation can be reaped by all, then it has to require democratic legitimacy.

This last consideration is particularly hard on Rawls's thesis, because if the theory of liberal peace is correct, then it fatally undermines Rawls's first requirement that hierarchical societies be peaceful. Unlike the Kantian thesis defended in this book, which advocates a liberal alliance as the only legitimate basis of international law, Rawls's "law of peoples" fails to meet the test of stability (liberal and nonliberal societies just cannot coexist peacefully) and is therefore nonviable. Nonliberal societies (and not just tyrannies) are war-prone. Representatives (of liberal and hierarchical societies alike) concerned with peace would therefore choose democratic representation, for the very reasons that Kant gave in *Perpetual Peace*. It is an open question how much of their conception of the good representatives of hierarchical societies would have to give up to accommodate democracy.

Gender Equality. Nobody could seriously accuse John Rawls of endorsing the oppression of women,[69] yet hierarchical societies, as portrayed in the essay, could, it seems, legitimately discriminate against them. Rawls decries the subjection of women in connection with his argument that global economic justice is more likely to be achieved by putting pressure on corrupt governments.[70] But Rawls's hierarchical societies, as he defines them, could validly discriminate against women in ways that Rawls himself would not accept and are, moreover, unlawful under current international law. Because a hierarchical society is not committed to treating persons as equal and free, its comprehensive conception of the good may confine women to subordinate roles.[71] In Rawls's definition of a hierarchical society, such exclusion would be permissible, as long as (1) the discrimination were sincerely held by officials, and (2) women were heard at some point in the political process of consultation. Yet according to widely accepted international law principles, discrimination against women is prohibited, and women have an equal right to participate in all forms of public life, including government.[72] International law is now quite clear that women may not be treated in certain ways, so Rawls's "law of peoples," in a manner surely unintended by him, lags behind positive international law. The notion of a decent nonliberal society that Rawls wants to introduce needs to be amended to accommodate Rawls's (and any decent person's) commitment to gender equality. Only then could such regimes come close to being members in good standing of the international society. It is easy to see that with these amendments in the direction of equality and freedom, hierarchical societies start looking quite like liberal societies.

Political Dissent. The third case is that of political dissenters. We saw that Rawls's only requirement of legitimacy is that those societies implement a system of "hierarchical consultation" where people, and especially the dissenters, are heard at least once. But once the government has made a political decision citizens have no right to free speech, which means they cannot validly dissent from the party line. The government can then say: "You've been heard already, we decided against your interests in a way that is consistent with our conception of justice, and now you may not speak against our decision." Take the current situation in China. Can the U.S. government complain about the human rights situation there? Certainly Marxism is a "comprehensive philosophical worldview" (which Rawls allows as analogue to the religious worldview). Maybe Rawls wants to say that Marxism is an unreasonable comprehensive doctrine, or that the Chinese government does not sincerely believe in it, or that they do not apply it fairly. Or maybe he would want to say that the current regime does not provide a "hierarchical system of consulta-tion" or that it violates "basic" human rights because, say, it arbitrarily imprisons or tortures people. All that may be empirically true, but I do not think it would be hard for the Chinese regime to meet the Rawls/Soper requirements of legitimacy while persisting in their suppression of dissent. Certainly they could say that neighborhood committees and party structures provide everyone with a chance to be heard at some point. If that is true, then criticism of their suppression of dissent, such as the one currently advanced by the U.S. government, is unwarranted. Dissent is a form of expression, and Rawls refuses to say that freedom of expression should be recognized by international law. To be sure, Rawls is correct that the First Amendment of the U.S. Constitution ought not be considered the international standard. But, here again, there is convincing evidence that international law "for the present age" goes far beyond the meager measure of protection of speech that Rawls is willing to recognize.[73] Rawls would have to say that liberal dissenters, such as the heroes of Tiananmen Square, are misfits in their own culture.[74]

There is no need yet to recite all the reasons why freedom of expression is an indispensable component of any decent political arrangement.[75] Free intellect is the engine of human progress and welfare, and I do not believe that *all* the reasons that support a universal recognition of free expression can be dismissed as biased or culturally bound. But even accepting, *gratia argumentandi*, that Rawls's conception of the law of nations is essentially correct and that hierarchical societies are internationally legitimate, there are two decisive reasons why even these societies must allow some freedom of speech and political dissent. First, if as Rawls suggests the hierarchical society must respect a modicum of liberty to be legitimate (defined, as we saw, as the "basic human rights" listed in articles 3 through 18 of the Universal Declaration), then that society has to recognize the freedom of citizens to debate whether or not that threshold, modest as it is, has been observed. Otherwise, experience shows that the condition of stability of political institutions will be seriously undermined and the hierarchical society will drift toward tyranny. Speech to question whether or not the government respects basic human rights is necessary for utilitarian reasons of the kind Mill gave, even accepting, for the sake of argument, that hierarchical societies are morally legitimate. There is no need to resort to (allegedly biased) ideas of autonomy and equal moral worth. Similarly, if the undemocratic hierarchical society implements a system of consultation, then it is natural to recognize the freedom to question whether or not that system has been fairly implemented. So even on Rawls's view, hierarchical regimes must tolerate the expression that relates to those regimes' conditions of legitimacy—in particular, the "basic human rights" and the hierarchical system of consultation. Perhaps citizens in a hierarchical society cannot criticize the government for doing a bad job or for enacting unjust tax laws, but they should be able to challenge practices that they believe depart from the conception of the good that the society entertains and that citizens and public officials both sincerely hold. In conclusion, even hierarchical societies must recognize a modicum of freedom of expression and dissent. If this is true, however, it is hard to see why it wouldn't be rational for hierarchical societies to allow for a broader right to free expression. The only reasons I can see against that are those that governments have given over the centuries to silence dissidents: dissidents are a threat to power, and it is more expedient to silence them by force than to confront them with rational argument.[76] Remember: behind all the talk about "sincerely held comprehensive conceptions of the good" and "enabling rights," the stark reality is that in hierarchical societies, as Rawls describes them, jails are full of dissidents. That there is no right to dissent means no less than dissent is prohibited, and that means that peaceful dissenters are imprisoned just for expressing their opinion. Such imprisonment will be legitimate, under Rawls's theory, as long as the dissenters have had a fair hearing at some point in the political process.

The second reason why hierarchical societies must allow for free expression is analogous to the one I indicated in connection with democratic representation, and was first suggested by Kant: if free debate is thwarted, there is a grave danger of the regime becoming war-prone. We saw in Chapter 1 that when public opinion has little impact on the government's decisions there is no opportunity for public debate on the moral and prudential reasons to make war. Psychologically, this insulation creates in rulers a sense of invincibility and megalomania. As Kant warned, when the government is undemocratic, its prerogatives and privileges remain intact in case of war.[77] Freedom of expression operates, therefore, as a moderating influence on the destructive and aggressive nationalist instincts that governments and people unfortunately tend to exhibit in international disputes. It follows that a state that does not recognize freedom of expression fails to meet the condition of international stability, or peacefulness, required by Rawls's system.

Here again, given what Rawls has written elsewhere about freedom of speech,[78] I do not believe that this harsh result was intended by him for international law. But if so, his definition of a decent nonliberal society has, once again, to be reworked to meet the considered moral intuition that the silencing of dissidents is intolerable. As with the case of equality discussed in the previous section, the nonliberal society needs to become more liberal to be decent.

The Question of War

At times Rawls gives the impression that his desire to treat hierarchical societies as members in good standing of the international community stems from his concern with peace.[79] The liberal argument that seems to worry Rawls is this: "Liberal regimes are the only ones that are legitimate. Therefore, it is morally justified to get rid of illiberal governments by whatever means, including force, whenever possible." But this worry confuses two different issues. It is true that the Kantian treats illiberal governments as outlaws, but *it does not follow that it is morally permissible to eliminate them by force whenever possible*. The legitimacy of a state or a government is only *one* of the reasons that precludes waging war. If a regime is legitimate, then it is prohibited to make war against it, come what may (liberal states do not wage war against one another anyway). But this is not true *a contrario sensu*: if a regime is illegitimate (i.e., it is unrepresentative and fails to respect human rights) there may still be powerful reasons why it would be unjustified to use force against that regime. For example, in Rawls's hierarchical societies, where the political system is authoritarian but not crassly tyrannical, the best course of action for liberal democracies is to use moral persuasion and diplomatic pressure to try to effect democratic change in those societies. War is excluded simply because it is disproportionate to the goal sought: experience shows that democratic change can in most cases be achieved by less drastic means. Even in cases where the regime is overtly tyrannical (as in present-day China) waging war would be wrong because of the impossibility or prohibitive cost of victory. So humanitarian intervention (i.e., the war to liberate oppressed populations) is subject to a number of constraints that counsel moderation in many cases *regardless* of the question of the legitimacy of the government. The Kantian should strive to expand the liberal alliance by those means that are best suited to the realities he has to face, reserving the use of force for the most serious cases of oppression where there is a genuine chance for victory and where the restoration of democracy and human rights is a realistic objective. The upshot is that we don't need to call an undemocratic regime that suppresses dissent and denies equality "legitimate," "reasonable," or "member in good standing" in order to conclude that it would be unjustified and unwise to eliminate that regime by force. Still, the relationship between liberal and illiberal states can only be a peaceful *modus vivendi* and not a community of shared moral beliefs and political commonalities.[80] Liberal states must try to help oppressed populations, and the best way to do this is to encourage and press for democratic change and full respect of human rights as are now embodied in the pertinent international instruments and, in egregious cases, act forcibly to rescue innocent victims of despotism.[81]

Conclusion

There are two John Rawlses. The first John Rawls is, I believe, the greatest political philosopher of this century. *A Theory of Justice* is a work that not only set the agenda for political philosophy but, as important, served as inspiration for many who were resisting oppression in many parts of the world. The second John Rawls moved toward a more relativistic, context-based conception of justice and political morality, where rights and liberties no longer have a foundation in higher principles or liberal views of human nature but are merely the result of the peculiar history and traditions of the West. It should be clear that deriving a rich notion of *international* human rights from such a relativistic conception is a very hard, if not impossible, task. The critique in this chapter can be interpreted, therefore, as a liberal reaction against the second Rawls, the one that took definitive shape in *Political Liberalism.*

At a different level, one of the functions of liberal international theory should be to suggest *improvements* to positive international law. Traditional international law has been notoriously obsessed with the sanctity of sovereignty and the prerogatives of governments. It is therefore only natural for liberals of all kinds (be they philosophers, politicians, or human rights activists) to attempt reformulations that mitigate the consequences of the quasi-absolute attachment to sovereignty that has characterized our discipline for several centuries. Rawls is absolutely right that the two main scourges of our era, aggression and oppression, are intimately tied to the classic notion of sovereignty. It is therefore surprising for the leading liberal philosopher to propose, at a time when more and more societies are finally adopting liberal constitutions, a theory of international law that is *regressive* when compared even to the modest accomplishments of the law of human rights. Of course that the conformity or otherwise with positive international law should not be the touchstone of acceptance of a philosophical theory. But it should certainly count against a liberal theory that in the tension between human rights and states' rights, between freedom and nationalism, between collective forms of oppression and the quest for human progress, between the individual and the government, the theory sides with rulers (provided they are not "demonic" tyrants) and not with people. It is as if Rawls believed that the human rights movement had gone too far in recognizing rights such as freedom of expression; those rights are, in some sense, too liberal.

The truth is that international human rights as they stand today have been greatly influenced by liberal principles. A plausible way to justify international human rights is to recognize that all human beings, regardless of culture and history, are born free and equal and have inherent dignity, as the Preamble of the United Nations Charter and article 1 of Universal Declaration of Human Rights do. The United Nations Charter was predicated upon this liberal premise. To suggest otherwise, to accept and recognize as legitimate regimes that, while not patently atrocious, suppress dissent, discriminate against groups *qua* groups, and lack democratic credentials, is to turn the clock back to the pre–World War II era. Quite apart from the fact that the assumptions made are per se unappealing, Rawls's result fails to match our considered *international* judgments. From here one can, by reflective equilibrium, do two things. Either one gives up promoting universal freedom of expression or democratic governance, as Rawls does, or one gives up the theory instead. If the theory does not justify an international principle that recognizes moral equality, freedom of expression and political dissent, and the right to democratic governance, then the theory ought to be discarded. This last solution is not only the one consistent with international human rights law as it stands today but, more important, is closer to any reasonable person's intuitions about the relationship between freedom and sovereignty.

Notes

1. See John Rawls, *A Theory of Justice* (1971) [hereinafter Theory of Justice].

2. For an examination of Rawls's early views on international law, see Fernando R. Tesón, *Humanitarian Intervention: An Inquiry into Law and Morality* 61–74 (2d ed. 1997).

3. John Rawls, "The Law of Peoples," 20 *Critical Inquiry* 36 (1993) [hereinafter Law of Peoples]. Rawls's seminal work is, of course, Theory of Justice, supra note 1. In his most recent book, *Political Liberalism* (1993) [hereinafter Political Liberalism], Rawls departs considerably from the original theory.

4. See Rawls, *Law of Peoples*, supra note 3, at 42, 58 ("a reasonable law of peoples for the present age").

5. See id. at 37. "What form does the toleration of nonliberal societies take in this case (i.e., in the law of nations)." Id.

6. See id. at 37, 66. On this point, therefore, he agrees with the thrust of this book, see Chapter 1.

7. See, e.g., Thomas Pogge, *Realizing Rawls* 246–259 (1989).

8. See Rawls, *Theory of Justice*, supra note 1, at 92.

9. See Rawls, *Law of Peoples*, supra note 3, at 55, 56. "[International human] rights do not depend on any . . . moral doctrine or philosophical conception of human nature, such as, for example, that human beings are moral persons and have equal worth." Id.

10. See id. at 43–50.

11. But, according to Rawls's recent version of his theory, this does not entail adherence to any particular comprehensive doctrine, in particular to metaphysical conceptions of personhood (such as religious, utilitarian or Kantian). See Rawls, *Political Liberalism*, supra note 3, at xvi, xvii–xviii, 29–35.

12. The principles governing the liberal alliance are listed in Rawls, *Law of Peoples*, supra note 3, at 46.

13. See Immanuel Kant, "To Perpetual Peace: A Philosophical Sketch" [1795], in *Perpetual Peace and Other Essays* 107, 107–118 (Ted Humphrey trans., 1983).

14. Rawls, *Law of Peoples*, supra note 3, at 47.

15. Id.

16. See id. at 49.

17. Rawls relies expressly on Hegel on this point. See id. at 58.

18. See id.

19. See id. at 50.

20. It is hard to understand what concept of "reasonableness" or "rationality" Rawls is now using. Consider the following: "One should allow, I think, a space between the reasonable or fully reasonable, which requires full and equal liberty of conscience, and the fully unreasonable, which denies it entirely. Doctrines that allow a measure of liberty of conscience but do not allow it fully are views that lie in that space and are not fully unreasonable." Id. at 53 n.27.

21. See id. at 51–52. The work relied upon is Philip Soper, *A Theory of Law* (1982).

22. See Rawls, *Law of Peoples*, supra note 3, at 51.

23. See id. at 52.

24. See id. at 52–53.

25. See, e.g., id. at 57.

26. See id. at 59 n.45.

27. See id. at 52.

28. See id. at 59 n.45.

29. Rawls first stated this position in John Rawls, "Justice as Fairness: Political not Metaphysical," 14 *Philosophy of Public Affairs* 223 (1985). See also Rawls, *Political Liberalism*, supra note 3, at xi–xviii.

30. It is worth noting here that in his recent book Rawls confined the domain of political liberalism to addressing the following problem: how is a democratic society possible given the fact that people hold incompatible reasonable comprehensive doctrines? See Rawls, *Political Liberalism*, supra note 3. His answer is to declare that political liberalism must be agnostic as to these doctrines. Citizens in liberal societies, however, still retain their status as free and equal, and as reasonable and rational. See id. at 19–20, 48–58. However, Rawls drops these last attributes for the law of nations, because he believes that its task is to devise principles that encompass liberal and nonliberal societies.

31. Rawls, *Law of Peoples*, supra note 3, at 59.

32. Id.

33. See id. at 67.

34. See id. at 59, 67.

35. See Charles Beitz, *Political Theory and International Relations* 143–153 (1979); Brian Barry, "Do Countries Have Moral Obligations? The Case of World Hunger," in 2 *The Tanner Lectures on Human Values* 25 (S. McMurrin ed., 1981).

36. The difference principle is the one that governs the distribution of wealth. It provides that: "Social and economic inequalities are to be arranged so that they are both: (a) to the greatest benefit of the least advantaged . . . and (b) attached to positions and offices open to all under conditions of fair equality of opportunity." Rawls, *Theory of Justice*, supra note 1, at 302.

37. A "Rawls-superior" move occurs when the situation of the worse-off is improved. Notice that how much the better-off gains in such move is irrelevant. So even under the highly redistributive global difference principle proposed by Beitz and Barry, the existence of an economic "gap" between industrialized and developing nations is not enough to justify wealth transfers.

38. Rawls, *Law of Peoples*, supra note 3, at 63.

39. Id.

40. See id. at 64 n.52. The work that Rawls relies upon is Amartya Sen, *Poverty and Famines: An Essay on Entitlement and Deprivation* (1981).

41. Rawls, *Law of Peoples*, supra note 3, at 63.

42. These liberal assumptions are the ones endorsed by Rawls in *A Theory of Justice* and, to a lesser degree, in *Political Liberalism*. As I pointed out, supra note 3, they need not entail a particular metaphysics of personhood, such as the one defended by Kant.

43. See Rawls, *Law of Peoples*, supra note 3, at 59, 66–67.

44. For a full discussion of statism, see supra Chapter 2.

45. Rawls, *Theory of Justice*, supra note 1, at 264.

46. Rawls, *Law of Peoples*, supra note 3, at 55.

47. Id.

48. See Immanuel Kant, *Groundwork for a Metaphysics of Morals* 57 (H.J. Paton trans., Harper Torchbook ed. 1964). There are, of course, important differences between the liberal assumptions in Rawls's theory and the metaphysical foundations of freedom found in Kant. Those differences are well explained by Rawls, see *Theory of Justice*, supra note 1, at 251–267. But while Rawls tries to avoid the metaphysical puzzles that Kant faced, both *A Theory of Justice* and *Political Liberalism* still retain important assumptions about moral persons: their capacity to have a conception of their good ("The Rational") and their sense of justice ("The Reasonable"). See, e.g., id. at 505; and Rawls, *Political Liberalism*, supra note 3, at 48–58. As I read *The Law of Peoples*, these two powers of moral personality are no longer universal.

49. See David Gauthier, *Morals by Agreement* (1986).

50. Rawls, *Law of Peoples*, supra note 3, at 53.

51. See id. at 54.

52. For a modern defense of this view, see Terry Nardin, *Law, Morality, and the Relations of States* (1983). See generally Michael J. Smith, *Realist Thought from Weber to Kissinger* (1986).

53. Rawls, *Law of Peoples*, supra note 3, at 57 (emphasis added).

54. For a convincing critique of Soper's theory, see Joseph Raz, "The Morality of Obedience," 83 *Michigan Law Review* 732, 744–749 (1985).

55. Id. at 746. Of course, Rawls would regard those examples as tyrannical, but the quotation illustrates the difficulties of placing much weight on the sincerity of rulers.

56. During the military dictatorship in Argentina (1976–1982) the government responded to criticisms by articulating a "worldview" according to which Argentine society was "Western and Christian," by which they meant some pre-Enlightenment medieval version of those words. Now I do not doubt that ridiculous and clumsy as such a "worldview" was, they sincerely believed in it: they were not merely cloaking their evil intents and their sadistic impulses. But from a human rights standpoint why should it matter whether or not the authoritarian government is sincere? Either free speech is a right to be recognized or it isn't but it should not depend on how sincere and earnest the censors are. In fact, experience shows that "true believers" are the most dangerous tyrants.

57. See Rawls, *Law of Peoples*, supra note 3, at 67. "Critical commentary [of hierarchical societies] in liberal societies would be fully consistent with the civic liberties and integrity of those societies." Id.

58. Id. at 61.

59. Id. at 68.

60. On this, see the enlightening discussion by the late Argentine philosopher Carlos Nino, *The Ethics of Human Rights* 38–43, 101–128 (Oxford, Clarendon Press 1991).

61. See Rawls, *Law of Peoples*, supra note 3, at 53 & n.29.

62. Given my view that Rawls's position on international human rights is no longer liberal, I am surprised that in this article he defends himself against possible charges that his endorsement of modest "basic human rights" may be ethnocentric, that is, biased in favor of Western culture. See id. at 57.

63. See Thomas M. Franck, "The Emerging Right to Democratic Governance," 86 *American Journal of International Law* 46 (1992).

64. As many commentators have emphasized, international human rights are the result of many philosophical doctrines, the two main ones being liberalism and socialism. See, inter alia, James Nickel, *Making Sense of Human Rights: Philosophical Reflections on the Universal Declaration on Human Rights* (1987); Henry Shue, *Basic Rights: Subsistence, Affluence and U.S. Policy* (1980).

65. See, e.g., Montevideo Convention on the Rights and Duties of States, 1933, article 1, *United States Treaties* 881.

66. See United Nations Charter preamble.

67. This proposition has been cited in numerous recent resolutions of the General Assembly and the Security Council, most recently in the resolutions regarding the situation in Haiti. I discuss the legal status of democracy at some length in Fernando R. Tesón, "Changing Perceptions of Domestic Jurisdiction and Intervention," in *Beyond Sovereignty: Collectively Defending Democracy in the Americas* 29 (Tom Farer ed., 1996).

68. For a full discussion and references, see Franck, supra note 63, and Gregory H. Fox, "The Right to Political Participation in International Law," 17 *Yale Journal of International Law* 539 (1992).

69. Rawls writes: "The same equality of the Declaration of Independence which Lincoln invoked to condemn slavery can be invoked to condemn the inequality and oppression of women." Political Liberalism, supra note 3, at xxix. Rawls thus aligns himself, as one would expect, with liberal feminism. For contrasting views about the usefulness of liberal and radical feminism in the critique of international law, see Hilary Charlesworth et al., "Feminist Approaches to International Law," 85 *American Journal of International Law* 613 (1991), and infra Chapter 6.

70. See Rawls, *Law of Peoples*, supra note 3, at 64.

71. See id. at 54 (members of hierarchical societies accept basic inequalities among them). I am convinced that those conceptions of the good that purport to deny human rights in the name of tradition are either misstatements of the traditions they purport to represent or simply self-serving rationalizations for oppression. One cannot but agree with Ann Mayer: "In reality, the world's Muslims have never been consulted about what rights they would like to have or about whether they truly prefer to be governed by so called 'Islamic' rights, norms that fall far below the protection guaranteed to non-Muslims under international law." Ann E. Mayer, "Universal Versus Islamic Human Rights: A Clash of Cultures or a Clash With a Construct?" 15 *Michigan Journal of International Law* 307, 404 (1994).

72. See, e.g., "Convention on the Elimination of All Forms of Discrimination Against Women" 19 *International Legal Materials* 33 (1979).

73. See International Covenant on Civil and Political Rights, Dec. 19, 1966, article 19, 999 *United Nations Treaty Series* 171, 6 *International Legal Materials* 368 (1977); African Charter on Human and Peoples' Rights, article 9, O.A.U. Doc. CAB/LEG/67/3, Rev. 5 (1981); American Convention on Human Rights, Nov. 22, 1969, article 13, reprinted in Organization of American States, Handbook of Existing Rules Pertaining to Human Rights in the InterAmerican System, OEA/Ser.L/V/II.60, Doc. 28, at 29 (1967); European Convention on Human Rights and Fundamental Freedoms, Nov. 4, 1950, article 10, 213

United Nations Treaty Series 222. See also Paul Sieghart, *The Lawful Rights of Mankind* 140–143 (1985) (while regulation of free expression may vary, the existence and stringency of the obligation to respect it is beyond doubt).

74. It is ironic that Rawls's article is excerpted from an Amnesty International Lecture: if his law of peoples were implemented, Amnesty International, whose main mandate is to put pressure on governments to release prisoners of conscience, would be largely out of business.

75. No one has articulated a philosophical defense of free expression better than John Stuart Mill. See John Stuart Mill, *On Liberty* [1859] 75–118 (Penguin Classic ed. 1974).

76. At the end of the article Rawls correctly asserts that democratic pluralism in liberal societies is the outcome "of human reason under free institutions [that] can only be undone by the oppressive use of state power." Rawls, *Law of Peoples*, supra note 3, at 68. I do not understand, therefore, his statement that the law of peoples "is simply and extension of these same ideas to the political society of well-ordered peoples." Hierarchical societies precisely use state power to silence the exercise of human reason.

77. Kant, supra note 13, at 113.

78. See, inter alia, Rawls, *Political Liberalism*, supra note 3, at 340–356.

79. See, e.g., Rawls, *Law of Peoples*, supra note 3, at 67–68 (a belief that liberalism is superior to other forms of political organization does not support a claim to rid the world of illiberal regimes).

80. Rawls correctly concludes that the relationship between well-ordered societies (that is liberal plus hierarchical) and tyrannical regimes can only be a *modus vivendi*. See id. at 61. For the reasons given in the text, I extend that conclusion to the relationship between liberal societies and illiberal ones.

81. Thus, I agree with Rawls that humanitarian intervention is permissible only in very serious cases, that is, in what we both call outlaw tyrannical regimes. By definition, Rawls's hierarchical societies, although illegitimate by my lights, have not reached the level of oppression that would justify abandoning peaceful methods of diplomatic pressure to effect democratic reforms.

5

Self-Determination, Group Rights, and Secession

Introduction

The Kantian theory of international law claims that the morally preferable international political system is the one agreed upon by democratic, rights-respecting nations. We saw in Chapter 1 that the Kantian theory rejects, on liberty grounds, proposals for a world state and promotes instead the establishment of an alliance of separate liberal states as the best foundation of international law. This solution, however, raises a difficult question: When does a group of individuals have the right to create its own sovereign state? Evidently the answer cannot simply be "when the state so created is legitimate according to the Kantian thesis, that is, it respects human rights and the government is democratic." For while it is true that a state ought to be liberal to be legitimate, it does not follow that any group of individuals who wish to create a liberal state can do so *anywhere, anytime* (unless it intends to create its own state in *terra nulla*). The creation of states is not governed only by liberal principles of legitimacy; those principles establish a necessary but not a sufficient condition for the justification of states. There are issues of territory and issues of equity that are not captured by a sole appeal to Kantian principles of legitimacy. That is why the problem of self-determination has to be examined separately.

The principle of self-determination has an important place in modern international law.[1] In political terms, the principle has been, and continues to be, a powerful motivating force. In ethical terms world opinion has regarded the claims by peoples in the colonies and other territories as morally compelling. Most would agree that the peoples of colonies and other territories (e.g., the Baltic Republics) that were unjustly annexed were morally *justified* in demanding independence from foreign rule. Yet the principle of self-determination resists easy handling. Under what circumstances can a group claim autonomy, special rights, or sovereignty? When can government legitimately resist self-determination claims? What are the obligations of third states? What *kinds* of moral reasons make such claims justified in some cases and spurious in others? There are no easy answers to these questions. From the standpoint of the Kantian thesis, it is easier to answer the question of the legitimacy of *existing* states. While, as we shall see, liberal legitimacy plays a preeminent role in the analysis of self-determination, the issue of when a group of individuals is justified in creating a state requires an examination of additional factors.

In this chapter I will examine the justification of self-determination under the assumptions of the Kantian thesis. The argument developed in the previous chapters took existing states and their boundaries as given. The legitimacy of those boundaries and of the creation of new states remained unexamined. One reason for that omission in most accounts of international ethics is that perhaps it is not possible or practical to argue for a *de novo* redistribution of land and people in our globe. But at the very least, it might be possible to find principles that govern the establishment of group rights and the creation of new states from the current distribution of world political power, that is, for cases of group autonomy and secession. That inquiry hopefully will help us understand the meaning and scope of the principle of self-determination, pinpoint more clearly the ethical reasons that support its endurance, and thus help us distinguish valid from spurious claims.[2]

The confusion surrounding self-determination stems from several sources. To the philosopher, there are theoretical and ethical puzzles about self-determination. Theoretically, it is hard to understand the meaning of a right held by a collective entity like the nation or the people. Because international lawyers formulate the right of self-determination in anthropomorphic terms (e.g., the "freedom" of a "people" to "determine itself") the philosopher understandably suspects that they might be guilty of a category mistake. If, as is true in the Kantian tradition, self-determination is linked to individual autonomy, and if autonomy can only be predicated of persons, in what sense does a collective entity determine itself? What do the emotionally loaded words "freedom" and "autonomy" mean when predicated of collective entities? From an ethical standpoint, liberalism insists that rights be predicated only of persons. Rights are moral and legal extensions of personhood. Hence, liberal theory distrusts assertions of rights held by collective entities because it is unclear what function they perform in normative political theory. In particular, it is unclear whether or not group rights can coexist with individual rights. If we add to these perplexities the indubitable fact that states have been historically responsible for the violation of individual rights, the need to examine the place of collective rights (and in particular the right of self-determination) in the Kantian theory of international law becomes apparent. The challenge is to offer a formulation of the principle of self-determination that responds to these concerns—a liberal theory of self-determination.

The argument in this chapter can be used to analyze all kinds of group claims, from special group rights to secession. While I mostly examine the justification for the right for a group residing in a territory to secede from a larger state and create its own political unit (independent state) in that territory, I use the reasoning to evaluate less drastic claims for group autonomy (such as group rights) as well.

I define the right of self-determination as *a majoritarian entitlement held by members of a group residing in a territory to determine its political status and organization in order to redress political or territorial injustice within the framework of respect for individual human rights and of the legitimate interest of outsiders.* This general right of self-determination, exercised through democratic vote, has two aspects. First, self-determination includes the right to determine *who* is going to rule the community (classical rights-constrained democracy or *internal* self-determination). Second, it includes the right to determine whether or not the community will be politically independent of other political units (national or *external* self-determination). In determining the appropriate cases where a community may establish group autonomy (including secession) I will show how the right of self-determination is subordinated to individual human rights in a crucial way. Observance of individual human rights constrains the majoritarian choices that a community may make. Thus, both democratic choices and national self-determination choices are limited within the confines of human rights observance. In contrast, where individual rights are not violated in a state, the collective right to national self-determination held by communities belonging to that state loses some of its force, and the legitimate interests of outsiders gain correspondingly in importance.

The main idea is that issues of political *organization* and social policy are properly decided by democratic vote. National self-determination is an issue of political coordination, as is the election of government. In contrast, the imperative to respect basic human rights is not a mere matter of political organization, of social coordination, where the decision could go one way or the other depending on probable results as measured by efficiency or expediency—as it would be the case if left to majoritarian aggregate preferences. The principle of respect for human rights is a genuine principle, in the sense that it trumps majoritarian preferences,[3] including claims of national self-determination. Therefore, whether or not human rights will be respected cannot be properly left to democratic vote. One corollary of this analysis is that the implementation of national self-determination may not properly take place at the cost of oppression and tyranny, even when the oppressors are a majority of the individuals in the territory in question. In addition, those exercising the right of self-determination (secessionists in particular) must be sensitive to the *legitimate* expectations and interests of outsiders. One must be careful, however, not to overstate the claims of outsiders—in particular claims by the parent state. Legitimate interests are either human rights reasons (e.g., the secessionists intend to oppress minorities) or reasonable and strong *prudential* objections to self-determination (e.g., the secessionists attempt to take with them resources that are vital to the economic survival of the larger state). Other reasons frequently given, such as the need to preserve national unity or territorial integrity, are often spurious.

Another corollary of my argument is that *ethnic* groups are note entitled to self-determination or special political status simply by virtue of the fact that they possess the ethnic trait (race, language, religion, etc.). Group rights, including secession, are justified (when they are justified) by other considerations, such as the need to escape injustice or the vindication of a legitimate territorial title. The argument in this book thus challenges the current emphasis on ethnic states as the basis for national self-determination.

The argument made here derives from a more general premise about politics: government is always instrumental to the interests and rights of individuals, and the question of *who* governs is subordinated to the much more important question of *how* people are governed.[4] So principles such as the supposed right to be governed by individuals of one's own race or religion are, under the liberal assumptions of this book, difficult to justify. If state and government are legitimate, that is, if the constitution effectively protects human rights and the government is democratic, complaining that nonetheless the individuals in government are not members of "my" ethnic group is irrational and, as experience shows, ultimately destructive. Thus, for example (and notwithstanding nationalist rhetoric), the demands by Africans under colonial domination that Europeans leave Africa are best understood as demands about remedying unjust conquest and ending unjust exploitation and subjugation, not as demands requiring racial identity between people and government. What was wrong about colonialism was that it was deeply unjust under liberal principles, not that it violated the "principle" that persons in government had to satisfy some racial (or linguistic or religious) test.

Thus understood, national self-determination, I suggest, cannot be explained by an independent normative notion of community. While we need to rely on some concept of communal property to explain the territorial component of group claims, the right of self-determination is as a by-product, albeit an important one, of individual liberty. A possible test to identify the groups entitled to secession is whether or not the group in question would have formed its own civil society, its own state, had it not been unjustly prevented from doing so. However, an answer to this question is not enough, for there are issues of equity arising out of reciprocal expectations created over time. In making a judgment about the legitimacy of secession various circumstances count, including the kind of interests and reasons advanced by the group and how seriously the interests of others are affected.[5] Yet even in cases where, all things considered, the group that democratically wishes to secede is not justified in doing so, it does not follow that the parent state has a right to *forcibly* resist the secession. The right to use force is reserved for a narrower class of cases.

The Inadequacy of the Current Law of Self-Determination

No area of international law is more confused, incoherent, and unsatisfactory than the law of self-determination. Under the pertinent international instruments, "All peoples have the right to self-determination; by virtue of that right they freely determine their political status and freely pursue their economic, social, and cultural development."[6]

I will not revisit here the history of the principle and how it developed mainly in connection with the decolonization efforts encouraged and sponsored by the United Nations.[7] While the wording itself may suggest two elements in the definition, it authorizes first the exercise by "people" of national, or external, self-determination—the right of peoples to "freely" determine their "political status."[8] In the first part of the sentence, the words "political status" refer to *international* political status, that is, the people's status vis-à-vis the other states and peoples of the world. The word "freely" means "without *outside* interference." The second part of the sentence provides that by virtue of the right to self-determination peoples "freely pursue their economic, social, and cultural development." At first sight, this right of peoples to pursue their forms of social organization follows logically from the first part of the right, the right to self-government. Writers are divided on whether the right to self-determination includes also the right to democratic rule, that is, a right of individuals and groups to elect their government by free suffrage, also called *internal* self-determination. While the classical view of self-determination did not include the right to democracy, the modern trend is to do so.[9]

According to most lawyers, it is crucial, in order to make this principle operational, to formulate an accurate definition of "people." International lawyers are divided into two camps. One contends that the only groups that have an unrestrained right of self-determination, that is, a right to statehood, are the colonial peoples and the populations of existing states.[10] Noncolonial substate groups (e.g., ethnic groups within a state) are simply minorities and thus not potentially entitled to statehood.[11] The second group of writers believes this definition to be too narrow and admits that groups within states may also be eligible if they meet some criteria of group identification (ethnicity, shared history, religion, or language). Ian Brownlie, for example, defines the principle of self-determination as "the right of a community which has a distinct character to have this character reflected in the institutions of government under which it lives."[12] In this view, if the character of the community is sufficiently distinct, then presumably it will be entitled to form its own independent state. Only with statehood will the distinctness of the community be sufficiently reflected in the institutions.

The pertinent texts do not settle this question. Resolution 1514 and the United Nations Covenants proclaim that *all* peoples have the right to self-determination.[13] But this statement either begs the question (because we don't know what a "people" is) or, if it has empirical content, it is obviously wrong: for example, the people of Arizona do not seem to be a good candidate for the right of self-determination. The term "people," therefore, must be a term of art; hence it is necessary to narrow down its meaning for purposes of determining the content of the right. There are clear cases where the right is applicable: the former colonies created as a result of European expansion. But outside the colonial context international law has left the issue unresolved. Standard reasoning seems to fall into a vicious circle: all peoples have the right to self-determination, but most groups are not peoples . . . only those who have the right to self-determination!

This brief discussion reveals how inadequate and underdeveloped international law is on this crucial matter. The first inadequacy, or rather contradiction, is that the pertinent instruments affirm at the same time the inalienable right of self-determination that peoples have and the right of existing states to preserve their territorial integrity.[14] The second shortcoming is the lack of criteria to know when a self-determination or secession claim is sound. A repetition of the requirement that the group be a people does not help much, since we are left at a loss to know when a group is a people. Many international lawyers have understandably given up and have resorted to one of their favorite all-purpose tools: the principle of effectiveness, which roughly holds that if a group fights and achieves its independence it must be recognized as such by other states, and then it becomes legally sovereign.[15] An international lawyer confronted with a secessionist movement reasons as follows. If the secessionists win, then they form their own state, which third states must recognize because it is effective (i.e., the new government effectively exercises political power over the population in the territory), and the right of self-determination has been exercised. If the government wins, then there is no new state, third states ought to refrain from recognition because the rebels have no effective government, and the right of territorial integrity has been vindicated. As a consequence, if our imaginary lawyer is consulted *in advance* about the dispute he has to say that there are no preexisting principles and that the outcome can only be decided in the battlefield![16] In my view, this is not law but antilaw. Such unconditional surrender to the most brutal realities of power politics has no place in a philosophy of international law: we want to know whether or not the secessionists are *justified* in their demands, regardless of whether or not they win the struggle. We want to know their reasons, and international law doctrine fails to provide any. In contrast, philosophers and political scientists have recently attempted to fill this gap. I will first examine the concept of group right. I will then review several theories of self-determination before turning to the one that I believe best responds to the various concerns that underlie the problem.

The Concept of Group Right

The analysis must begin with an examination of the concept of group (or collective) rights. Are collective rights a distinct category within a liberal theory of rights? Some influential writers, such as Allen Buchanan and Will Kymlicka, think so.[17] In their view, liberal theory has unjustifiedly neglected group rights and should therefore be reformulated to make room for them. Under this view, liberal theory must countenance a notion of group rights that is irreducible to traditional liberal notions of individual rights. Notwithstanding this irreducibility, supporters of collective rights claim that recognizing such rights does not necessarily do violence to liberalism's central commitments—in particular, the commitment to individual rights and the normative primacy of the individual.

I believe that this attempt to vindicate group rights alongside individual rights is misguided. For what their proponents call group rights are really instances of *social policies* that they believe should prevail over claims of individual rights. I do not attempt to demonstrate here whether or not in a particular instance it is morally justified to secure a collective goal (be it called group right or social policy) that is partially inconsistent with individual rights. Rather, my point is purely conceptual: the meaning of the word "right" in the expression "collective rights" is different in crucial ways from the meaning of the same word when talking about individual rights—in fact, it is the precisely the opposite.

How do defenders of group rights define them? A collective right is, for them, a claim asserted not on behalf of an individual but of a group. Collective or group rights are defined as rights that have three characteristics.[18] First, they are held by groups, not by individuals. Second, they can only be exercised collectively or on behalf of the collective (usually through some mechanism of political representation). And finally, the good secured by the right will be available to all or most members of the group. Thus, for example, the right of a group to preserve its language (as distinct to the individual right to speak a language of one's choice) is a right that is exercised on behalf of the group by its representatives, say, by enacting the laws necessary to preserve the group's language. In addition, the good secured by the right, namely the preservation of the group's language, will be available to all members of the group, including its future members.

As a preliminary matter, there are some rights that look like group rights but are not. Sometimes a claim of collective right can be understood as a shorthand for a claim advancing individual rights or benefits or interests for the *individuals* who belong to the group in question. For example, a claim that women should enjoy equal opportunity to run for office is simply a claim about each individual woman's right to run for office under the same conditions as men. This is not a right that the collective entity "women" have but a right belonging to each individual woman. The only collective aspect of this individual right is that the right-holders are identified by their having certain characteristics—in this case, physical characteristics—that not all human beings possess. Even in cases where the asserted right is not one related to formal notions of equality, it can still be analyzed as a cluster of individual rights or benefits. Suppose someone asserts that Latinos have a right to receive preferential treatment for government jobs. What is meant by this is that each individual Latino has the right to receive such preferential treatment. Now this kind of right is collective in the obvious sense that the way to identify its holders is group membership, but it will still be the case that the right of the group can be properly reformulated, without any loss of meaning, in terms of individual rights. Any such right may or may not be plausible or defensible, but its analysis does not create problems other than those encountered in the analysis of individual human rights.

Defenders of group rights, however, do not have in mind these cases. Some collective rights, we are told, cannot be analyzed in terms of individual rights.[19] A collective right is conceived as a right to realize some state of affairs that, it is thought, can only be a group attribute. Take for example the right to language preservation, one of those identified as characteristic and definitive of ethnic groups. Such a right, we are told, is necessarily held by the group, by the community. It does not seem appropriate to disaggregate this collective right into individual linguistic rights. Nor does such a right seem to depend upon individual preferences of the members of the group.

To show why the idea of group rights is misleading, let us start with a definition of right that is typical of deontological liberalism—the one suggested by Ronald Dworkin.[20] On this view, to say that someone has a right to X is to say that he has a moral reason to effect X that, at some point, trumps the pursuit of social utility or other collective or aggregative goals. The justification for upholding the right resides in a principle that predates the assertion of the right in a particular instance and thus outweighs other arguments, especially prospective utilitarian arguments. Sometimes, of course, the collective goal may prevail over the right in question; but for a claim to be called a right it has to have *some* threshold value where it trumps other considerations, in particular the pursuit of the general welfare.[21] Now, if this definition of right is accepted, then it is plain that we cannot call just any claim that competes against an individual right also a "right." Suppose that we recognize that people have the right to free speech but that this right can be limited for pressing reasons of national security. We can say, rhetorically, that society has a right to national security, but under the theory under consideration that would be inaccurate. What we say is that individuals have the right to free speech but that the threshold value of that right, high as it is, doesn't allow it to prevail against the social policy of urgent national security. Another technical way of describing the difference is that rights are nonaggregative and distributive, whereas social policies are aggregative and nondistributive.

What I would like to focus on is the following question: Are group rights genuinely deontological (i.e., "trumping" rights) in the sense that individual rights are deontological (i.e., "trumping" rights)? Or are they instead simply social policies that sometimes prevail over individual rights? It will help if we focus on a concrete example: the so-called collective right to preserve a language—such as, for example, the collective right of Québec to preserve French language in that Canadian province. The argument for recognizing that right might run as follows: the community Québec has a distinctive character (in the sense explained by Margalit and Raz), and one of the distinctive features is that it speaks French in a largely Anglo-speaking country, Canada. Because the preservation of French is crucial to the endurance of Québec as a distinct community, the Québécois authorities should be allowed to enact legislation mandating, say, the exclusive use of French in public places. This (so the argument goes) is a matter of right for the community of Québec, but it is a collective right, not an individual one. As such the right concerns a collective good, that is, a good that, if secured, will be available to most or all members of the community. And it is a right the implementation of which is delegated by the group to some agent, the provincial government, through a mechanism of democratic representation.

The first question to ask is: who is the right asserted against? In other words, who (if any) has the corresponding obligation? The answer, of course, is more complex than the answer we would give to a similar question concerning an individual right. Because the right to the preservation of the indigenous language is a collective right, it has a double dimension: internally, the community asserts the right against the dissenters within Québec, that is, against those who want to speak English in public places.[22] Externally (and for defenders of collective rights this is perhaps its most important aspect), the right is asserted against higher centers of authority, for example, the central government of Canada.[23] This is tantamount to saying (so the argument suggests) that Québec is asserting its right against Canada, group against group. To use Dworkin's metaphor: the right of Québec to language preservation trumps the interest of Canada to, say, have a multilingual system.

This analysis, however, is highly misleading. When closely examined, the exercise of the collective right of preservation of French in Québec is nothing more than an *attempt to grant powers to the provincial Government to thwart individual rights that Canadian citizens would normally have.* Suppose the democratic lawmakers in Québec enact legislation imposing French in all public places, banning the use of other languages. It wouldn't matter how many people wanted to speak English, because the government would be enforcing a right that pertains to the "nation." The dissenters would have lost a right to free speech that they would normally have in the absence of the restricting legislation. So internally, a collective right is simply a prerogative or *carte blanche* granted to governments to thwart rights or preferences that individuals would have but for the existence of the collective right. The so-called collective right to language preservation is a power granted to the government to impose restrictions on the speech of dissenters within the group. Now such restrictions might or might not be morally justified, all things considered. But why are they even called a collective right? The original meaning of rights was that they constituted barriers against the government; they were deontological restrictions on the pursuit of the general welfare. Why not simply say that there is a greater collective interest (language preservation) that prevails on these facts over freedom of speech?

A possible answer by supporters of group rights is to emphasize the external dimension of the right in question, mentioned above. In our example, the collective right of Québec to preserve the French language is asserted against the Canadian government. Since the Québecois are a minority in Canada, their group right is a deontological restriction on the wishes of the Canadian majority represented by the Canadian government. So (the argument concludes) the group right has a "trumping threshold" just as the individual right has a "trumping threshold" against the pursuit of social policy. This symmetry, however, is only illusory. For the interest of the

Canadian government (which represents, indeed, the majority) is *simply to protect the individual right to speak English that individuals would normally have under the Canadian Constitution*. The federal government is, one would assume, the guarantor of individual rights, and its interest in not seeing the Québecois legislation enacted is simply the interest in protecting Canadian citizens against majoritarian unconstitutional encroachments upon those rights. The argument that what we have here is a collective right of Québec to speak French that trumps the contrary interests of the Canadian government is *exactly* like the argument made by some states in the U.S. South some decades ago to the effect that states's rights (i.e., state legislation mandating racial segregation) ought to trump the pursuit of racial equality by the federal government. The point here is that not just any claim can be called right and not just any claim can be called policy. The collective interest in protecting individual rights is not just another policy in the Dworkinian sense. And the social policy, say, of language preservation, is not another right held by the community, qualitatively equivalent to the individual right that the policy purports to suppress.

So on a classic liberal analysis of the concept of right, collective rights are not rights but aggregative social policies considered particularly weighty by their supporters. Collective rights lack the deontological bite, as it were. Why do many people, then, defend the idea of collective rights? The reason might be simply rhetorical. The rhetoric of rights is extremely powerful. As many have pointed out, to say that a certain claim is a matter of right is to give the most powerful moral reasons in favor of that claim. Rights-talk is the heaviest artillery of our moral arsenal. In light of this usage, those who advocated an expansion of governmental power (such as the one exemplified by Québec's collective right to language preservation) had considerable difficulty in justifying those proposals, since liberals would insist that, in most cases, individual rights may not be lightly sacrificed in the pursuit of social policies. From the standpoint of rights-based liberalism, the burden of proof is always on those who advocate the primacy of a social policy over the (individual) right with which it competes. So defenders of expanded governmental power then decided to avail themselves of the persuasive, emotional connotations of rights language. The situation would no longer be described as right versus policy, where the burden would be on those who favor the policy, but rather as right versus right—the (individual) right of free speech versus the (collective) right of cultural preservation, where presumably there would be no burden of proof on either side.

Collective rights, then, reveal an ugly face: they are assertions of governmental (regional, tribal) power to cancel individual rights—what Kymlicka calls "internal restrictions."[24] Once again: I am not here claiming that the linguistic question in Québec should be resolved in favor of individual freedom of speech and against the attempts to impose the French language. Nor am I claiming that strong prudential considerations, such as the need to manage conflict, may not justify the establishment of special group rights. It may well be that these are cases where the social policy is urgent enough to outweigh the individual rights with which the policy competes. The claims on behalf of the community are claims to limit individual rights, and the clash must be decided, like all moral matters, on its merits. What I am claiming is, first, that those communal claims cannot be called rights in the same sense that deontological liberalism defines rights; and second, that, for that reason, the establishment of such arrangements is subject to a high level of scrutiny to make sure that they do not impinge too much on traditional human rights, including the right to political participation. For liberals, the burden of proof is on those who purport to deny the individual right, and while the decision to call these arrangements "group rights" may be ultimately simply a verbal preference, such a linguistic decision should not strengthen the merits of the claim.

Theories of Self-Determination

Group rights, then, are simply weighty social policies that sometimes, it is thought, prevail over individual rights. But this is a mere conceptual point and does not resolve the normative question. Someone who claims, for example, that ethnicity has moral currency can still claim that groups should be accorded these prerogatives, no matter what one calls them. So, when should groups (ethnic or otherwise) be accorded autonomy, even sometimes statehood? There have been many answers to this question. I will now review some of them and then suggest that the only justification for special group rights, including forms of political autonomy, is that such arrangements are necessary to remedy specific *injustices* suffered by the group in question. Ethnicity plays no role in such justification, except indirectly.

The Nationalist Thesis

The nationalist argument for self-determination makes two claims. First, groups entitled to self-determination are identified by nonvoluntary factors; second, as a matter of right, political and ethnic boundaries must coincide.[25] The nationalist thesis seems to be implicit in the broad language of the applicable international instruments,[26] at least if "peoples" are defined as ethnic groups. This view has a suspect *pedigree*, as it is directly anchored in an organicist theory of the nation, in a definition of the nation as distinct from the state. This line of thought is quite old and has been given various versions of varying degrees of plausibility. But its flaws are quite obvious and have already been pointed out by commentators.[27] The first one is the difficulties associated with the definition of people or nation. If a people (nation) is defined by reference to shared history, there is the problem of historical discontinuity. History is ever changing and different groups participate in the history of a nation or state—not to mention the epistemological difficulties of choosing, say, political history over social, economic, or other kinds of history as constitutive of the social identity of the nation in question. If a people is instead defined by reference to ethnicity, then multiethnic states lack legitimacy, since their association is not based on the cultural traits that the nationalists favor. The same objections apply to language, religion, and similar factors.

But the most devastating objection against the nationalist thesis is its potential for exclusion of, and hostility toward, those persons that do not possess the trait in question (race, language, history, or religion). Ethnic identity as a political normative principle has a double face. In its kind face, the principle seems to stand for inclusion and vindication of some lofty cultural trait (religion, history, race) of which the members of the group are proud. But in its unkind face, the principle endorses ethnic homogeneity. And this can only be achieved, as Ernest Gellner puts it, if the group "either kills, expels, or assimilates all nonnationals."[28] Many kinds of evil practices, from Nazi genocide to Turkey's massacres against Armenians, to modern ethnic cleansing, have been advanced in the name of the nationalist principle understood in this way, and the connection is far from coincidental. If I believe that, say, my race is the foundation of the bonds of citizenship, then I will not feel a strong political obligation toward those persons who, though living in the same territory, have a different race. And from that view it is but a small step to the view that I do not have any moral obligation to them and can therefore treat them as means to my ends, as things. Indeed, one could go farther and suggest, with Gellner, that the very concept of nation is spurious: the ideology of nationalism engenders nations, not the other way around. Thus, languages and cultures are invented and reinvented selectively to justify particular political arrangements.[29] For those reasons, it is hard not to agree with Allen Buchanan's view that the pure nationalist principle, notwithstanding its popularity in some circles, is one of the least plausible arguments for self-determination and group rights. The moral costs of implementing the principle (understood in this way) are prohibitive.[30]

The Soft Communitarian Thesis[31]

The defense of a group right to self-determination need not, however, reach the extreme illiberal conclusions of nationalism. Some writers have tried to explain self-determination by appealing to reasonable notions of community that do not completely lose sight of liberal values. This more moderate view, which I here call soft communitarianism, still places value in the group as something distinct from the individual, and regards collective rights as irreducible to individual rights. The best effort in this regard is contained in an article by Arvit Margalit and Joseph Raz.[32] Their thesis can be summarized as follows. The right to self-determination is grounded in the wider value of self-government. Self-government, however, is justified not as an end in itself but instrumentally, that is, by reference to the well-being of its members. Only certain groups (called "encompassing groups") qualify as holders of the right to decide whether or not it will be self-governed. Encompassing groups are those that meet a list of more or less stringent communitarian requirements. Thus, the group has a common character and a common culture that encompasses many varied and important aspects of life, so that the possibilities to lead a meaningful life are seriously reduced if they are denied access to these features of communal life. These include mutual recognition and self-identification among members of the group through those nonvoluntary features shaped through a relatively long period in the group's history. In short: groups that qualify are those that have pervasive cultures, where the value of self-identification for members of the group is crucial to their individual well-being.[33]

Margalit and Raz add some important qualifications to this definition. When a group qualifies, it can exercise the right to determine whether it will be self-governed (e.g., form an independent state), but that decision must be made with regard to other interests of members of the group, of minorities within the group, and of outsiders. Because self-determination is instrumental, the case for it is sensitive to counterarguments relevant to its justification.[34] For example, if a group seeks political autonomy and, along with legitimate reasons, the members of the majority intend to oppress minorities or women, then their case is fatally undermined.[35] Similarly, self-determination loses its moral force if it is sought for the wrong reasons, such as controlling certain economic resources.[36]

With respect to the manner of exercising this right, Margalit and Raz conclude that, because the decision is irreversible, it should require more than mere majoritarian vote: there should be an overwhelming majority of members of the group wishing to pursue self-government.[37] Finally, the authors claim that the right to self-determination is not reducible to liberal notions of political consent. Self-determination "is a group right, deriving from the value of a collective good, and as such opposed in spirit to contractarian-individualistic approaches to politics or to individual well-being."[38]

This view of self-determination is thus a mixed one. By asserting that the value of self-government is purely instrumental, Margalit and Raz reject a purely nationalist approach to self-determination. As we saw, the extreme nationalist view treats individual rights, interests, and well-being as *derivative* of, and consequently subordinated to, the original notion of community. While Margalit and Raz reject this approach by focusing instead on the value of self-government for the *individual* well-being of members of the group, they still believe that the issue of self-determination is independent of other issues of political morality. In this sense, their view closely resembles that of Michael Walzer, for whom communal integrity takes precedence over other matters of political morality, even though it is ultimately a function of the rights and interests of individuals.[39] On balance, I believe their model is predominantly communitarian and not liberal for two reasons. First, the traits that define an encompassing group (and thus entitle it to self-determination) are largely nonvoluntary. This naturally undermines liberal insistence on consent and the honoring of individual preferences as the bases of political institutions. Second, and related, self-determination is a *group* right and, as such, linked to notions of collective, not individual, good. This is reflected in the fact that it is the group's collective will that counts, not individual opinions or objections to self-government.

The soft communitarian view attempts to reconcile liberal intuitions linked to the inherent worth of individual human beings with the undeniably communitarian thrust that underlies the concept of self-determination—the foremost group right, the group right *par excellence*. I suggest, however, that the authors' concessions to communitarianism are unnecessary and that the seemingly unsolvable dilemma of group rights can be explained within the framework of liberal political theory. In addition, their argument unduly neglects the question of territorial rights, and in doing so, fatally begs the question of determining the appropriate democratic unit—that is, the unit entitled to create an independent state.

The first problem with the argument under discussion is connected with the claim that goals and relationships, essential for individual well-being, are culturally determined. For the authors, "familiarity with the culture determines the boundaries of the imaginable," thus making all possible choices by individuals culturally confined. Culture is what provides the context for meaningful choice. What this means is that the prosperity of the culture is important for the well-being of the members. According to Margalit and Raz "If the culture is decaying, or if it persecuted or discriminated against, the options and opportunities open to its members will shrink"[40] But this premise, essential to the argument, is problematic.[41] The Kantian tradition, as well as other versions of the liberal tradition, provide alternative explanations of rational choice where the cultural component is factored in as part of the choice itself rather as some predetermined brute fact. In other words, for the Kantian theory, choices by people in a culture (for example, to participate in the group's religion) count only if they are in some sense voluntary. An important assumption of liberalism is that we can detach ourselves from any particular communal practice: we are able and must be allowed to evaluate, revise, and eventually reject cultural practices.[42] An emphasis on nonvoluntary foundations of the bonds of citizenship runs counter to the liberal ideal that the liberal democratic community cannot be based merely on force but rather on some form of consent. Perhaps consent is simply our ability to revise and reject what is given to us from birth. Even on this weak definition of consent, membership in a culture is, for the Kantian, chosen by the individual, not imposed upon her. This foundational disagreement between liberals and communitarians is a much discussed topic today, and I will not attempt to address it fully here. I shall confine myself instead to showing where the soft communitarian position leads to problematic or counterintuitive results with regard to the issue of self-determination and special group rights.

Consider Margalit and Raz's discussion of the decay of cultures. There are two possibilities according to them: a culture may be persecuted or discriminated against, or a culture may decay. The first case poses no need to resort to group rights. If members of a group are persecuted or discriminated against, then this is simply a violation of individual rights for which liberal theory has a sufficient answer without any need to resort to collective rights. The solution may very well be to recognize a legal right to self-determination to the group, but this will occur not because the group has a pervasive culture or because there is an independent moral status of the group above and beyond that of individuals but simply because their human rights are violated and they are, perhaps, justified in seeking their liberation through special group rights, even perhaps secession.

Yet what does it mean to say that the culture is decaying (as opposed to its being persecuted)? That the culture is decaying means simply that its members do not care much about the culture, that they voluntarily choose social arrangements and rituals other than those constitutive of the original culture. The culture of the group is decaying not because the majority discriminates against the group but because its members (say, the youth) prefer another (perhaps more cosmopolitan) culture. But if this is the case, what can be the argument for coercively preserving the culture, for example by recognizing greater autonomy from the larger unit so that the group leaders can impose the culture by law? Presumably the idea here is that the culture needs to be preserved and that this can only be achieved through self-determination and self-government. But there are problems with this suggestion. For one thing, if the culture is decaying as a result of people's voluntary choices, preservation of the culture is not likely to be assured by self-government since people will likely continue making the same choices (Canadian sovereignty doesn't make Canadians less inclined to buy American goods or listen to American music). If this is the case, the only way for the new sovereign government to preserve the culture is by the use of state power aimed at frustrating people's choices. So self-determination or special group rights as a solution to a culture's spontaneous decay often will justify the adoption of laws aimed at thwarting voluntary choices by members of the group in a manner inconsistent with those persons' autonomy. Self-determination and special group rights in these cases may thus lead to unduly repressive policies.

A possible argument in favor of preserving the culture in cases of spontaneous decay draws from the literature on public goods.[43] Sometimes, it is argued, people make individual choices unaware that the result of others making similar choices is not something they would want, could they express the preference for a collective result. For example, I am a Latin American but speak to my sons in English for reasons of convenience. If somebody asked me: "Do you want Spanish to be preserved in the Latino community?" I'd say yes. However, because the only way in which Spanish is going to be preserved in the Latino community is if people like me speak in Spanish to their children, there is an inconsistency between my individual choice (speaking in English) and my preferred result for the group (that Spanish be preserved). Perhaps I am just unaware of the consequences of my individual choice, in which case I will choose differently once I am made aware of those collective consequences. Or perhaps (more likely) I hope to *free ride* on the other members of the group: I don't believe that my speaking Spanish will make a difference because I am confident that all the other Latinos will do, collectively, whatever is necessary to preserve the language in the community.[44] So I can get the benefits of the public good in question (preservation of Spanish language) without incurring the costs. But if everyone does the same thing, then there will be no Spanish spoken, that is, no public good provided. (A public good, such as, let's suppose, the linguistic identity of a community, is defined as one that has non-exclusiveness, that is, it cannot be privately supplied because suppliers cannot exclude people who don't pay, and nonrivalry, that is, one person's consumption of the good does not lessen the amount of it available to others).

If this is the case (so the argument goes) then we are confronting a case of *market failure*. Because of partial ignorance and free riding problems, the collective result is not what the majority (or even perhaps all) of the members of the group want for the group. In specialized language: "the failure of the group to cooperate to produce a collective good may be collectively, but not individually, suboptimal from the point of view of self-interest."[45] The time has come, it is then argued, for coercive intervention: the government needs to have special powers to correct the market failure. Rolf Sartorius describes this view well:

> The strong hand of government will typically be required to lead individuals to make decisions whose collective effects will be mutually advantageous rather than mutually detrimental. The power to tax is, in this view, the power to compel individuals to contribute to the purchase of public goods that they would not be motivated to purchase for themselves. The power to make and enforce laws backed by coercive sanctions is, in this view, the power to provide individuals with reasons to act in ways that satisfy the general schema. "If everyone (or a sufficiently large number of people) acted that way, everyone would be better off."[46]

In the case of spontaneous decay of pervasive cultures, the soft communitarian argument is that self-determination and even secession might be needed to empower a government that will correct the market failure and enact into law the preferences for the public good (preservation of the culture) held by members of the culture. Coercion is needed to prevent defection, which in turn is caused both by the fact that the first preference of individuals is to defect while others cooperate and by the lack of assurance against defection by others. Thus, the public goods argument presumes the legitimacy of helping people do what they want to do (preserve the culture) but cannot do without the government's help.[47]

This is a sophisticated argument, and its appeal rests on the fact that it relies on the idea of rational choice. The argument, however, encounters serious difficulties. One is that it assumes without proof that *force* can be justified as a solution to the public goods dilemma.[48] It does not follow from the fact that there is a public goods dilemma that it is morally justified to use governmental coercion to supply the public good in question. The reason for doubting that it can be is the following. The interests that different people have in the public good can vary widely. In particular, "that a good exhibits characteristics of nonexclusiveness and nonrivalry in consumption does not guarantee that a given person has an interest in it."[49] Some people simply *don't care* about the public good in question. It is true that *if all* cared, then it might be justified to use coercion to do away with free riding. In this case, because every member of the community would like to see the good produced (the language preserved), they will be more than happy to have the state prevent defection. But surely there are those who refuse to contribute simply because they don't want the good, and the public goods analysis mistakenly assumes those people away.[50]

This objection shows that there is both a false premise and a non sequitur in the public goods argument. The false premise is that all members of the group want the public good in question, either with or without their contribution.[51] As we saw, this assumption is false, as there are people who are interested neither in producing nor in consuming the good. The non sequitur is to say that because a good is public government intervention is justified in order to supply it. In fact, I suspect that defenders of group rights need an *independent* justification to force some people (the "honest holdouts") to help pay for other people's projects. Advocates of coercion must show not only that the public good is *public* but also that it is indeed a *good.* Thus, the public goods argument alone fails to justify special governmental powers or group rights.

At any rate, the public goods argument sounds strange because of the difficulty in discerning structures of preferences different from the ones expressed in the market. If someone acts on an individual preference that, if universalized, would corrode the group's culture, then what does it mean to say that she also has the preference that the culture not be corroded? It seems that she cannot have it both ways: whatever people's motives (including, but not limited to, free riding) they are presumably aware of the alternatives and prefer to do those things that collectively result in the demise of the culture. Why, then, enforce the counterfactual choice that the agent decided *not* to make? Again, my guess is that those who make the market failure argument have decided *in advance* that the collective goal is worthy, and so their true reason to favor that goal does not really depend on the existence of the market failure.

The gist of the liberal position is that, in principle, a free society must privilege individual choice and that arguments to the contrary carry the burden of proof. A liberal regards a group's cultural symbols as important insofar as the members themselves regard those symbols as important. Leaders of an ethnic group do not have a right that their culture survive if a majority of its members do not want it to survive. So if a culture is discriminated against (this, by the way, is a misnomer: only individuals can be discriminated against), it is a case where the right to equal treatment of the members of the culture is being violated. If, however, the culture is decaying spontaneously, it is hard to see how that fact would justify special group rights or secession from a liberal state.

The final problem with the thesis here examined is that it unduly neglects the territorial issue: self-government over a territory implies title over that territory. Therefore, appeal to the nonvoluntary communitarian traits that, according to Margalit and Raz, define encompassing groups cannot resolve the question of self-determination. A group may be encompassing and have a pervasive culture yet lack title over the territory. If this is so, then the group is not entitled to self-determination. This view has been forcefully advanced by Lea Brilmayer, and to it I now turn.

The Territorialist Thesis

Lea Brilmayer has argued that, contrary to what transpires from the legal debate, secessionist claims (and, I add, other claims for group autonomy) involve, first and foremost, disputed claims to territory.[52] Group traits emphasized by communitarians, such as ethnicity, simply serve to identify the people making the territorial claim. As a result, the strength of a separatist claim "does not depend primarily on the degree to which the group in question constitutes a distinct people."[53] Claims to territory do not flow automatically from ethnic distinctiveness, and oppression of the group can be remedied by removing or reforming the oppressors (perhaps through revolution), not by granting permission to set up a new state.[54] Brilmayer encourages groups seeking autonomy to make their territorial claims explicit instead of subordinating them to the current self-determination rhetoric.[55] The territorial approach focuses on the history of the dispute rather than on whether the secessionists are a people. According to Brilmayer, the standard account of self-determination fails to appreciate that secessionists (and other groups seeking lesser forms of political autonomy) typically seek to remedy historical wrongs.[56] Under this interpretation, "a different set of questions must be addressed in order to evaluate the merits of a separatist movement": a territorial approach to secession and special group rights focuses not on factors such as whether the group considers itself a people or whether they have the same race or language but on territorial equities. The questions then are: How immediate was the historical wrong? How alive has the claim been kept? Are there new settlers? Has there been "adverse possession"? How serious was the wrong, that is, was the territory conquered or was the settlement gradual instead?[57] Brilmayer concedes that the answers to these questions aren't any easier than the answers to the questions posed by the traditional approach, but at least she concludes they are the right questions.

Brilmayer's argument is an important contribution to the topic. Furthermore, her view gets some support from the leading case on self-determination: the Western Sahara advisory opinion.[58] One of the issues in that case was whether Morocco or Mauritania had title over the Western Sahara. The International Court of Justice concluded that neither did and, consequently, the principle of self-determination was applicable.[59] *A contrario sensu*, a finding of title would have legally prevented the people of Western Sahara from voting themselves into independence.[60] The Court's view, therefore, is very close to Brilmayer's: a determination of the status of the territory is a determination of title, not merely of wishes.

Brilmayer's analysis is incontrovertible—as far as it goes. The territorial analysis proves that having a valid territorial title is an important factor in the evaluation of self-determination claims. There are a couple of problems, however. The first one is that government exercises its authority over both territory and people, and while rightly drawing our attention to the neglected territorial issue, the territorial argument, in my judgment, goes too far if it implies that having the territorial title (difficult to show as that may be) is a *sufficient* justification for special group rights, including secession. In other words, while Brilmayer is absolutely right in criticizing both the consent and communitarian versions of self-determination with their misplaced emphases on personal factors, the justification of legitimate political authority involved in ethnic disputes must, under liberal theory, go beyond matters of territorial title. Moreover, having territorial title does not serve as a *necessary* condition for self-determination either. There may be cases where recognizing special group rights for ethnic groups may be the only viable way to escape serious forms of oppression. Under the primacy of human rights presupposed by the Kantian thesis, the urgency of escaping oppression may justify special group rights, even secession, notwithstanding the absence of title.

The reverse is also true: self-determination for the purpose of violating human rights is illegitimate. Suppose that people in one of the territories now part of Russia wish to secede. Suppose further that the secessionist leaders intend to create a rigid dictatorial state founded on the restoration of the principles and practices of Stalinist Marxism.[61] Let us assume that the group has a valid territorial title founded in a legitimate historical grievance against Russia. Under the thesis defended in this book, the issue of human rights takes precedence over the territorial title. The government of Russia has a moral obligation to protect the citizens of the territory (who, until the secession is consummated, are under Russian jurisdiction) against the incoming abuses that can be reasonably expected under the planned Stalinist regime. The territorialist approach would have to disregard the question of human rights in favor of the question of territory, and that seems questionable from a moral standpoint. Governmental power is both authority over territory and authority over people, and just as the soft communitarian and pure voluntarist views (see below) neglect the former, the territorial view neglects the latter. And this problem does not disappear by pointing out that a majority of the citizens of the territory has voted to secede, because oppression cannot be legitimized by majority vote. A liberal does not merely ask: "Is this territory yours?" Rather, the liberal follows the question with a second one: "And just what do you intend to do in that territory?" Territories are not mere objects of titely; they are *loci* for rights.

The second problem with the territorialist thesis is this: what do we mean when we say that a *group* has title over a territory? There are several possibilities. The first is to say that people who *live* in a territory have title over it. But this cannot be right. Certainly, to put forth an autonomy claim, the claimants must have a territory available, and in most cases it will be the territory where they live. But this is surely different from the question of title. The inhabitants of California do not have a title over California just because they live within its confines. The federal claim is that

California is first and foremost U.S. territory and that for that reason California may not seek autonomy or secede. The very claim of those who oppose secession is that those who live in the territory may not lawfully take it. The current claim of the Russian government is that Chechnya is part of Russia as a matter of territorial sovereignty. The secessionist Chechnyans claim, in contrast, that the territory was unlawfully annexed by Russia. Presumably they do not consider themselves entitled to secession just because they live there. So while perhaps living in a territory is a physical precondition for self-determination claims, it is not dispositive of the question of title.

A second alternative is to derive territorial sovereignty from private property. A group has title, under this view, when its members hold legitimate titles of property over land that, when added together, constitute the group's title over the territory. This approach seems consistent with libertarian theories of natural property rights. Property rights are antecedent to government, and the latter's authority is created to protect them. But this view misconstrues the notion of territory. The rights of a group over a territory is not the sum of private property rights but rather the *locus* of the exercise of authority derived from the social contract. And this holds even accepting, for the sake of argument, that the libertarian explanation of the state is adequate. On a libertarian view, individuals create the state to fulfill minimal functions of protection against crime and external enemies.[62] Thus, for example, the government's authority over my private land is superimposed to my property right over the same land.

Another possibility is to draw from the international law principles regarding title to territory. According to customary international law, there are several ways in which a state can lawfully acquire title, but peaceful and uninterrupted occupation is, with some exceptions, as good as title.[63] Customary law has also developed the notion of *critical date*, that is, the date on which the question of title was crucial. This is in most cases the date when the dispute arose between two states about sovereignty over the territory. The critical date is important for evaluating the legal meaning of acts of sovereignty that occurred after that date. In general, critical date analysis considers the period leading up to the critical date as the most important to decide title. Acts of open and peaceful display of sovereignty in the period leading up to the critical date are, therefore, decisive for the determination of what state has title over the territory in dispute. Can this analysis help to decide questions of self-determination? The main problem with customary international law is that it is only relevant to disputes among *states*. Because self-determination involves claims by groups that are not states international law regarding title is of little help. For example, it is obvious that the Soviet Union exercised open acts of sovereignty in Chechnya over a long period of time. This sovereignty was accepted by other states, but it does not help us solve the issue of whether or not the territory was unjustly taken from the Chechnyans. Thus, international law is helpful in interstate territorial disputes, but because of its traditional emphasis on state sovereignty it begs the question of the justice of territorial takings by states of land that belongs to groups that are not states.

Nonetheless, an analogical use of some international legal concepts such as critical date may help. For example, a relevant question is whether or not the Chechnyans were an independent state, or on their way to becoming one, at the time when the Russians took over the territory. Another relevant question is whether the Chechnyans consented at the time to become part of Russia. Under critical date analysis, events leading up to the critical date will be the most important for determining title. For example, the critical date in the Chechnyan dispute would be in principle the date when the Russians annexed the territory. But if such an event occurred a long time ago, the group's claim will be weakened. In other words, the more recent the unjust territorial taking the stronger the claim will be. Here, considerations of political stability affect territorial claims. This is analogous to the insistence of customary law on occupation and display of sovereignty. In short, the international law principles may be useful provided that they shake off their statist bias and also take into account territorial claims of substate groups.

Yet another possibility is to analyze territorial injustice as a form of unlawful usurpation of power. What does it mean to say that a group (say, Latvia) has title over the Latvian territory? Perhaps what we mean is this: there was in the past a government in Latvia that was, in some sense, legitimate. At some point, the Soviet army invaded and forcibly replaced that sovereign with a new one. The change of sovereign would be analogous to an unconstitutional change of power. To say that Latvians have a title over the territory is to say that the group (Latvia) has a right to restore the original sovereign over the territory. However, what if the original sovereign was itself morally illegitimate (i.e., a tyrannical regime?). It seems odd to persist with the thesis of unlawful usurpation, for the old sovereign would not be any more legitimate than the new one.

In order to give some room, as I do, to the territorialist thesis, it is not necessary to choose between these different possibilities. It is sufficient for the argument defended here to accept that groups may have a collective title over land, determined perhaps by long occupation. After all, it *does* make sense to say "this group, the Armenians, have lived in this territory, Armenia, for a period long enough to create a title, so that whether or not they form a separate state, it is their territory."

The Pure Voluntarist Thesis

The foregoing discussion has shown that both the communitarian and territorial views fail to take fully into account important concerns. The communitarians do so by overemphasizing group traits over individual rights and preferences, the territorialists by overemphasizing title to territory over human rights. What about the view that there ought to be an unlimited right for groups to organize themselves as they see fit, even to secede? According to this view, people ought to have an unlimited right freely to establish whatever political associations they wish to establish, including sovereign states. Harry Beran has defended such a view,[64] and it seems to have been supported by Judge Harry Dillard in his separate opinion in the Western Sahara case.[65] For Beran, a right to secession follows from liberalism's commitment to freedom and popular sovereignty. Because liberalism regards the justified civil society as that which comes as close as possible to being a voluntary scheme, people ought to be able freely to choose their political associations.[66] But states are not and should not be immutable, so "a commitment to the freedom of the self-governing choosers to live in societies that approach as closely as possible to voluntary schemes, requires that the unity of the state itself be voluntary."[67] As a result, liberalism must grant "territorially concentrated groups" the right to form their own state.[68]

Beran is right that under liberal theory *some* form of consent forms the basis of political obligation.[69] However, as the previous discussion shows, even if the liberal premises are accepted, the view neglects the territorial question. For what does Beran mean by "territorially concentrated" groups? This cannot mean groups in the communitarian sense, for what matters to Beran are people's voluntary choices, not their involuntary group traits such as ethnicity. As Lea Brilmayer shows, that the group living in a territory merely *wishes* to secede will not have shown that it can lawfully take the territory. Government by consent does not include a right to opt out, but merely requires a right to democratic participation.[70] And because of the neglect of territorial title, Beran's argument begs the question of what is the relevant group to consult: group leaders will answer that their group is the relevant one, members of the larger unit that the larger unit is. So it seems that Beran does not resolve this question, unless what he means by "territorially concentrated groups" is groups that have the title to territory. If so, his argument is identical to Brilmayer's: if a group owns the territory and wishes to secede, it should in principle be allowed to do so.

There is another problem with Beran's thesis. We saw that, for him, the right of unlimited secession follows from the ideas of popular sovereignty and freedom. Yet, to be consistent with the conceptions of freedom it espouses, Beran's view has to require *unanimity* in order to secede (or to establish a group right). Otherwise, the majority in the group would be establishing a new authority over the dissenters within the group. And why can't they exercise in turn a right to secession? Again, the expression "territorially concentrated groups" is suspect. If that entity has the right to self-determination, so do subgroups, and so do individuals. Popular sovereignty is not very useful if we have not identified the *populus*. Even if we have, popular sovereignty does not sit well with the other idea put forth by Beran: individual freedom.

Injustice as a Rationale for Collective Rights

Violation of Human Rights and Territorial Injustice

The first justification of special group rights (and, in appropriate cases, secession) is when those who inhabit the region are subject to serious injustice and when other remedies (say, democratic remedies) are unavailable. What counts, however, as a serious injustice? Here writers differ. Allen Buchanan treats as injustices the violation of group rights,[71] the need to prevent genocide,[72] and the need to escape what he calls "discriminatory redistribution."[73] Yet there is one more obvious form of injustice: the serious violation of *individual* human rights, even if it does not reach genocidal proportions. Oppression may be directed against the group as such or against all the citizens of the state. In either case, the government has lost its legitimacy, and citizens have a right to free themselves from oppression. An important proviso, however, is that other means of redress (and in extreme cases, revolution) be unavailable. Maybe the persecuted group cannot enlist a sufficiently large number of votes (or revolutionaries); maybe even the majority in the state acquiesce in the human rights violations. In these cases, it should matter little whether or not the group has a legitimate historical grievance over the taking of territory, that is, whether the group is also a victim of territorial injustice, although if it is, its case will of course be strengthened. Brilmayer objects that the remedy for mistreatment is better treatment, not secession.[74] However, if peaceful reform or violent revolution within the state cannot achieve better treatment, then special group rights, and sometimes secession, are morally preferable to the preservation of state unity that countenances oppression. As a recent commentator describes this model: "citizens have only a right not to be treated unjustly, not a primary right to political self-determination that permits secession in the absence of injustice."[75] The right to self-determination is derivative of the right not to suffer injustice and not independent of it. However, when it applies, it trumps the territorial integrity of the state.

The second justification for collective rights and self-determination is, as we saw, the redress of a territorial injustice such as an invasion and annexation. We saw also that this rationale is always properly limited by deontological constraints, by the observance of human rights.

I will now discuss a possible justification for self-determination and special group rights, which, on closer analysis, is wanting: discriminatory redistribution.

Discriminatory Redistribution

An alleged form of injustice suggested by Allen Buchanan as a possible justification for secession (or other forms of self-determination) is discriminatory redistribution. This is defined as "taxation schemes or regulatory policies or economic programs that systematically work to the disadvantage of some groups . . . in morally arbitrary ways."[76] According to Buchanan, discriminatory redistribution can occur even when the state respects individual rights and group and minority rights, including the right to democratic representation. This form of injustice may call into question the legitimacy of political authority with regard to the group that is victimized.

This, however, is a dubious justification for self-determination and special group rights. If no rights are being violated, then all the group can complain about is that it ended up losing in the democratic process. If so, either it has title to territory or it does not. If it does, its sole will should suffice (this does not mean that the question of title is a straightforward one). If it does not have title over the territory, then its claim is no different from the claim of any group that ends up losing in the democratic process: the farmers, the auto industries, the homeless, and so on. In other words: the claim that a disadvantaged group is the victim of discriminatory redistribution is tautologically true of any economic program adopted in a democratic political system that respects individual rights and abides by the strictures of democratic fairness. If the state is just in the liberal sense (and again, this may be hard to determine) then there is no residual claim of injustice by those whose interests (not rights) have been thwarted in the democratic process. Here the remedies should be democratic, and there seems to be little merit in the suggestion that if the group has an ethnic identity then it should be given a special shield against adverse democratic decisions. To be sure, if our liberal theory of justice mandates economic redistribution, and if the laws of that country do not provide for such redistribution, then people who live in a territory and who happen to be the victims of that economic injustice may be entitled to self-determination in order to escape the injustice (just like any other case of violation of human rights). A violation of economic rights that cannot be redressed through the democratic process or by other means may leave no alternative but the creation of some form of political autonomy. Of course, it is not enough that the region be economically disadvantaged in a general sense (e.g., southern Italy); rather the economic arrangements must fail to satisfy the minimal requirements of liberal justice for the majority of the people who inhabit the territory, and self-determination (special group rights, political autonomy, or secession in extreme cases) is the only realistic remedy to that injustice.

Conclusions

The discussion suggests that there are three factors to be considered in the moral evaluation of self-determination claims. The first is the moral urgency to escape serious *political* injustice against a group. In this case, self-determination, autonomy, group rights, and even secession may be the only viable forms of political reorganization to end the injustice. The second is the need to remedy past *territorial* injustice against the group (along the lines suggested by Brilmayer). Political injustice occurs when members of the group are denied human rights; territorial injustice occurs when the group's governance over the territory has been forcibly replaced by outsiders. Certainly, the need to redress an unjust territorial taking provides a good justification for self-determination rights for a group, on the condition that the group itself intends to observe human rights. Nevertheless, a group escaping oppression is justified in seeking political autonomy whenever revolution or other means of political reform are unavailable, even if it does not have title. So title to territory is a sufficient justification for self-determination only in the case of a liberal group seeking autonomy within a liberal state. In other cases, the preservation and protection of human rights should take precedence.

The third factor is the need to take into account the *legitimate interests* of third parties, in particular, of people in the parent state. Those legitimate expectations of third parties, however, ought always be either *moral* reasons (e.g., a fear that larger autonomy for the group would impair the democratic institutions in the parent state) or *strong prudential* reasons (e.g., a danger that larger group autonomy will jeopardize a vital food supply). The reasons usually given by international lawyers to oppose secession and self-determination, such as the need to respect the territorial integrity of the state, are suspect. There is no right to territorial integrity independent of the legitimacy of the state that rules over that territory, and there is nothing morally important in keeping the territory together, as it were. Here, as elsewhere, traditional international law is highly anthropomorphic: because the preservation of *bodily* integrity is morally important, lawyers assume that preservation of the "body" of the state, the territory, is equally important. Similarly, there seems to be something intrinsically sobering about the death of a person (even of one who deserves to die), but there is nothing intrinsically wrong with the "death" of a state (think about East Germany). A person has inherent dignity, whereas the state is simply a form of political organization. The "life" of a state is entirely dependent on the rights and interests of the people who populate it. The state is not a person, and the territory is not a body. A territory is the *locus* of political organization and thus the space where persons exercise their moral rights. A society needs a territory, but it does not follow that a specific territory is required by principles of justice.

How are these factors to be weighed against one another cannot be determined by any fixed formula. Some consequences follow, however:

1. Liberal principles of justice act as deontological constraints over self-determination claims.
2. Groups (including ethnic groups) are never morally entitled to create a despotic state.
3. The establishment of group rights (and other forms of group autonomy) cannot take place at the cost of the violation of the rights of members of the group.
4. Conversely, self-determination (including secession) as the only viable means to escape oppression is justified.

5. The exercise of the right of self-determination and secession must take into account the legitimate interests of third parties, in particular the parent state.

I showed that group rights are best describes as aggregative social policies. While the implementation of those policies carries dangers of restrictions on people's freedoms, nothing in my argument precludes the establishment of *legal* group rights or other forms of group autonomy for weighty pragmatic or prudential reasons, such as the need to avert ethnic conflict.[77] What I have tried to show is that, while legal collective rights may sometimes be an appropriate remedy, they are never required by justice. They are not supported by principled, deontological reasons or by the popular public goods argument. There are no *moral* collective rights—at least none that are consistent with rights-based liberalism.[78]

The issue of ethnic identity and the rights associated with it raise profound questions about our commitment to freedom and equality. An assertion of group rights founded in common race, religion, or language, challenges liberalism's commitment to universality and its emphasis on human *commonality*. Equal rights of citizenship is, for liberals, blind (to color, language, and so on). The assumption behind the political relevance of ethnic identity is that there is a right to be governed by members of one's own race (or language and the like). But that cannot be right, notwithstanding rhetoric to the contrary. If a government is morally legitimate under liberal principles, why should it be important that the officials "look like me"? What was wrong with colonialism was not that the ruler of the colony was white. What was wrong was that the government was morally illegitimate because it did not respect human or democratic rights; it had been established for the purpose of subjecting the inhabitants of the colonies to political and economic exploitation. These are liberal-individualistic reasons to condemn colonialism. The recognition of special group rights and self-determination is linked to, and dependent upon, the imperatives to respect human rights and promote social justice.

Notes

1. See generally Antonio Cassesse, *Self-Determination of Peoples* (1995); Rein Mullerson, *International Law, Rights and Politics* (1994); *Le droit des peuples a disposer déux mêmes: Mélanges offerts a Charles Chaumont* (1984); and Micha Pomerance, *Self-Determination In International Law and Practice* (1982).

2. There is not much philosophical literature on the question of national self-determination. Notable exceptions include Allen Buchanan, *Secession: The Morality of Political Divorce from Fort Sumter to Québec* (1991); and Avit Margalit & Joseph Raz, "National Self-Determination," 87 *Journal of Philosophy* 439 (1990). On group rights generally, Will Kymlicka has written two important books: *Liberalism, Community and Culture* (1989) [hereinafter Liberalism] and *Multicultural Citizenship* (1995) [hereinafter Multicultural Citizenship].

3. See Ronald Dworkin, *Taking Rights Seriously* (1977).

4. See 1 Karl R. Popper, *The Open Society and Its Enemies* 120–122 (2d ed. 1966).

5. This is, essentially, Allen Buchanan's position, discussed supra. See Buchanan, supra note 2, at 127–162.

6. Article 2, Resolution 1514 (XV) article 1; United Nations Covenants.

7. A thorough treatment of the history of the principle can be found in Cassesse, supra note 1, at 1–159.

8. This interpretation is supported, inter alia, by the work of the Human Rights Committee under the United Nations human rights covenants. See id. at 62–63, and references therein.

9. See, e.g., id. at 52–54, 101–108; Thomas Franck, "The Emerging Right to Democratic Governance," 86 *American Journal of International Law* 46 (1992). But see Mullerson, supra note 1, at 69 (expressing serious doubt as to whether the right to democratic rule applies to oppressed populations that do not have ethnic status).

10. See, e.g., Antonio Cassesse, "The Self-Determination of Peoples," in *The International Bill of Rights* 92, 95 (L. Henkin ed., 1981); James Crawford, *The Creation of States* 101 (1979); Mullerson, supra note 1, at 74–75.

11. See Mullerson, supra note 1, at 74–75.

12. Ian Brownlie, "The Rights of Peoples in Modern International Law" in *The Rights of Peoples* 1, 5 (James Crawford ed., 1988). See also Christian Tomuschat, "Self-Determination in a Post–Colonial World," in *Modern Law of Self-Determination* 1, 16–17 (Christian Tomuschat ed., 1993).

13. Declaration on the Granting of Independence to Colonial Countries and Peoples, General Assembly Resolution 1514 (XV), December 14, 1960, United Nations General Assembly, 15th Session, Supp. 16 (A/4684) at 66; United Nations Covenant on Civil and Political Rights, article 4, 999 *Unites Nations Treaty Series* 171 (1966).

14. See Resolution 1514, paragraph 8; United Nations Covenants article 1.

15. See H. Johnson, *Self-Determination Within the Community of Nations* 50 (1967) (secession is not a matter of right but of success or failure); Bos, "Self-Determination by the Grace of History," 15 *Nederlands Tijdschrift Voor International Recht* 362, 372 (1968); Kaur, "Self-determination in International Law," 10 *Indian International Law Journal* 479, 493 (1970).

16. Some commentators saw this fatal flaw in the traditional view. See Lee Buchheit, *Secession* 45 (1978) (we can only discern the legitimacy of separatist movement by hindsight).

17. See Kymlicka, *Liberalism*, supra note 2; Buchanan, supra note 2.

18. See Buchanan, supra note 2, at 74–75.

19. For discussion of the distinctions inherent in the concept of collective rights, see Kymlicka, *Multicultural Citizenship*, supra note 2, at 34–48. While I agree with Kymlicka's distinction between internal restrictions and external protections, and, as the text demonstrates, I also share his skepticism for the former, I am less optimistic about his contention that the liberal tradition can accommodate group rights with ease.

20. See Dworkin, supra note 3, at xi–xii, 90–100.

21. Id. at 92.

22. This is what Kymlicka calls "internal restrictions." See Kymlicka, *Multicultural Citizenship*, supra note 2, at 35–48.

23. Id. This is what Kymlicka calls "external protections." He wants to downplay the internal coercion presupposed by group rights, and emphasize the external aspect. But it is hard to think of many group rights that do not involve a claim by the group leaders to restrict

the individual rights of its members.

24. Id.

25. See Buchanan, supra note 2, at 48.

26. Article 2, Resolution 1514 (XV). Article 1; United Nations Covenants.

27. See, e.g., Buchanan, supra note 2, at 49–50.

28. Ernest Gellner, *Nations and Nationalism* 2 (1983).

29. Id. at 55–56. He adds: "The cultural shreds and patches used by nationalism are often historical inventions." Id.

30. See Buchanan, supra note 2, at 48.

31. I call the position I am about to discuss soft communitarianism to distinguish it from stronger forms of communitarianism such as the ones defended by Charles Taylor, Michael Sandel, Alasdair MacIntyre, and others. I am indebted to Carlos Rosenkrantz for calling my attention to this point.

32. Margalit & Raz, supra note 2.

33. Id. at 442–447.

34. Id. at 451.

35. Id. at 459–460.

36. Id. at 459.

37. Id. at 458.

38. Id. at 456–457.

39. See Michael Walzer, "The Rights of Political Communities," in *International Ethics* 165, 181 (Beitz et al. eds., 1985).

40. Margalit & Raz, supra note 2, at 449.

41. There is a voluminous literature devoted to this debate between liberals and communitarians. The best liberal response is, in my view, Kymlicka, *Liberalism*, supra note 2. See also Derek L. Phillips, *Looking Backward: A Critical Appraisal of Communitarian Thought* (1995).

42. See Liberalism, supra note 2, at 50–51.

43. For a representative collection of essays, see *The Theory of Market Failure: A Critical Examination* (T. Cowen ed., 1988).

44. On free riding, see Garrett Cull, "Moral Free Riding," 24 *Philosophy and Public Affairs* 3 (1995).

45. Id. at 4.

46. Rolf Sartorius, *The Limits of Libertarianism* 104–105 (1980).

47. See David Schmidtz, *The Limits of Government: An Essay on the Public Goods Argument* 82 (1991).

48. Here I follow Schmidtz, id. at 82–107.

49. Id. at 83.

50. These are called by Schmidtz the "honest holdouts." Id. at 84.

51. In classic public goods dilemmas, each player's first preference is to have the good without paying for it (for example, the Québecois who wants to live in a French culture but be able to speak English whenever he finds it convenient). Such person is a free rider. Each player's second preference is to have the good and pay for it. The criticism in the text is that often people who refuse to contribute for the good fall in neither category: they just don't want the good.

52. Lea Brilmayer, "Secession: A Territorial Reinterpretation," 16 Yale *Journal of International Law* 177 (1991).

53. Id. at 178.

54. Id. at 188.

55. Id. at 189.

56. Id. at 191.

57. Id. at 197–201.

58. Advisory Opinion No. 61, Western Sahara, 1975 *International Court of Justice* 12 (Oct. 16).

59. Id. at 68.

60. Judge Dillard expressly rejected this implication in his concurrence. See id. at 122.

61. There are some indications that in the current crisis in Chechnya, authoritarian secessionists are attempting to break away from increasingly liberal Russia. See "Yeltsin Must Learn that Democracies Cannot Be Glued Together by Force," *The Economist*, December 25, 1994, at G4 ("Chechnya is more like a gangster republic fighting a Russia which has usually been willing to abide by popular decision").

62. See generally Robert A. Nozick, *Anarchy, State, and Utopia* (1974).

63. For the classic statement of the theory of acquisition of territory, see Island of Palmas Case (Netherlands v. United States), 2 *Reports of International Arbitral Awards* 829 (M. Huber, arbitrator, 1928).

64. Harry Beran, "A Liberal Theory of Secession," 32 *Political Studies* 21 (1984). I read Christopher Wellman as proposing a similar view: "*any* group may secede as long as it and its remainder state are large, cohesive, and geographically contiguous enough to form a government that effectively performs the functions necessary to create a secure political environment." Christopher H. Wellman, "A Defense of Secession and Political Self-Determination," 24 *Philosophy and Public Affairs* 142 (1995). Thus, for this author the freedom to secede is normatively preeminent, and it is limited only by pragmatic reasons (size, etc.).

65. Advisory Opinion No. 61, Western Sahara, 1975 *International Court of Justice* 12 (Oct. 16) ("It is for the people to determine the destiny of the territory and not the territory the destiny of the people").

66. Beran, supra note 65, at 25.

67. Id.

68. Id. at 26.

69. For a brief discussion of the general problems with this view, see Buchanan, supra note 2, at 71–73.

70. Brilmayer, supra note 53, at 185.

71. See Buchanan, supra note 2, at 40.

72. Id. at 64–67.

73. Id. at 38–45. Under "Rectifying Past Injustices," Buchanan includes the territorial argument introduced by Brilmayer.

74. See Brilmayer, supra note 53, at 188.

75. See Wellman, supra note 65, at 157.

76. See Buchanan, supra note 2, at 40.

77. See the penetrating essay by Horacio Spector, "Communitarianism and Collective Rights," 17 *Analyse and Kritik* 67, 88 (1995). Spector's position is quite close to the one defended in this book.

78. See id. at 79–82. Spector makes the following powerful point: "[Individual] autonomy is especially important because it involves the exercise of second-order capabilities which tell us whether a preference we have is appropriate or not, compatible or incompatible with our nature. . . . And it is this rational ability that the communitarian

weakens or replaces directly by the preference of her community (or its authorities)." Id. at 82.

6

Radical Challenges: Feminism and International Law

Introduction

During the past several years, jurisprudence has been enriched by the contributions of feminists. Until recently, however, international law had not undergone a sustained feminist critique, but this gap is now slowly being filled.[1] This chapter presents a reply to the feminist critique from the standpoint of the Kantian thesis. Although much of my argument engages more general issues in feminist theory, it would be impossible, within the scope of this book, to address every important political, cultural, biological, epistemological, and metaphysical issue raised by the various feminist critiques of traditional jurisprudence. I therefore confine the analysis to arguments directly relevant to international law, focusing on the analogies and contrasts between the differing feminist approaches to international law and the Kantian theory of international law defended in this book.

The feminist critique of international law contains many disparate strands of theory that must be disentangled. One difficulty with that critique is that it conflates divergent arguments from very different (and often irreconcilable) camps within feminist theory. In this chapter I try, therefore to separate, analyze, and evaluate these interwoven but uncongenial threads of feminist thought.[2] In examining the liberal and radical feminist approaches to international law, I distinguish three different levels of criticism. The first level concerns *the processes* of international lawmaking, the second addresses the *content* of international law, and the third attempts to derive a critical theory from the (purported) nature or inherent qualities of liberal international legal institutions. These critiques are treated differently, in complex ways, by radical and liberal feminism. Yet on all three critical dimensions, my conclusion is the same: although *liberal* feminism has important things to say about international law and relations, *radical* feminism is inconsistent both with the facts and with a view of international law rooted in human rights and respect for persons.

Liberal and Radical Feminism

The international law theory defended here is founded on the idea of the individual as rational and autonomous. Kantian liberals regard individuals as capable of rational choices, possessed of inherent dignity, and worthy of respect.[3] We saw in Chapter 1 that liberal states, the members of the liberal alliance, are those nation-states with democratically elected officials, where human rights are generally respected. Liberal internationalism assumes a right to democratic governance and holds that a state may not discriminate against individuals, including women.[4] This principle is, of course, a centerpiece of the international law of human rights.[5] A corollary of the Kantian thesis is that illegitimate governments may not be embraced as members of the liberal alliance.

Liberal feminists rely on liberal principles of domestic and international law to end abuses against women. Very succinctly, liberal feminism is the view that women are unjustly treated, that their rights are violated, and that political reform is needed to improve their situation, thereby allowing them to exercise autonomous choices and enjoy full equal status as free citizens in a liberal democracy.[6] The governing international principles are the imperatives of human rights, nondiscrimination, and equal opportunity for women, as envisioned in articles 1(3), 8, and 55 of the United Nations Charter.[7] When a state discriminates or deprives women of these human rights, it commits an injustice, a violation of international human rights law for which it is responsible.[8] Radical feminists agree with liberal feminists that the situation of women must be improved. They believe, however, that liberal institutions are themselves but tools of gender oppression and that women are exploited by men in unsuspecting ways.[9] Radical feminists believe that existing states are hierarchically structured according to gender, and that gender hierarchy necessarily infects the process of legal reasoning itself.[10] They claim that the actual choices of women only *seem* to be autonomous and free; in reality they are *socially* determined. Human beings are not, as liberals would have it, separate, rational entities capable of individual choice but rather beings that to an important degree are defined and determined by their social—and particularly gender—relationships.[11] Under radical feminist theory, no woman is truly free, not even in the otherwise freest of societies.

Three Feminist Critiques of International Law

In light of the differences in feminist theory it will be convenient to set forth three feminist critiques of international law and the central claim associated with each: (1) *the processes* of international lawmaking exclude women; (2) the *content* of international law privileges men to the detriment of women; and (3) international law, as a patriarchal institution, *inherently* oppresses women, marginalizes their interests, and submerges their experiences and perspectives. I will address each of these critiques in turn.

The Processes of International Lawmaking Exclude Women

Feminists criticize the international lawmaking process for depriving women of the access and opportunity to take part in lawmaking in two important ways. First, feminists argue that women are *underrepresented* in international relations, that is, in high positions in international organizations, in diplomatic services, and as heads of state and government.[12] Second, they contend that because of this underrepresentation, the *creation* of international law is reserved almost exclusively to men. Women are thus effectively prevented from participating in the processes of international lawmaking.[13]

There is no doubt that there are relatively few women heads of state, diplomats, or international organizations officials.[14] Is this state of things, however, an injustice? And how can the statistical underrepresentation (whether or not it is an injustice) be redressed? It is useful, in addressing these issues, to distinguish, first, between legitimate and illegitimate governments (in the sense defined in Chapters 1 and 2), and second, between governments and international organizations.

Let us consider first the case of illegitimate, undemocratic governments, as I define them in this book. Plainly, it does not make sense to criticize a dictator, say, for not appointing enough women to his government or diplomatic corps. To do so would constitute a contextual *category* mistake: blaming a dictator who has taken and held power by means of torture and murder for not appointing a woman as ambassador to the United Nations is like blaming a burglar ransacking your home at gunpoint for not having asked your permission to use the telephone. The normative context of a burglary is one in which it does not make sense to insist on compliance with the norms of courtesy. Likewise, the normative context of a tyrannical state is one in which it does not make sense to ask the tyrant to appoint more women (or men, or blacks, or Catholics).[15] In such a case, the government is illegitimate in the first place, so its appointments are morally invalid regardless of the sex of the appointees. If an illegitimate government consists of a group of men systematically excluding women, this is of course an injustice, but it is one that is subordinated to the greater injustice of tyranny, which by definition includes the illegitimacy of origin and the violation of human rights. Discriminating against women aggravates the injustice of tyranny; it therefore makes sense to put pressure on *all* governments to refrain from sexist practices. The analysis, however, does not work the other way around: tyranny is not cured by the tyrant's celebration of diversity, as it were. Even in cases where human rights abuses (other than exclusion from government) are primarily directed at women, suggesting that what we need is more women as international representatives of dictators is absurd on its face. The only remedy, here as elsewhere, is to get rid of the tyrants and secure human rights.

Put differently, in a tyrannical state the *agency* relationship between people and government, the vertical social contract, has broken down.[16] Therefore, the tyrant cannot legitimately address the question of the sex of his political appointees because he does not represent anybody. The women he decides to appoint to office to achieve gender balance are likewise blighted by the original illegitimacy. A partial reply to the complaint that women are underrepresented in international relations, then, is that it is not sensible to start addressing that issue *globally* without addressing also the issue of democratic legitimacy.

More interesting is the case of full members of the liberal alliance, states with democratically elected officials where human rights are generally respected. Assuming a right to democratic governance,[17] a state may not discriminate against women in their exercise of that right.[18] The governing principle, then, is the imperative of nondiscrimination and equal opportunity for women, along the lines suggested by the pertinent international instruments, themselves inspired in articles 1(3), 8, and 55 of the United Nations Charter.[19] Therefore, if the under-representation of women results from governments preventing them from exercising their right to political participation, that is an injustice, a violation of international human rights law for which the state is responsible. A similar analysis holds for a state that discriminates against women in its processes for admission to the diplomatic service. Such discrimination is contrary to the mandates of international human rights law.[20] This conclusion follows from both liberal feminism and the Kantian theory of international law.

Radical feminists, however, seem to believe that there is a global injustice even where, as a result of democratic elections held in independent, rights-respecting states, it is mostly men who are elected to government, or if in such states mostly men traditionally seek admission to the diplomatic service. An example is the discussion by Hilary Charlesworth and her associates of the Women's Convention.[21] They strongly criticize the Convention for assuming that men and women should be treated alike, which is the liberal outlook.[22] The view is that sexism is "a pervasive, structural problem."[23] Further, it is male dominance that lies at the root of the structural problem and that must be addressed as a means to reach the structural issues. But what are the authors' suggestions? If we descend from the abstract slogan that liberal equality is just the men's measure of things, how do feminists suggest rewriting each of the rights recognized by the Convention to meet their concerns? Take article 7, for example, which directs states to eliminate all discrimination against women in the political and public life of the country.[24] Would a radical feminist rewriting of this article require states to *appoint* women, regardless of popular vote?[25] Would it impose a 50 percent gender quota for elected positions or force women who do not want to run for office to do so?[26] These are not just rhetorical questions: given the radical feminists' rejection of rights discourse and formal political equality, it is difficult to imagine what a radical list of international women's rights would look like.

That said, the Kantian theory of international law does not preclude domestic electoral arrangements designed to heighten the probability of electing women in a given state. This is no different from gerrymandering for the purpose of strengthening the vote of minorities or other groups in some states.[27] Here again, international law cannot go beyond mandating democratic governance and nondiscrimination in a general way. Local conditions will vary, and in states where women have been previously excluded from politics it may be permissible and desirable to adopt preferential electoral arrangements. Such measures, when properly tailored, do not do violence to the international law principle of nondiscrimination and the right of all citizens to participate in public life.

This analysis holds with even more force for the permanent staffs of international organizations. There would be nothing wrong with the United Nations, for example, attempting to achieve a gender balance in the composition of its administrative staff, much in the way the organization attempts to maintain a geographical and even ideological balance.[28] In this case there is no competing legitimate sovereignty principle, and the organization would not be impairing individual or collective choices in legitimate states (i.e., liberal democracies)[29] if it attempted to hire officials under such a scheme.

In sum, imposing on states the duties of nondiscrimination and equal opportunity, and permitting affirmative measures where appropriate, is the only way to redress the underrepresentation of women as state agents consistent with full respect for democratic and individual choices.[30] Likewise, in international organizations it may make sense, depending on the circumstances (past discrimination, goals of the organization), to push to achieve a gender balance in the composition of the organization's personnel.

The Content of the Rules of International Law

In addition to criticizing the processes of international lawmaking, many feminists argue that the *content* of international law privileges men to the detriment of women.[31] The claim that the content of international law favors the interests of men may incorporate either or both of the following arguments: first, international law rules in general are "gendered" to privilege men;[32] second, international rules such as sovereign equality and nonintervention protect states, and states are instrumental in disadvantaging or oppressing women.[33] The latter claim, in turn, may intend either or both of the following: first, international law is too tolerant of violations of women's rights *by governments*;[34] second, international law is too tolerant of violations of the rights of women *by private individuals* within states, such as physical abuse by men in the home.[35]

In response to the first point, I find little plausibility in the claim of some feminists that the specific content of international law rules systematically privileges men. Positive international law is a vast and heterogeneous system consisting of principles, rules, and standards of varying degrees of generality, many of a technical nature. Rules such as the principle of territoriality in criminal jurisdiction, or the rule that third states should in principle have access to the surplus of the entire allowable catch of fish in a coastal state's Exclusive Economic Zone are not "thoroughly gendered"[36] but, on the contrary, gender-neutral. It cannot be seriously maintained that such norms operate overtly or covertly to the detriment of women. The same can be said of the great bulk of international legal rules.[37]

Feminists are correct, however, on their second claim that international law overprotects states and governments. International law, as traditionally understood, is formulated in exaggeratedly statist terms. Statism, the doctrine that state sovereignty is the foundational concept of international law, repudiates the central place accorded to the individual in any liberal normative theory; by extension, it often results in ignoring the rights and interests of women within states. This criticism is identical to the one made in this book. The Kantian thesis insists upon disenfranchising illegitimate governments. Likewise, there is little doubt that the government of a state that denies women status as equal citizens is illegitimate, just as the apartheid regime in South Africa was illegitimate. Feminists are right, in short, in challenging statism.

Yet radical feminists also attack liberalism. Insofar as this attack is predicated on the perception that liberal philosophy and the liberal state oppress women, it must be met with a philosophical and political defense of the liberal vision. But if the feminist attack on liberalism is predicated on the belief that statism, as an assumption of international law, is necessarily entailed by liberalism, the answer is simply that this is a mistaken inference. I showed in Chapter 2 why statism is at odds with liberalism. The Kantian thesis (certainly the most liberal international legal theory) rejects statism because the latter protects illegitimate governments and is thus an *illiberal* theory of international law. The whole point of this book is to challenge absolute sovereignty as an antiquated, authoritarian doctrine inhospitable to the aspirations of human rights and democratic legitimacy.

Liberal feminism and the Kantian theory of international law join in rejecting statism. Indeed, one of the most valuable contributions of feminist international legal theory is the attempt to disaggregate states, to pierce the sovereignty veil and inquire about real social relations, relations among individuals and those between individuals and government within the state. This is also the thrust of the Kantian thesis.[38] When the veil of state sovereignty is lifted, liberal feminists find that women are unfairly treated (i.e., their rights are violated) in most or all states. This injustice is compounded by the fact that it often takes place in spheres shielded from the reach of domestic and international law. Beneath the sovereignty veil, two different situations become relevant: violation of women's rights *by the government,* and violation of women's rights *by private persons* (notably, abuse by men in the home and the workplace). From the standpoint of the international law of human rights, the violation of women's rights by governments does not present difficulties distinct from the violation of other human rights.[39] Liberal and radical feminists are at one here in condemning discrimination against women. Discrimination is a violation of international human rights law for which the state is internationally responsible.

The violation of women's rights by private persons or groups raises more difficult issues because, as feminists rightly point out, the boundaries between public and private action are blurred. Indeed, radical feminists contend that the very distinction between public or state action and private action is indefensible because it is male biased and harmful to women.

It will be convenient here to treat separately what seems to me one of feminism's most persuasive points: the modern state affords excessive legal protection to the family.[40] Family "autonomy," as the legal basis of the private social domain, has legitimized the domination of women and children by men. This oppression ranges from outright brutality to subtler ways of socializing women within the family; for example, by more or less coercively convincing women that their place is in the home, thus preventing them from pursuing other options. For some feminists, the fact that the family is legally treated as a semienclosed unit to a greater extent than other legal relationships, and the fact that modern governments are, consequently, slow in intervening in internal family affairs, make states, in different degrees, accomplices in this injustice. International law in turn protects states by imposing a strong duty of nonintervention in internal matters.[41] So there are two layers of legal immunity enjoyed by men who oppress women: domestic law, which treats the family as the man's castle, and international law, which likewise leaves the state (with its many men's castles) largely shielded from external scrutiny.

I think that feminists, radical and liberal, are right in decrying the excessive prerogatives enjoyed by men within the family. The law should punish the victimization of women, and culprits should not be allowed to hide behind the "family unit," a politically defined space where men may unjustly dominate and sometimes even victimize women and children. Toleration of this sort of abuse does not, however, arise from *liberalism,* for *group* autonomy (state sovereignty, family autonomy) is an *illiberal* notion. Kantian liberalism insists that our moral principles derive from *individual* dignity and autonomy. Every person holds individual rights that are not forfeited by membership in the family group. Therefore, a liberal state must recognize and enforce the rights of women and children within the family and protect their rights. Just as the principle of state sovereignty must be set aside to protect citizens whose rights are violated by their government, so the principle of family autonomy must be set aside to protect the rights of members of the family.

At this point, the international lawyer may raise an objection. Why cannot *domestic* law address the question of abuse of women? Why should *international* law provide a remedy for the acts of private individuals?[42] Surely many offenses (e.g., murder or rape), heinous as they are, are not criminalized by international law. International law, the traditionalist would claim, is primarily concerned with rules of state behavior. These rules do include human rights standards, but these standards can only be violated by state officials. Crimes committed by private individuals against fellow citizens fall instead within the purview of the ordinary criminal law. It is true that in special circumstances certain crimes committed by private individuals are directly regulated by international law: piracy and genocide are examples. However, most common offenses, including men's offenses against women, belong (it is argued) in the province of the state. The state, through its criminal and civil legislation, has the power to prevent and redress those injustices.

This reply, however, is too hasty, because it begs the question of why international law should be content with a few injunctions against governmental coercion and why it should not instead impose some *positive* obligations on states to criminalize certain actions. To take an extreme example, imagine a state where rape is not criminalized. Unscrupulous men could go about taking advantage of women and terrorizing them; everyone would live in constant fear. I am not sure we would even call this Hobbesian jungle a *state;* it would certainly not be a civilized state in any meaningful sense, and it would be ludicrous for the government to escape international scrutiny by arguing that the legally permitted acts of rape are not being perpetrated by state officials. Liberal theory must therefore postulate an affirmative obligation *in international law* on the part of the state to have a reasonably effective legal system in which assaults against life, physical integrity, and property are not tolerated.[43] Thus, a state is in breach of its international obligations not only if it violates human rights in the traditional sense but also if it fails adequately to protect its citizens— if it fails to punish enough, as it were.

In this regard, the case *X and Y v. The Netherlands,*[44] decided in 1985 by the European Court of Human Rights, is instructive. The litigation arose from an unintended gap in Dutch criminal procedure that left a sixteen-year-old mentally retarded victim of rape unable to initiate criminal proceedings.[45] The legal guardian of the victim brought the case to the Court alleging violation of her right to privacy under article 8 of the European Convention. The applicant claimed that the loophole in Dutch law amounted to a failure to protect the mentally handicapped woman's right to privacy (in this case, against sexual assault). The Dutch government responded, *inter alia,* that article 8 could not be interpreted to *require* a state to legislate specific rules of criminal procedure in cases where the applicant had been victimized not by state officials but by a private individual and where civil remedies were available.[46] The government argued that the Convention accorded to the states the task of determining the appropriate mix of civil and criminal penalties for a wrongful act.[47] Nevertheless, the Court agreed with the applicant, reasoning that the European Convention entailed positive as well as negative obligations on the part of the state.[48] The loophole in Dutch criminal law, while unintentional, amounted to an omission by the Dutch state that resulted, in this case, in the violation of the right to privacy of the applicant and where tort remedies were insufficient.[49] The Netherlands was thus held in breach of article 8 of the Convention and ordered to pay reparation.[50]

This decision by the oldest and most effective international human rights court demonstrates that it is possible for international law to mandate that states provide remedies for violations of human rights by private individuals. The international law of human rights need not be concerned only with direct human rights violations by public officials. Feminists are therefore right to criticize the international law rule of state attribution according to which only acts by public officials implicate the international responsibility of the state. Such a rule does not properly protect human rights, because it does not account for the failure of states to enact or enforce domestic legislation protecting women from abuse within the family. To the extent that such acts of violence are treated by domestic law as purely internal family matters, a state, by putting women at an unfair risk within the home, fails to treat them with respect and dignity and thus violates the central tenet of the Kantian theory of international law.[51] The state, in that case, finds itself in a situation virtually identical to that of the Dutch government in *X and Y v. The Netherlands.*[52] This is not for the dubious conspiratorial reason that the state is an inherently oppressive patriarchal entity and thus is, in some convoluted way, an active accomplice of the wife beater; rather it is because the government has failed in its duty to protect a group of citizens (women) against serious assault, thus putting them at an unfair risk.

There are also cases where governments openly encourage or tolerate groups of private individuals who violate the rights of women or other groups. In some countries, for example, religious guards patrol the streets to ensure that women, under the threat of severe physical punishment, abide by a set of strict rules that reinforce and help perpetuate women's official status as inferior citizens.[53] Unlike the Dutch case of an unintentional loophole, here the state sanctions the inferior status of women and encourages the squads in their actions. In such a case, the situation is even more closely analogous to direct human rights violations by state officials.[54] In both cases there is a positive, affirmative breach of an international obligation. There is, however, an important moral, if not legal, difference between active governmental complicity in human rights violations by individuals and mere negligent failure to enact appropriate protective legislation. In the first case there might be reasons for declaring a government morally illegitimate; in the second case the state is merely out of compliance with an international obligation. Although the boundaries between direct governmental action and mere omission may be hard to draw, there is nothing to prevent international law from establishing standards that states must meet in the enactment and enforcement of their criminal law. Feminism and Kantianism thus agree that international law, in addition to imposing traditional negative constraints on governmental coercion, must impose affirmative duties of legislation and enforcement in order to deter and punish private individuals (e.g., men in their homes) who violate the rights of others (including, but not limited to, women).[55]

It is in light of these considerations that one must evaluate the criticism of the Convention Against Torture put forth by Charlesworth and her associates. They deplore the fact that the Convention is limited to *official* torture, that is, torture by governments or under color of government authority.[56] By imposing this require-ment, they argue, the Convention does not reach affronts to women's dignity (e.g., battery) typically sustained by them in the home.[57]

In one sense, this objection misses the point of the Convention. It is one thing to assert, properly, that governments have a duty, through legislation, to punish the violation of their citizens' physical integrity by private individuals. It is a very different thing to imply, as the authors seem to do, that because the Convention Against Torture is concerned with *official* torture it therefore permits states to leave private crimes unpunished. Official torture is a worthy object of prohibitive legislation in its own right, as anyone who has witnessed government oppression will agree.[58] Governments have been among history's most egregious culprits in violating human rights. There is ample reason for human rights conventions to deal specifically with official torture. There is something particularly evil in governmental violations of human rights, for in those cases the government has turned its awesome coercive power against the very citizens who have entrusted their protection to it. This is the age-old evil that most human rights conventions, including the Convention Against Torture, are meant to address. Radical feminists are wrong, I think, in drawing the alarmist inference that a hidden purpose or effect of these conventions is to free states from their other international obligations, including the obligation to protect the rights of women against invasion by private individuals. Yet the point that state complicity or inaction in the face of private torture should have been included in the Convention is unexceptionable. As I indicate above, under the liberal theory of international law governments that tolerate the violation of women's rights by private individuals should not be allowed to hide behind the claim that such conduct is outside the purview of the international law of human rights.[59]

The question then returns to which acts or omissions amount to state complicity. The radical feminist claim is that the reluctance of a government to intervene in internal family affairs amounts to complicity. We saw that if domestic law fails to criminalize or punish the behavior of husbands who torment their wives the state should be held accountable by international law.[60] There are, of course, degrees of government negligence, and lines must inevitably be drawn. Nevertheless, the traditional international law requirement that states take reasonable steps to prevent and punish crimes seems to me an entirely appropriate standard.

Although even the most liberal states may have been remiss in the past in this regard (and there is surely much yet to be done, especially in the Latin American democracies), most democratic, rights-respecting states have laws that prohibit and punish the abuse of women. Where that legislation is enforced in good faith, holding such states nonetheless internationally responsible for the instances of abuse of women that still occur is like holding states internationally responsible for, say, murders that are committed every year notwithstanding the states' good faith efforts at crime prevention. It is one thing to hold a state in breach of international human rights law if it knowingly tolerates the behavior of wife beaters (or death squads or the Mafia) or if it fails to enact or enforce appropriate protective legislation, as in the Dutch case. It is a very different thing to hold a state responsible when, despite reasonable legislation and law enforcement, crimes are still committed by private persons.

I would go further: from a human rights standpoint, it is a mistake to strive for perfect (or even near-perfect) crime control.[61] For in such a system, effective deterrence would be achieved by criminal codes imposing harsh punishments, such as death, for minor offenses, and the law would be enforced by an aggressive and intrusive police force with broad powers of arrest and seizure. Citizens of a liberal democracy, concerned with limiting rather than enlarging state power, would rightly reject legislation so severe and law enforcement machineries so efficient as to ensure the punishment of *all* wife beaters, just as they would a system that ensured the punishment of all murderers. Even granting that the problem today lies in too little rather than too much state intervention against the abuse of women, there is surely a point at which the costs of more law enforcement will outweigh the benefits. But where should the line be drawn? What do radical feminists propose? When the rhetorical dust settles, it is difficult to tell exactly how radical feminists intend to deter private violence against women while curtailing the power of the (putatively) oppressive patriarchal state.

Both radical and liberal feminists generally agree that the statist orientation of traditional international legal theory tends to the detriment of women. A truly liberal theory of international law, on the Kantian model, rejects statism as impermissibly solicitous of rights violations by states and unresponsive to the justified claims of all persons, including women, to dignity and equal treatment. The rejection of statism entails scrutiny not only of the official acts of states but also of their complicity and even omissions in the protection of human rights. The notion that liberalism entails statism is therefore misconceived; the logic of liberal internationalism requires that international law limit absolute sovereignty to improve the situation of women, insofar as women remain deprived of equal respect and dignity.

The Radical Claim of Inherent Oppressiveness

I will now respond to the third feminist critique of international law, the claim that international law is inherently oppressive of women. Some feminists argue that because current international law derives from European, male, liberal legalism, its very form and structure are inherently patriarchal and oppressive. In response to this contention, I first argue that the foundations of the "inherent oppressiveness" thesis are faulty, that nothing in the philosophic "nature" of a state makes it oppressive or nonoppressive, and that the radical feminists' nominalism only serves to obscure differences between states that defenders of women's interests ought to care about. I then examine and defend two institutions of liberal political thought proffered by some radical feminists as constitutive of inherent liberal oppression: the public-private distinction and the liberal emphasis on individual autonomy. Against these philosophical attacks, the positive justification of the Kantian thesis presented in this book views it as a bundle of *normative* commitments rather than deductions from some arcane masculinist metaphysics. Finally, I examine the methodological strictures entailed by the Kantian normative commitments and criticize radical feminists for abandoning them, and with them, the liberal norms of objectivity and intellectual integrity.

A number of radical feminists argue that states are inherently patriarchal entities—again, bothering little with distinctions between liberal and illiberal governments. Perhaps radical feminists believe that the governments of liberal democracies are, to paraphrase Marx, mere committees to handle the interests of men. If an interest of men was to secure the continuing oppression of women, and if the state were now and forever a property of men, then the international law principles of sovereign equality and nonintervention would indeed operate systematically to the detriment of women. Of course, under these assumptions no truly legitimate state or government currently exists; all appear in this light as simply men's devices to perpetuate their domination of women. Under this view, states are patriarchal entities; governments (even formally democratic ones) represent the male elites of those entities; and international law abets this tyranny by securing the sovereignty of states. These assertions hold true—equally true—for all states.

It is significant, in this regard, that Charlesworth and her associates do not seem particularly concerned about violations of women's rights by particular governments, even though in many countries women are *officially* discriminated against and sometimes even horribly mutilated with official endorsement or complicity.[62] This omission is related, I believe, to the inherent oppressiveness thesis. Identifying and opposing egregious human rights practices simply holds less *philosophic* interest for the radical feminist than unmasking patriarchal oppression as a pervasive (albeit often invisible) evil. Moreover, defending the *rights* of the oppressed against their government already presupposes the acceptance of rights discourse and runs the risk of treating women as equal citizens, something radical feminists expressly refuse to do.[63] Their obsession with male dominance leads radical feminists to the grotesque proposition that the oppression of women is as serious in liberal democracies as in those societies that institutionally victimize and exclude women.[64] For feminists to try to improve the condition of women in even the freest societies is a commendable goal, because liberal democracies are not free of sexist practices. This is very different, however, from claiming that liberal democracies and tyrannical states are morally equivalent in the way they treat women. Such an assertion not only perverts the facts; it does a disservice to the women's cause.[65]

The sweeping radical thesis that states are inherently oppressive is not only politically counterproductive but also philosophically untenable. The assertion that a social arrangement is unjust or oppressive is contingent; it depends not only on the theory of justice that is presupposed but on the facts as well. Oppression does not follow from the definition of "state"; it is not therefore inherent in the social organization we know as the modern state. Oppression may be defined as occurring when an individual or a group unjustly prevents others from exercising choices, and this may or may not occur in a particular case. Viewing oppressiveness as a necessary rather than contingent property of states is undoubtedly an epistemological convenience for the radical; there is no need to bother with scrutinizing the political practices of *actual* states. Unfortunately, the product of this sort of inquiry can be nothing more than nominalism: metaphysics in, metaphysics out.

One problem with the claim that states are inherently patriarchal entities is that it is not subject to empirical disconfirmation. It is true that some radical proponents of the patriarchy thesis believe in the (perhaps utopian) possibility of a non-patriarchal world.[66] Short of utopia, however, the patriarchy thesis holds the oppressiveness of states beyond the need of empirical validation. To be sure, not all propositions have to be testable to retain philosophical credibility. Metaphysical statements, definitions, or moral assertions, for example, are not testable.[67] But the claim that states are inherently oppressive structures is neither an analytic truth, nor a pure deontic ought-statement, nor a transparently metaphysical claim with no apparent referent in the world of facts. Rather, the claim purports to be descriptive of actual social relations, and as such it must be subject to interpersonal methods of empirical validation.[68] As we have seen, the radical's metaphysics attempts precisely to avoid such validation: the thesis admits no contrary proof.

The inherent oppressiveness thesis is connected with a radical notion of social determinism; that notion, too, admits of no degree or gradation and lies beyond dispute. For at least some radical feminists there may be a possible *future* world in which women will be emancipated, but there is currently no society, no marriage, no relationship in which women are free in any meaningful sense. Even in the freest societies (the Western liberal democracies) where most choices by women are apparently free, radical feminists insist either that such choices are not really autonomous because women have been socialized to make them or that there is no such thing as autonomy anyway.[69] Indeed, even consensual sexual intercourse is regarded by some of them as oppressive.[70] Accordingly, every social fact is interpreted in the light of this premise, which is itself immune to challenge. Like Marxists before them, radical feminists see their theory of gender oppression and hierarchy confirmed in every single social event, for the good reason that no single fact counts as a counterexample.[71] No improvement in women's condition counts as a move toward liberation; states remain patriarchal entities, and women remain oppressed regardless of progressive legislation or other significant advances. No amount of reform will placate the radical feminist.

So the sweeping definition of the state as inherently oppressive of women is, in my view, factually false because there are or could be states where women are not oppressed;[72] it is also morally irresponsible because it trivializes tyranny. States come in many moral shapes. In some states women are oppressed; in some others blacks are oppressed; whites are persecuted in a few; in still other states members of a particular religion, speakers of a certain language, or foreigners may be mistreated; and in some states almost everyone is oppressed. The radical feminist's insistence on the inherent oppression of women by the state succeeds only in blurring the distinction between freedom and tyranny; for the purposes of the "inherent oppressiveness" thesis, a state where the government murders and tortures women is in the same moral category as one where there is a statistical gender imbalance in the public employees roster.

A final problem with the theory of inherent patriarchal oppressiveness is that even in skilled hands it tends to stray dangerously close to a deservingly discredited form of social thought: conspiracy theory.[73] A feminist conspiratorial theory of the state attempts to explain social phenomena by suggesting that men, interested in preserving patriarchy, have in some manner devised and implemented a plan to perpetuate the subjugation of women.[74] Of course, one cannot deny that there is something exhilarating in postulating a *total* explanation of society or the universe: every occurrence can be effortlessly explained by reference to the One Great Conspiratorial Premise,[75] and we are relieved of trying to discover and understand complex causal chains of social events. But an explanation of the complexities of human history by reference to a pervasive, sinister, transgenerational, yet invisible cabal surely need not, and ought not, be taken seriously.

There are two fast and effective ways to undermine a conspiracy theory. One is simply to deny that such a conspiracy ever took place, shifting the (rather weighty) burden of persuasion to the conspiracy theorist. The second is to observe that, even if a conspiracy actually took place, conspirators on the social stage very rarely consummate their designs—let alone effect their ends over the course of centuries. As Sir Karl Popper has perceptively shown, this is often the case with social action, conspiracy or no conspiracy, because of the *effets pervers* (the unintended consequences) of social action.[76] Even if men in fact conspired to achieve the current world, they could not possibly have anticipated every consequence of their machinations.

A conspiratorial explanation of the modern state is not only impoverished and simplistic;[77] but also overlooks both the magnitude and the direction of the social forces unleashed when the universality of human rights was proclaimed by the "bourgeoisie."[78] Feminists, radical and liberal, are correct that many of the early architects (and stewards) of liberalism supported the exclusion of women from many of the benefits of liberty. This, however, was the precipitate of a mistaken anthropology, not a mistaken ethics.[79] Once the prejudice against women was exposed as such, the universality of liberal moral theory, logically entailed by the belief in the inherent dignity of *all* persons, acquired a life of its own and resulted in an astonishing improvement of the predicament of women in free societies. Given the egalitarian consequences of the Enlightenment and the liberal revolutions that it inspired, one is hard pressed to describe the modern liberal state and the international alliance of liberal states as inherently oppressive of women. More plausibly, they have been the matrix of women's liberation.

Radical feminists have sought support for the idea that liberal institutions are inherently oppressive in the fact that much of liberal theory and law has relied on a distinction between public and private spheres of society. Feminists have contended that the public-private distinction is something of a fake, an ideological construct designed to devalue women and their work by confining them to the (less prestigious) private domain.[80] Insofar as feminists seek access for women to markets, politics, and other areas of the public sphere, their efforts fully accord with the imperatives of Kantian liberalism. But when radical feminists reject a person's free choice of a life in the public or private sphere they merely seek to impose their own preferences upon others and should be resisted in the interest of the ideal of equal dignity, which mandates respect for the considered choices of others. Feminists rightly criticize the coercive *confinement* of women to the (presumably less valued) private sphere.[81] From making this valid observation, however, to rejecting wholesale the distinction between public and private law there is an expansive logical gap, and the latter assertion seems to me misguided. Radical feminists, having discovered that the identification of women with the private domain is unjust, conclude that we should give up altogether the distinction between private and public law.[82]

The concept of family privacy makes sense (notwithstanding the justified feminist critique already discussed) insofar as it remains derivative of *individual* rights and autonomy, in the same way that state sovereignty is derivative of individual rights and autonomy. Liberals, unlike communitarians, ground family privacy in individual autonomy and freedom, not in the primacy of the group over the individual. The duty of the state not to interfere with the family (provided the rights of family members are protected) is thus a simple extension of the duty to respect voluntary arrangements entered into by individuals. Even a radical feminist, I assume, would agree that if the state sent agents to take children away for reeducation, or to make sure that sexual intercourse was practiced in the officially sanctioned manner, it would violate a private familial space.[83] A consequence of accepting an autonomy-based family privacy is that the distinction between private and public may well reflect in many cases a rational division of labor between the sexes achieved through noncoercive, voluntary arrangements.

More generally, individual freedom *requires* separation between the private and public spheres, because the distinction simply derives from the imperative of *individual* privacy required by any but the most totalitarian theories of law. For liberals, the power of the state is always limited, and individuals should be legally allowed to make choices in their personal and economic lives free of governmental coercion. This elementary idea (and not some conspiracy to oppress women) lies at the basis of the much maligned public-private distinction. Far from being "an ideological construct rationalizing the exclusion of women from the sources of power,"[84] the public-private distinction is a centerpiece of any constitutional system that protects human rights.[85]

In light of this obvious and, in my view, conclusive reply, why must radical feminism insist upon such an extreme account of the public-private distinction? The answer, again, lies in the ideology. The private, autonomous sphere that radicals challenge is but a travesty of liberalism's insistence on individual self-determination free from governmental coercion. Radical feminists align liberal autonomy with a conception of the family as a Dantesque place where the physically stronger husband victimizes weaker family members. Calling wife abuse an instance of family autonomy is as offensive as calling Saddam Hussein's genocide of the Kurds an instance of Iraqi self-determination. Family autonomy is the least liberal part of the "liberal" theory that radical feminists believe they are challenging. Just as the Kantian thesis is unsympathetic to absolute nonintervention in the domestic affairs of the state, so it is unsympathetic to absolute non-intervention in family affairs (or church affairs or school affairs) when the individual rights of members of the community in question are threatened. Genuine liberal theory refuses to tolerate a private domain in which the strong can victimize the weak with impunity.

Another fertile source of speculation about the idea of inherent oppressiveness is the liberal emphasis on individual autonomy. A number of radical feminists have attacked the notion;[86] some believe that women do not relate to autonomy but instead to emotional connectedness and that abstractions about sovereignty, states, governments, and even human rights therefore ignore women's experiences and exclude their perspectives.[87] This position is common to feminists and communitarians, but where feminists use it to recommend an ethics of care instead of, or alongside, an ethics of justice, communitarians use it instead to exalt communities—including those that, from a liberal or feminist standpoint, oppress people.[88]

What is distinctively feminist about this radical critique is the view that the law's reliance on concepts such as autonomy, rights, and justice is a fundamentally masculine trait. As one commentator described the radical feminist position, "Liberalism has been viewed as inextricably masculine in its model of separate, atomistic, competing individuals establishing a legal system to pursue their own interests and to protect them from others' interference with their rights to do so."[89] The argument, analogous here to the communitarian critique, is that this masculine jurisprudence has unduly emphasized rights over responsibilities, autonomy over connectedness, and the individual over the community. The radical implication seems to be that the basis of liberalism is unsound, that its foundation rests upon an unsupported masculinist metaphysics.

It is true that the idea of the self as rational and autonomous is central to the Kantian theory of international law, which regards individuals as capable of independent, rational choice, possessed of inherent dignity, and worthy of respect. These propositions together form the cornerstone of the theory. The Kantian thesis therefore happily concedes the charge by radical feminists and communitarians that it exalts the individual over the community—this is indeed the central tenet of liberalism.[90] These Kantian premises also form the basis of international human rights law; indeed, it would be difficult to make sense of that body of law if they were discarded.[91] In the international arena, legitimate states are the ones that recognize and honor individual autonomy, and a just international legal system is likewise one that embodies a basic respect for human rights, that is, an imperative to treat people with dignity and respect.

I will first respond to the claim that the autonomous self is a distinctively masculine concept and should therefore be rejected as biased. Feminist critics may mean two different things by this assertion: that men created the theory of autonomy or that it is a reflection of how men typically think or feel and thus excludes women.[92] Neither version of the claim defeats the liberal commitment to individual autonomy; both confuse the *context of origin* with the *context of justification* of a theory. It is perfectly possible to concede that the concept of autonomy is masculine in origin or mental makeup but that it is also the *correct* position to hold. *Who* created the theory or *how* it came about or whether men or women think more about it may be interesting historical or anthropological questions, but they are irrelevant to whether or not the theory is justified. Dismissing liberalism as distinctively masculine because it was formulated by men or because it is a masculine way of thinking is like dismissing the theory of relativity as distinctively Jewish because it was formulated by Albert Einstein. Indeed, if I were persuaded by radical feminists that the feminine way of thinking about political philosophy is illiberal, I would do my best to *keep* women from power. But, of course, the claim that women think about morality in less liberal ways is as false as the claim that men think about morality in more liberal ways.[93] Liberals, it seems, give women more credit than do their radical defenders.

Radical feminists, like communitarians and other radicals, believe that the liberal assumption of autonomy is mistaken because the self is not autonomous but rather socially constituted.[94] This point (which for some reason has become almost undisputed among radicals and even among many of their detractors) is overdrawn. Among other things, it overlooks the undeniable capacity of human beings to overcome the constraints of history, tradition, and social pressures, including state coercion, to challenge existing values and follow their own lights.[95] In addition, the claim is self-refuting, because if choices are socially constituted, presumably the choices of illiberal dissenters who challenge liberalism (the latter being the predominant philosophy in the West) are not excepted from this deterministic postulate. Radical feminists cannot just say that liberal society conditions everybody's choices *except the radicals' own choices.* One cannot hold a theory whose very formulation contradicts its central premise. The radicals' theorizing would not be possible if values and choices were entirely socially constituted: only people in Teheran, not in Berkeley, would be able to challenge liberalism.[96]

Kantian liberalism is a normative, not a metaphysical, proposition. Even if, *grátia argumentandi,* the claim that choices are socially determined is conceded, the concession need not affect the moral force of liberalism. The normative injunction to respect autonomy amounts to this: people make choices, they care about them, and we must respect them (within the framework of the coercion presupposed by the social contract), *even* if those choices are, in a Laplacean sense, biologically or socially determined. Liberals claim that, regardless of the response to the ultimate metaphysical question of social or biological determinism, a distinctive characteristic of human beings is their capacity for what for all purposes looks like rational choices and that such a capacity *must be respected* by fellow citizens and by the government. This is a moral claim, not a metaphysical one.[97]

Another way of making the same point is this: we *don't know* the right answer to the old philosophical controversy about the extent to which our choices are socially or biologically determined. Morality, however, requires us to act *as if* people were rational and autonomous. Freedom of the will is thus postulated as a logically necessary prerequisite of the best principles of individual and political morality.[98] Therefore, in attempting to answer the metaphysical question, we risk error on the side of liberty, as it were: if we treated persons *as if* they were social or biological robots (and we do not have a positive proof that they are robots), the set of moral and political principles constructed on such an assumption would be truly terrifying.[99] We must treat people as if they possessed free will because that is the right thing to do, and this requires the rejection of radical determinism. Our belief in treating persons with dignity and respect should determine our answer to the controverted metaphysical question, not the other way around. Liberals thus reject radical determinism for *moral* reasons.

Radical feminists, by contrast, ignore, disparage, or assume away the actual choices of women when it is convenient for them to do so—for example, the choice of some women to stay in the home.[100] Because radical feminists believe homemakers' choices to be degrading, they conclude that those are not real choices but rather are forced by socialization.[101] Leaving aside the disdain for family, motherhood, and heterosexuality associated with this claim,[102] the form of argument itself is highly suspect. One cannot just pick those choices that one approves of ideologically as being real choices and discount those that do not fit one's preferred utopia as merely apparent. From a Kantian standpoint, there is an imperative to respect people's rational, autonomous choices. If the individual's autonomy has been impaired by coercion or fraud, then of course it will not be a real choice. Absent coercion or fraud, however, the choice of a homemaker to devote herself to the family ought to be valued and honored.[103]

A liberal feminist, however, might reply as follows: the Kantian theory insists that choices be rational, and the Kantian idea of rationality is indeed complex.[104] It would certainly be a mistake to portray Kant's categorical imperative as a command to respect any preference: irrational choices are not deserving of respect. Hence, the liberal feminist may conclude, the choices of the homemakers are irrational, comparable perhaps to the choices of people who knowingly surrender their rights to a tyrant.

Such a view, however, depends on the a priori decision that the family is a less valued and important domain—a most controversial premise, especially for feminists. There is a good case to be made for the proposition that choosing to stay in the home is a rational choice for many women.[105] What should be rejected is the superstitious prejudice that the woman's role, predetermined by God or by Nature, must be the home. There is nothing in the liberal account of morality or human nature that a priori excludes or mandates home, factory, or Parliament as the place where a woman finds her self-realization.

While some radical feminists accuse liberalism of promoting socially determined choices in the guise of autonomy, others claim that the liberal emphasis on respect and autonomy does not leave room for an ethics of care and compassion.[106] This is an unjustified charge against liberalism. As many commentators have shown, rights-based liberalism is perfectly consistent with the flourishing of human emotions such as love and compassion.[107] The very idea of inherent dignity and respect for persons requires us to put ourselves in the place of other people, thus understanding their claims as equal moral beings.[108] In this way, the empathetic consideration of other "selves" and the understanding of the circumstances of others are intrinsic to moral and political reasoning.[109] Difference is not discarded but rather factored into our normative judgments.

What Kant was justly concerned about was the fact that people often do terrible harm to others out of love. He claimed, consequently, that duty is a surer guide to moral behavior.[110] For Kant, inclination and emotion are just biological natural facts and, as such, contingent and unreliable.[111] Duty, on the contrary, can be dispassionately (though not infallibly) ascertained by the exercise of reason and is, as such, accessible to every human being *regardless* of his inclinations. This position does not exclude love and compassion, it just refuses to make them the foundation of morality. The Kantian cautionary message is quite plausible: until that time when universal love (mandatory love?) is achieved, civil society will rest on firmer ground in mandating simply respect.

Liberalism does not espouse any particular theory of psychological personality.[112] People make choices (even if they are, in some general sense, determined) and care about them. The categorical imperative directs us, and governments, to respect those choices, at least when they are rational (where "rational" means *both* universalizable and respectful of the dignity of others).[113] The arguments against liberalism, therefore, need to focus on this *normative* thesis, that is, they must show why individual autonomy ought *not* be respected, at least under specified circumstances. Certainly radical feminist critics of international law would have to support at least a significant dismantling of international human rights law, because that body of law relies expressly on the principles of liberal autonomy and the equal dignity of all persons, men and women. My suspicion (although this may be unduly optimistic) is that these critics do not want to take us all the way in this direction.

Science, Method, and Objectivity

The radical abandonment of the normative premises of liberalism must inevitably raise questions of method, because the intellectual values that guide research and debate in the Western world arose, and exist, within liberalism. For the liberal, questions of intellectual ethics are vital and the commitment to intellectual integrity is fundamental. These values have been challenged by radical feminism: for example, some feminists reject the objective standpoint as nothing more than a masculine posture and the scientific method as merely a set of male verification criteria.[114] This sort of methodological rejectionism deserves our most determined opposition. It represents an obscurantist, pre-Galilean repudiation of even the most elementary ground rules for testing the validity of empirical claims. It is a troubling commentary on the radical feminists' dogmatic irrationalism and should have no place in any serious debate about these issues.

Rejecting the scientific method wholesale is not simply bad epistemology, however; it has vast political consequences. In the radical's world, because there is nothing even approaching objective truth, rational argument becomes simply another means to achieve one's objectives. In its most extreme form, antiliberal radicalism views people (and governments) as relieved from constraining rational argument and therefore free even to suppress knowledge in the pursuit of higher ends.[115] The world is just an arena for struggle; there is no independent value in truth or objectivity. Even in its lesser forms, the radicals' self-consciously partisan method allows them to cite data supporting their position (thus showing deference to empirical validation) but to ignore contrary data.[116] The sole objective of radical feminism is the emancipation of women; truth is a value insofar as it contributes to that effort.[117]

In contrast, liberals regard free intellect as the engine of human progress, and intellectual integrity as an unconditional ethical commitment—rather than a political value to be weighed against others. Honesty for the Kantian is part of the categorical imperative to respect other rational beings by not using them manipulatively as means to other ends. The liberal commitment to rational discourse encompasses both science and morality.[118] If we abandon it, as radicals urge, we jeopardize not only the path to knowledge and scientific progress but also our freedoms.

The moral predicament ensuing from such radical relativism is also illustrated by the radical feminist attitude toward rights. Even while endorsing a thoroughgoing attack against rights, some radical feminists nevertheless recommend that international human rights discourse be preserved because it is an accepted means of challenging existing law.[119] They may mean two different things by this assertion. They may hold the hypocritical view that they do not really believe in human rights but that rights discourse is a strategically expedient means to persuade powerholders to relinquish their power. Not the least of this view's difficulties is that the feminist will not be terribly effective in persuading the powerholder to relinquish his power if he knows that she is insincere in her appeal to rights. The radical cannot convince the powerholder *at the same time* of the truth of the radical theory and of the existence of the injustice, so she has to fake a belief in justice and rights, knowing that a liberal powerholder is committed to recognizing the rights of the intolerant as long as they are kept from actually destroying liberal society.[120]

At the very least, this advocacy of rights for purely strategic purposes calls into question the integrity of the theory upon which such advocacy is predicated.

The far preferable view is the one defended by liberal feminists: rights discourse is accepted not for strategic reasons but for the *moral* reasons supplied by the Kantian theory of international law. Individuals should be respected and allowed to flourish autonomously. The liberal theory of international law rejects male privilege and insists that women be treated with equal dignity, much in the way promised by the United Nations Charter.[121] Legitimate states are those that honor that categorical moral imperative as an essential constitutional principle, and individual moral action consists in treating other rational persons as worthy of respect in every realm of human endeavor—including the practices of public research and debate.

The theory of inherent patriarchal oppression is both philosophically untenable and politically counterproductive. By positing a category into which all states equally fall, radical feminists diminish (or, indeed, erase) the differences between relatively oppressive and relatively humane states. By proceeding on metaphysical grounds, they insulate their theory from empirical inquiry and criticism. Kantian liberalism, by contrast, is not a hermetically sealed conceptual system but rather a set of normative commitments based on individual autonomy and respect for freely chosen social arrangements. Nothing in liberalism militates against human solidarity in voluntary social arrangements or compels solicitude for abusers of human rights. Liberalism strives toward an ideal of universal human flourishing and does so by methods respectful of individual autonomy, human dignity, and the right to equal treatment.

Conclusion: Defending the Liberal Vision

Legal theory has been much enriched by feminist jurisprudence. Feminists have succeeded in drawing attention to areas where uncritically received legal theories and doctrines have resulted in injustices to women. International law should be no exception, and the contribution of Charlesworth and her associates will rightly force international lawyers to reexamine features of the international legal system that embody, actually or potentially, unjust treatment of women.

Much of the radical critique is commendably compatible with a committed liberal feminism. For example, radical feminists are correct to urge international organizations to try to achieve gender balance in their internal appointments. Radical feminists are also right in challenging statism and a notion of family autonomy that countenances state complicity or inaction in the face of mistreatment of women by private individuals. Privacy and state sovereignty must be wedded to democratic legitimacy and respect for individual human rights, including the rights of women. All of these goals are easily justified under the Kantian theory of international law.

Yet the basic assumptions of the radical feminist critique are untenable and must be rejected with the same energy and conviction that we reserve for the rejection of other illiberal theories and practices. Radical feminism exists at a remove from international reality because it exempts itself, by philosophical fiat, from critical examination and empirical verification. It wrongly assumes that *oppression* belongs to a category of thought accessible to pure philosophic speculation and thus renders scrutiny of real human rights practices superfluous. Perhaps most ominously, radicalism "unprivileges" the imperatives of objectivity, placing the demands of intellectual integrity and responsible political dialogue on a normative par with other, more political agendas.

When we move from the philosophical domain to political realities there is even more reason to resist the radical feminist agenda. Radical feminists have joined other radicals in attacking liberalism; indeed, their whole case rests upon the supposed bankruptcy of liberal society, upon the inadequacy of the kind of civil society mandated by the Kantian theory of international law. But is the oppression of women correlated to liberal practices? The answer is, emphatically, "no." The feminist claim that male domination is an inherent part of liberal discourse[122] and that liberal institutions are therefore inevitably oppressive of women is patently false.

The truth is that the situation of women is immeasurably better in liberal societies, Western or nonWestern. The most sexist societies, in contrast, are those informed and controlled by *illiberal* theories and institutions.[123] These societies are much more exclusive of women than liberal societies (and most of the Western societies are liberal). Thus, naive assertions such as that "decision-making processes in [non-Western] societies are every bit *as exclusive* of women as in Western societies"[124] merely reflect the warped starting premise that free societies and tyrannical ones[125] are, in some deep reality, morally equivalent. As we have seen, this sort of depth only obscures. The failure to reckon with the facts on record by those claiming to be concerned with the plight of women amounts to serious moral irresponsibility.

The situation of women in liberal societies reveals that liberalism has not yet fulfilled its promise to women of equal dignity. Liberalism is an ideal only partially realized, and its progress can at times seem painfully slow. Yet notwithstanding its imperfections, liberalism remains the most humane and progressively transformative system of social organization known to our time. Its aspiration to universal human flourishing is worthy; its principles of respect, equal treatment, and human dignity are sound. The great, pervasive injustices of the present arise not from liberalism, but from illiberal alternatives and, sometimes, from the lack of resolve to press the liberal vision to its ultimate resolution. Those who would dispirit that resolve, even while wrapped in banners of liberation, deserve our most wary and searching scrutiny.

Notes

1. See, inter alia, Hilary Charlesworth et al.,"Feminist Approaches to International Law," 85 *American Journal of International Law* 613 (1991).

2. There are other schools of thought within the feminist movement. Particularly noteworthy is relational, or cultural, feminism, inspired by Carol Gilligan. Carol Gilligan, *In A Different Voice: Psychological Theory and Women's Development* (1982); see also Suzanna Sherry, "Civic Virtue and the Feminine Voice in Constitutional Adjudication," 72 *Virginia Law Review* 543 (1986). In this chapter, however, I will discuss only liberal and radical feminism, in part because they seem to me the two alternatives that are truly irreconcilable. Moreover, Charlesworth and her associates do not rely on relational feminism as part of their critique of international law. Cf. Charlesworth et al., supra note 1, at 615–616 (discussing sympathetically Gilligan's work but refusing to adopt the "different voice" premise).

3. See supra, Chapter 1.

4. See generally Thomas M. Franck, "The Emerging Right to Democratic Governance," 86 *American Journal of International Law* 46 (1992).

5. See Convention on the Elimination of All Forms of Discrimination Against Women, December 18, 1979, articles 7–8, 19 *International Legal Materials* 33 (entered into force September 3, 1981) [hereinafter Women's Convention]; Convention on the Political Rights of Women, opened for signature March 31, 1953, articles 1–3, 27 *United States Treaties* 1909, 193 *United Nations Treaty Series* 135 (entered into force July 7, 1954); Inter-American Convention on Granting of Political Rights to Women, opened for signature May 2, 1948, article 1, 27 *United States Treaties* 3301, *Treaties and Other International Acts Series* No. 8365 (entered into force March 17, 1949).

6. For a useful survey of liberal feminism, see Alison M. Jaggar, *Feminist Politics and Human Nature* 27, passim (1983). For two excellent examples of modern liberal feminist scholarship, see Susan Moller Okin, "Reason and Feeling in Thinking about Justice," in *Feminism and Political Theory* 15 (Cass R. Sunstein ed., 1990); Diana T. Meyers, "Personal Autonomy and the Paradox of Feminine Socialization," 84 *Journal of Philosophy* 619 (1987).

7. United Nations Charter articles 1(3), 8, 55.

8. Id.

9. For examples of characteristic radical feminist legal theory, see Catharine A. MacKinnon, *Feminism Unmodified* (1987) [hereinafter Feminism Unmodified]; Catharine A. MacKinnon, *Toward a Feminist Theory of the State* (1989) [hereinafter Toward a Feminist Theory]; Robin West, "Jurisprudence and Gender," in *Feminist Legal Theory: Readings in Law and Gender* 201, 202 (Katherine T. Bartlett & Roseanne Kennedy eds., 1991). One of the boldest claims of some radical feminists is that *sexuality is* socially determined. See Catharine A. MacKinnon, "Desire and Power," in *Feminism Unmodified* (1987) [hereinafter Desire and Power].

10. See Catharine A. MacKinnon, "Difference and Dominance: On Sex Discrimination," in *Feminism Unmodified* 40 (1987) [hereinafter Difference and Dominance].

11. See, e.g., Martha Minow, *Making All the Difference: Inclusion, Exclusion, and American Law* 194 (1990).

12. Charlesworth et al., supra note 1, at 622.

13. Id.

14. See id. at 16 n.56.

15. See Gilbert Ryle, *The Concept of Mind* 16–18 (1949) (introducing the concept of category mistakes).

16. See supra, Chapter 3.

17. See generally Franck, supra note 4.

18. See id.

19. United Nations Charter articles 1(3), 8, 55.

20. The case law of the European Court of Human Rights applies the test of reasonableness and objectivity to determine whether a governmental distinction between groups is justified under article 14 of the European Convention on Human Rights. European Convention for the Protection of Human Rights and Fundamental Freedoms, 213 *United Nations Treaty Series* 221 [hereinafter Human Rights]; see Belgian Linguistic (No. 2), 1 *European Court of Human Rights* (ser. A) at 252 (1980); see also Marckx v. Belgium, 2 *European Court of Human Rights* (ser. A) at 330 (1979). Thus, a regulation prohibiting the government from sending a female diplomat to a country where women are much more likely to be assaulted or killed may be justified. General discrimination against women in the admission to the foreign service, however, is not. An interesting case is whether a government is justified in refusing to send women diplomats to countries where host governments dislike seeing women in any public positions primarily because they deny the women in *their* state access to such positions. In principle, democratic nations should refuse to honor the illegal discriminatory practices of other governments.

21. Charlesworth et al., supra note 1, at 631–634.

22. Id. at 631–632.

23. Id. at 632 (citing MacKinnon, Difference and Dominance, supra note 10, at 34 ("Man has become the measure of all things")).

24. See Women's Convention, supra note 5, article 7.

25. This sort of *global* affirmative action suggestion is untenable and impracticable. The problem with such a global requirement becomes quickly apparent. Imagine the United Nations requiring a country preparing to hold a democratic election to choose a female president, under threat of sanctions. This is completely different from the question of the permissibility under international law of *domestic* affirmative action programs designed to redress *de facto* inequalities of women. See id. article 4 (allowing temporary affirmative action programs provided they do not result in states maintaining separate standards). Whatever the laws of individual states on this issue, international law allows for such programs through the margin of appreciation left to states, at least when the programs are not extreme.

26. Cf. Charlesworth et al., supra note 1, at 623 (discussing the fifty percent figure for "professional jobs held by women" in international organizations and agencies). Interestingly, the authors use expressions such as the "silence" or "invisibility" of women instead of the term "injustice." Id. Analogous criticism is sometimes heard in the United States when critics complain, for example that the U.S. Senate is 98 percent male. Whatever the faults of the Senate or individual senators, this criticism is misguided. Each senator has democratic credentials, having been elected to the Senate by a free democratic choice of the electorate. I cannot, therefore, see any real injustice, unless feminists are suggesting that women are being prevented from voting or from running for office. It is also unclear how radical feminists intend to address this problem. A perfectly sensible way would be to mobilize the electorate to get more women elected (politically, this requires convincing voters that the candidate's sex is an important consideration). The impracticality of other alternatives, such as a constitutional amendment imposing a 50 percent quota for women in the Senate, is self-evident.

27. I am indebted to Lea Brilmayer for calling my attention to this point.

28. Thus, Charlesworth and her associates seem to be correct on this point. Charlesworth et al., supra note 1, at 625.

29. Again, I purposefully confine this discussion to legitimate states, because in my view envoys of illegitimate governments should not be allowed to represent their states, come what may. See supra, Chapter 1 (recommending that the United Nations require democratic legitimacy of representatives before admitting them to the organization).

30. Radical feminists do not accept even the possibility of free individual or collective choice in today's society. I address this issue below.

31. See Charlesworth et al., supra note 1, at 625.

32. Id. at 621–622.

33. Id. at 622 (citing Betty Reardon, *Sexism and the War System* 15 (1985)).

34. Charlesworth and her associates do not make this point expressly. See infra notes 72–75. For an account of violations of women's rights, see generally Amnesty International, *Women in the Front Line: Human Rights Violations Against Women* (1991).

35. Charlesworth et al., supra note 1, at 629.

36. Id. at 614 (stating that "international law is a thoroughly gendered system").

37. By the assertion that international law rules are gendered, feminists, especially radical feminists, may also mean that by virtue of being part of the liberal state system, international law rules are bound up with patriarchy, and therefore *inherently* oppress women. This line of reasoning is considered and rejected below.

38. See sources cited supra note 2.

39. See Laura Reanda, "Human Rights and Women's Rights: The United Nations Approach," 3 *Human Rights Quarterly* 11 (1981). See generally Malvina Halberstam & Elizabeth F. Defeis, *Women's Legal Rights: International Covenants an Alternative to ERA?* (1987).

40. See, e.g., Catharine A. MacKinnon, "Privacy v. Equality: Beyond Roe v. Wade," in *Feminism Unmodified* 93, 100–102 (1987) (maintaining that the law of privacy, conceived as promoting women's bodily autonomy, paradoxically protects activities tending toward the subjection of women).

41. See Charlesworth et al., supra note 1, at 625, 627.

42. See, e.g., Nigel Rodley, "The Evolution of the International Prohibition of Torture," in *Amnesty International, The Universal Declaration of Human Rights 1948–1988: Human Rights, the United Nations and Amnesty International* 55, 63 (1988). Whereas private criminal acts are handled under domestic criminal law, torture becomes a matter of international concern generally only when a government sanctions acts by its own law enforcement officials and personnel. Id.

43. The classic statement of the argument for criminalizing violent acts, as opposed to making them compensable only, is Robert A. Nozick, *Anarchy, State, and Utopia* 65–71 (1974). Nozick contends that if violent, wrongful acts were simply compensable, people would constantly fear violence against them. Compensating for this fear would not be possible, and, therefore, states instead forbid and punish violent acts criminally to alleviate general apprehension. Id.

44. X and Y v. The Netherlands, 91 *European Court of Human Rights* (ser. A) at 8 (1985).

45. Under Dutch law, initiating criminal proceedings in statutory rape cases required the filing of a complaint by victims over the age of twelve. For victims under twelve years old, a parent could file the complaint. Dutch law, however, had no provision allowing a parent of a mentally incompetent victim *over* the age of twelve to file a complaint on the victim's behalf. See id. at 9–10.

46. Id. at 11–12.

47. Id.
48. Id.
49. Id. at 13–14.
50. Id. at 16.
51. I owe to Jeffrie Murphy the idea of unfair risk in this context.
52. X and Y v. The Netherlands, 91 *European Court of Human Rights* (ser. A) at 8 (1985).
53. See *Middle East Watch, Empty Reforms: Saudi Arabia's New Basic Laws* 36–37 (1992); cf. Amnesty International, *Iran: Women Prisoners of Conscience* (1990) (concerning imprisoning Iranian women for nonviolent political activities).
54. Cf. United States Diplomatic and Consular Staff in Tehran (United States v. Iran), 1980 *International Court of Justice* 3, 29 (May 24) (holding that the Iranian government's approval of the seizure of the United States embassy makes Iran internationally responsible).
55. Cf. Women's Convention, supra note 5, articles 2, 3 (mandating legislation to eliminate gender discrimination).
56. Charlesworth et al., supra note 1, at 628 (citing United Nations Convention Against Torture and Other Cruel, Inhuman or Degrading Treatment or Punishment, General Assembly Resolution 39/46, United Nations General Assembly Organ, 39th Session, Supp. No. 51, at 197, United Nations Document A/RES/39/708, reprinted in 23 *International Legal Materials* 1027 (1984), revisions reprinted in 24 *International Legal Materials* 535 (opened for signature Feb. 4, 1985; entered into force June 26, 1987)).
57. Id. at 629.
58. See generally *Comisión Nacional Sobre La Desaparición De Personas, Nunca Más* (9th ed. 1985) (documenting human rights abuses in Argentina).
59. The same situation occurs when death squads operate in face of a government's inaction or complicity. See Amnesty International, *Amnesty International Report 1990* 86–89 (1990) (describing death squad activities in El Salvador). Here again, one cannot avoid this problem by *defining* "human rights violation" as a behavior that can be carried out only by a state official. Not only is it impossible to draw normative conclusions from definitions, but, from the standpoint of political theory, a private citizen may violate an individual's rights as much as the government. In fact, under social contract theory, it is precisely the danger of rights invasions by individuals that motivates persons in the state of nature to create the state.
60. See supra notes 56–58 and accompanying text.
61. See Jeffrie G. Murphy & Jules L. Coleman, *Philosophy of Law* 119 (2d ed. 1990).
62. See, e.g., Kay Boulware-Miller, "Female Circumcision, Challenges to the Practice as a Human Rights Violation," 8 *Harvard Women's Law Journal* 155 (1985).
63. See Charlesworth et al., supra note 1, at 631–632 (criticizing the Women's Convention for assuming that men and women are the same). Charlesworth and her associates do not want to be treated "equally" if such treatment is judged against a male standard. Id. The authors rely extensively on the work of MacKinnon for this point.
64. See id. at 616–621 (arguing that although women's situations differ in the Third and First Worlds, they are united by the common phenomenon of male domination).
65. Another reason for this moral equivalence thesis stems from a curiosity in the history of radical thought. Radical feminists are leftists, and one of the mottos of the left is solidarity with the Third World. Therefore, radical feminists feel more comfortable criticizing the imperialist West than acknowledging that in many Third World societies women are seriously mistreated. The anti-Western bias of Charlesworth and her associates

is clear in their brief reference to female circumcision. They delicately refer to "the tension between some First and Third World feminists over the correct approach to the issue of female genital mutilation." Charlesworth et al., supra note 1, at 619 n.39. The extraordinary practice of criticizing the liberal West while offering solicitude for genital mutilation suggests the root of the "tension" all too well: one cannot at the same time be a feminist and be sentimental about the Third World.

66. See MacKinnon, *Toward a Feminist Theory*, supra note 9, at 249 (envisioning a theory of the state based on "a new relation between life and law").

67. Metaphysical statements, roughly speaking, are those without any referent in the physical world; for example, statements about a transcendent God may be metaphysical. Analytic truths are circular statements in which the predicate can be logically derived from an analysis of the subject; hence, the statement "all bachelors are male" can be derived from the definition of "bachelor" (an unmarried adult male), and no empirical confirmation is necessary. Finally, "ought" statements, commands, questions, and other utterances that do not assert a state of the world may not require verification.

68. For a classic rejection of metaphysics in legal and social thought, see Felix S. Cohen, "Transcendental Nonsense and the Functional Approach," 35 *Columbia Law Review* 809 (1935).

69. For an interesting discussion of this issue, see Linda C. McClain, "'Atomistic Man' Revisited: Liberalism, Connection, and Feminist Jurisprudence," 65 *Southern California Law Review* 1171 (1992).

70. See MacKinnon, Desire and Power, supra note 9, at 60; see also Andrea Dworkin, *Intercourse* (1987).

71. See, e.g., MacKinnon, Difference and Dominance, supra note 10, at 40, 42.

72. If a nonoppressive state is even imaginable, then "oppression" cannot follow from the definition of "state"; for a nonoppressive state would be a contradiction in terms, like a square circle.

73. In a passage as much reminiscent of Hobbes, Locke, and Rousseau as it is of the Book of Genesis, MacKinnon announces a quasi-conspiratorial radical feminist creation story: "Here, on the first day that matters, dominance was achieved, probably by force. By the second day, division along the same lines had to be relatively firmly in place. On the third day, if not sooner, differences were demarcated, together with social systems to exaggerate them in perception and in fact, *because* the systematically differential delivery of benefits and deprivations required making no mistake about who was who. Comparatively speaking, man has been resting ever since." MacKinnon, Difference and Dominance, supra note 10, at 40 (emphasis in original). The idea that (even physical) sex differences precede gender differentiation is called into question. MacKinnon presents our perceptions of differences between the sexes as merely ideological constructs designed to legitimate oppression: "if gender is an inequality first, constructed as a socially relevant differentiation in order to keep that inequality in place, then sex inequality questions are questions of systematic dominance, of male supremacy, which is not at all abstract and is anything but a mistake." Id. at 42. Of course, not all feminists endorse (or even flirt with) a conspiratorial explanation of the state. I follow here, *mutatis mutandis,* 1 Karl R. Popper, *The Open Society and Its Enemies* 94–95 (2d ed. 1966). Popper views conspiracy theories as secular echoes of the superstitious belief that Homeric gods determine the outcome of battles.

74. Thus, MacKinnon writes, "Speaking descriptively rather than functionally or motivationally, the strategy is first to constitute society unequally prior to law; then to design the constitution, including the law of equality, so that all its guarantees apply only to those

values that are taken away by law; then to construct legitimating norms so that the state legitimates itself through noninterference with the status quo. Then, so long as male dominance is so effective in society that it is unnecessary to impose sex inequality through law, such that only the most superficial sex inequalities become *de jure,* not even a legal guarantee of sex equality will produce social equality." *Toward a Feminist Theory,* supra note 9, at 163–164. Speaking descriptively, MacKinnon's strategy seems to be to hide the careful qualifiers in the sweep of language (note the introductory phrase), and reap the rhetorical benefits of the conspiratorial assertion not quite made.

75. In radical feminist theory, men play the role that the capitalists, the Learned Men of Zion, the imperialists, the communists, etc., have played in various other conspiracy theories. Conspiracy theories, however, do become important when people who hold them are in power, for in that case they will spend most of their energies in a counterconspiracy against nonexistent conspirators. Popper, supra note 73, at 95. For an almost pristine example of a conspiracy theory, the military Junta in Argentina (1976–1984) believed that the world's outrage over their human rights violations was the result of a "well-orchestrated anti-Argentine campaign" waged by communists led by Amnesty International.

76. See id.

77. See Neil MacKormick, "Law, State, and Feminism: MacKinnon's Theses Considered," 10 *Law and Philosophy* 447, 450 (1991) (arguing that MacKinnon's conspiracy theory gets out of hand).

78. The use of the term "bourgeoisie" by Marxists and their progeny to refer to liberals is already derisive. It portrays those who have struggled and died to secure the liberties we enjoy as merely greedy merchants intent on peddling their wares.

79. See Barbara Herman, "Integrity and Impartiality," 66 *Monist* 233, 234–240 (1983).

80. Charlesworth et al., supra note 1, at 625–627; see also Privacy v. Equality, supra note 40, at 99–102; Carole Pateman, *Feminist Critiques of the Private/Public Dichotomy in Public and Private Social Life* 281 (Stanley I. Benn & Gerald F. Gaus eds., 1983).

81. See Charlesworth et al., supra note 1, at 625–630.

82. See, e.g., MacKinnon, *Toward a Feminist Theory,* supra note 9, at 193–194.

83. Indeed, this is the position taken by many feminists on abortion and other matters of reproductive autonomy.

84. Charlesworth et al., supra note 1, at 629.

85. What should we put in the place of a law that distinguishes between private and public spheres? Should all law be public law?

86. See, e.g., Charlesworth et al., supra note 1, at 617 (citing Sandra G. Harding, *The Science Question in Feminism* 165–171 (1986)). For a discussion on the point of "separateness" versus "connectedness," see generally Minow, supra note 11. For an excellent reply, compare McClain, supra note 69, at 1171 (arguing that the feminist view supporting "connectedness" inaccurately portrays contemporary liberalism).

87. West, supra note 9; Minow, supra note 11.

88. See Marylin Friedman, "Feminism and Modern Friendship: Dislocating the Community," 99 *Ethics* 275, 277–281 (1989).

89. McClain, supra note 69, at 1173.

90. It is a gross caricature to portray liberalism as encouraging an ethics of selfishness and lack of concern for others.

91. For example, the United Nations Charter has a remarkably Kantian emphasis on the "dignity and worth of the human person." United Nations Charter preamble.

92. See generally Minow, supra note 11. For the view that women think differently about morality, see generally Gilligan, supra note 2.

Some feminists argue that women, because of their nurturing nature, are more pacific than men, and that international law would therefore be more effective in curbing war if women had a greater role in its creation and implementation. See Charlesworth et al., supra note 1, at 628. For a survey of the literature, see Micaela Di Leonardo, "Morals, Mothers, and Militarism: Antimilitarism and Feminist Theory," 11 *Feminist Studies* 599 (1985); cf. Barbara Stark, "Nurturing Rights: An Essay on Women, Peace, and International Human Rights," 13 *Michigan Journal of International Law* 144 (1991) (correlating international recognition of basic economic, social, and cultural rights with women's increased participation in public life and with the promotion of peace). Stark's suggestion, however, is distinct from the "women are more peaceful" thesis because, for her, peace is promoted by the recognition of certain "nurturing rights." Id. at 147. Her views are thus closer to liberal feminism.

The view that women are more peaceful is arguable. Women can be as ruthless and belligerent as men. The curious reader may consult Jessica A. Salmonson, *Encyclopedia of the Amazon: Women Warriors from Antiquity to the Modern Era* (1991). Indeed, feminine war prowess is assumed by some feminists when arguing for allowing women to participate in combat.

93. Again, I am aware that perhaps there is no way of proving this, because every example of a liberal woman, the majority of women in the West, is dismissed by the radical feminist. For some radical feminists, neither liberal nor conservative women "speak" for women. See, e.g., MacKinnon, Difference and Dominance, supra note 10.

94. There are sharp differences among radical feminists about the import of this claim. MacKinnon believes that this condition is unacceptable because women's apparently free choices are not really free but coerced. MacKinnon, *Feminism Unmodified*, supra note 9. West, however, contends that the biological fact of material connectedness (a form of biological determinism) grounds the feminine way of thinking about ethics. West, supra note 9.

95. See Bernard Williams, *Ethics and the Limits of Philosophy* 113 (1985).

96. The current revolt against liberal values in the academic West shows that people can challenge tradition and cherished societal values—vindicating, ironically, the liberal view. The point is that people are capable of making choices that are not socially determined.

97. See Ronald Dworkin, *Law's Empire* 441 n.19 (1986) (arguing that liberals are tolerant because it is the right thing to do, not because of a belief in psychological "separateness"); see also McClain, supra note 69.

98. See Immanuel Kant, *Groundwork of the Metaphysics of Morals* 115–116 (H.J. Paton trans., 3d ed. 1965). I am indebted to Jeff Murphy for calling my attention to this point.

99. Radical feminists could reply that the principles built on the assumption of freedom have themselves been terrifying for women in practice. The only recourse is to the facts, and the facts suggest that terror travels with illiberalism. See Amnesty International, supra note 34.

100. On this, see the excellent discussion in Meyers, supra note 6.

101. See, e.g., Catharine A. MacKinnon, "Not by Law Alone: From a Debate with Phyllis Schlafly," in *Feminism Unmodified* 21–31 (1987).

102. See id.

103. See Meyers, supra note 6, at 621–624.

104. See Roger J. Sullivan, *Immanuel Kant's Moral Theory* 23–30 (1989).

105. It would be pointless to cite support for this proposition because its truth depends upon a definition of free will which radical feminists will not accept, regardless of how many instances one provides of actual homemakers who are happy with their choices and are fulfilled by their life plans. Nevertheless, uncoerced choices by homemakers ought to be valued. Failure to do so strips countless homemakers of their dignity and fails to account for "the sensitivity and imagination that childcare requires." Meyers, supra note 6, at 621. Suggesting that working in the home may be a rational choice for many women is totally different from suggesting that women are biologically inclined to make such choices. Kantian liberalism regards the latter idea as either false or irrelevant.

106. For a thoughtful article on this issue, see Sally Sedgwick, "Can Kant's Ethics Survive the Feminist Critique?" 71 *Pacific Philosophical Quarterly* 60 (1990).

107. For an excellent defense of Kant against radical objections, see Herman, supra note 79, at 234–240; see also McClain, supra note 69. Sedgwick concludes that although it is true that radical feminists have mischaracterized Kant, Kant's categorical imperative universalizes the male identity, causing feminist doubts to remain. Sedgwick, supra note 106. This claim assumes too narrow an interpretation of the categorical imperative, however. The categorical imperative is above all an injunction to treat others with dignity and respect, not a simple logical requirement of universalizability of moral judgments. See John Rawls, *A Theory of Justice* 251 n.29, 257 (1971) (contending one should avoid interpreting Kant's writings as merely providing formal requirements for moral judgments); see also Jeffrie G. Murphy, *Kant: The Philosophy of Right* 65–86 (1970) (stating that Kant's morality is not only formal, but also includes ends, purposes, and values).

108. See Okin, supra note 6, at 29–32.

109. Modern liberals expressly disavow an interpretation of liberalism that would exclude care and concern for others. See, e.g., John Rawls, "Kantian Constructivism in Moral Theory," 77 *Journal of Philosophy* 515 (1980); see also Dworkin, supra note 97, at 441–444 n.20 (finding sympathy for tort victims is consistent with liberalism).

110. See Kant, supra note 98, at 61–67.

111. Id. at 63–64.

112. See, e.g., Ronald Dworkin, *A Matter of Principle* 203 (1985).

113. These are the two first versions of Kant's categorical imperative. See Sullivan, supra note 104, at 149–211.

114. See, e.g., MacKinnon, Desire and Power, supra note 9, at 54 (rejecting the scientific method as a "specifically male approach to knowledge"). Charlesworth and her associates seem to accept this idea. See Charlesworth et al., supra note 1, at 613 (emphasizing "the permanent partiality of feminist inquiry" (quoting Harding, supra note 86, at 194)); see also id. at 617 (challenging male "epistemology" and calling for a more emotive approach to science (citing Harding, supra note 86, at 165)).

115. During the military dictatorship in Argentina, the Junta prohibited the teaching in schools of the set theory of numbers on the ground that it was collectivist.

116. See, e.g., Neil Gilbert, "The Phantom Date Rape Epidemic: How Radical Feminists Manipulated Data to Exaggerate the Problem," *Los Angeles Daily Journal*, July 17, 1991, at 6.

117. Thus, even though MacKinnon's "critique of the objective standpoint as male" disavows the scientific method and the "male criteria of verification" it embodies (Desire and Power, supra note 9, at 54) she is rather fond of citing statistics and empirical research to support her arguments. See, e.g., id. at 1, 41.

118. The late Argentine philosopher Carlos Nino has provided a cogent defense of human rights based on moral discourse. See Carlos S. Nino, *The Ethics of Human Rights* (1992).

119. See Charlesworth et al., supra note 1, at 634–638.

120. See Rawls, supra note 107, at 216–221.

121. Charlesworth and her associates, apparently ignoring their earlier disparagement of this liberal assumption as male biased, end their article with the following Kantian sentence: "To redefine the traditional scope of international law so as to acknowledge the interests of women can open the way to reimagining possibilities for change and may permit international law's promise of peaceful coexistence and *respect for the dignity of all persons* to become a reality." Charlesworth et al., supra note 1, at 645 (citing the United Nations Charter preamble) (emphasis added).

122. Or, as Charlesworth and her associates put it, "European, male discourse." Id. at 619. The frequency with which radicals use the adjective "European" derisively is bewildering. I suspect this is a renewed form of the sentimental prejudice that the Third World is simple, noble, and oppressed, while the First World is sophisticated, evil, and imperialistic.

123. See generally Amnesty International, supra note 34.

124. Charlesworth et al., supra note 1, at 618 (emphasis added).

125. Of course, I am far from suggesting a correlation between Third World and tyranny. While there may be now a very high correlation between Western societies (including here most of the former Soviet republics) and liberalism, the reverse is not true: a rapidly growing number of Third World states are liberal. Also, some culturally Western states are part of the Third World in terms of their economic development.

Index